CERVANTINE BLACKNESS

**IBERIAN ENCOUNTER
AND EXCHANGE
475–1755 | Vol. 10**

SERIES EDITORS
*Erin Kathleen Rowe
Michael A. Ryan*

The Pennsylvania State
University Press

The Iberian Peninsula has historically been an area of the world that fostered encounters and exchanges among peoples from different societies. For centuries Iberia acted as a nexus for the circulation of ideas, people, objects, and technology around the premodern western Mediterranean, Atlantic, and eventually Pacific. Iberian Encounter and Exchange, 475–1755 combines a broad thematic scope with the territorial limits of the Iberian Peninsula and its global contacts. In doing so, works in this series juxtapose previously disparate areas of study and challenge scholars to rethink the role of encounter and exchange in the formation of the modern world.

ADVISORY BOARD
*Paul H. Freedman
Richard Kagan
Marie Kelleher
Ricardo Padrón
Teofilo F. Ruiz
Marta V. Vicente*

OTHER TITLES IN THIS SERIES
Thomas W. Barton, *Contested Treasure: Jews and Authority in the Crown of Aragon*

Mercedes García-Arenal and Gerard Wiegers, eds., *Polemical Encounters: Christians, Jews, and Muslims in Iberia and Beyond*

Nicholas R. Jones, *Staging* Habla de Negros: *Radical Performances of the African Diaspora in Early Modern Spain*

Freddy Cristóbal Domínguez, *Radicals in Exile: English Catholic Books During the Reign of Philip II*

Lu Ann Homza, *Village Infernos and Witches' Advocates: Witch-Hunting in Navarre, 1608–1614*

Adam Franklin-Lyons, *Shortage and Famine in the Late Medieval Crown of Aragon*

Sarah Ifft Decker, *The Fruit of Her Hands: Jewish and Christian Women's Work in Medieval Catalan Cities*

Kyle C. Lincoln, *A Constellation of Authority: Castilian Bishops and the Secular Church During the Reign of Alfonso VIII*

Ran Segev, *Sacred Habitat: Nature and Catholicism in the Early Modern Spanish Atlantic*

A. Katie Harris, *The Stolen Bones of St. John of Matha: Forgery, Theft, and Sainthood in the Seventeenth-Century*

CERVANTINE BLACKNESS

NICHOLAS R. JONES

THE PENNSYLVANIA STATE UNIVERSITY PRESS
UNIVERSITY PARK, PENNSYLVANIA

Publication of this book was made possible with the assistance of the Frederick W. Hilles Publication Fund of Yale University.

Library of Congress Cataloging-in-Publication Data

Names: Jones, Nicholas R., 1982– author.
Title: Cervantine Blackness / Nicholas R. Jones.
Description: University Park, Pennsylvania : The Pennsylvania State University Press, 2024. | Series: Iberian encounter and exchange, 475–1755 series ; vol. 11 | Includes bibliographical references and index.
Summary: "Uses a close reading of the work of Miguel de Cervantes to critically examine the default approaches to the exploration, and exploitation, of Black bodies, Black characters, and Black content in early modern Spanish cultural and literary criticism"—Provided by publisher.
Identifiers: LCCN 2024035087 | ISBN 9780271098777 (hardback) | ISBN 9780271098784 (paperback)
Subjects: LCSH: Cervantes Saavedra, Miguel de, 1547–1616—Criticism and interpretation. | Black people in literature. | LCGFT: Literary criticism.
Classification: LCC PQ6324.Z5 J66 2024 | DDC 863/.3—dc23/eng/20240829
LC record available at https://lccn.loc.gov/2024035087

Copyright © 2024 Nicholas R. Jones
All rights reserved
Printed in the United States of America
Published by The Pennsylvania State University Press,
University Park, PA 16802-1003

The Pennsylvania State University Press is a member of the Association of University Presses.

It is the policy of The Pennsylvania State University Press to use acid-free paper. Publications on uncoated stock satisfy the minimum requirements of American National Standard for Information Sciences—Permanence of Paper for Printed Library Material, ANSI Z39.48-1992.

Contents

LIST OF ILLUSTRATIONS   vii
ACKNOWLEDGMENTS   ix

Prologue: The Scramble for Blackness   1

Meditation 1: Cervantine Blackness   21

Meditation 2: Granular Blackness and *Don Quixote*   45

Meditation 3: Rethinking Luis   73

Meditation 4: Cervantes Unhinged   101

Epilogue: To Cervantes with Love   137

NOTES   143
BIBLIOGRAPHY   161
INDEX   183

Illustrations

1. Caricature of Cecil John Rhodes, 1982   7
2. Starowieyski, *Teatr Dramatyczny, Sala Prób, Cervantes, Teatr Cudów*, 1968   14
3. Bronze bust of Cervantes. Golden Gate Park, San Francisco, 2020   23
4. Fragonard, *Don Giovanni Confronting the Stone Guest*, circa 1830–35   31
5. Godinho, *Coat of Arms of the Manicongo Kings*, 1548   57
6. *African Kızlar Ağası*, source unknown, 1682   82
7. Moráis, *Portrait of Joanna of Austria*, 1551 or 1552   106
8. Goya y Lucientes, *Duchess of Alba with María de la Luz*, 1794–95   106
9. Canals, *La toilette*, circa 1903   107
10. Yorùbá subgroup facial cicatrizations, 1958   110
11. Facial cicatrizations among Africans in Cuba, 1969   111
12. Fraser, illustration of "El prevenido, engañado," 1963   116
13. Fraser, illustration of *Desengaño Cuarto*, 1963   130
14. Walker, *Testimony*, print 2, 2005   141
15. Walker, *Testimony*, print 3, 2005   141

Acknowledgments

Cervantine Blackness is a labor of love that has been generously promoted and supported by an exhaustive number of international and transoceanic centers, interlocutors, institutes, and think tanks that—before, during, and "after" the worldwide COVID-19 pandemic—have welcomed me with open arms to deliver lectures and direct workshops at their respective colleges and universities. While the list of names is extensive, you know who you are, and I thank each of you from the bottom of my heart for believing in me and this project. I am also enormously grateful to my colleagues, students, and mentors at Yale University, as well as to those with whom I worked at the University of California, Davis. I also thank the incomparable and inimitable professors Jesús R. Velasco, Mary Malcolm Gaylord, and E. Michael Gerli for encouraging me to pursue this project on Miguel de Cervantes.

I have infinite gratitude for my editor extraordinaire Eleanor Goodman and IEE Series editors Erin Kathleen Rowe and Michael A. Ryan! You all are a dream team, and I've adored conspiring with you over the past years. I am over the moon to have had this second opportunity to work with you in this fruitful capacity. My debts at Penn State University Press also extend to the external anonymous readers who reviewed the manuscript, as well as the Press's conscientious editorial, marketing, and production teams. A heartfelt thanks goes to Amyrose McCue Gill and Lisa Regan for their consultant work during the project's embryonic stages. Thank you goes to Esteban Crespo Jaramillo and Adam Mahler for pouring your meticulous and painstaking work into this monograph's bibliography and index. I send infinite gratitude to Matylda Figlerowicz for assisting me with the book's Polish-to-English translations. No book reaches its completion and its most realized execution without a collective of individuals working conscientiously and creatively behind the scenes. I owe an additional hearty thanks to Sikkema Jenkins and Company and the Yale University Art Gallery for allowing me to reproduce artwork from their archives. Your care, experience, knowledge, intuition, and wisdom has made *Cervantine Blackness* better than I could have ever imagined. It's been a humbling journey and an enriching treat to grow and mature with you, as I've learned how to better trust my instincts and voice.

PROLOGUE
The Scramble for Blackness

> Idle Reader: I only wanted to offer it to you plain and bare, unadorned by a prologue. For I can tell you that although it cost me some effort to compose, none seemed greater than creating the preface you are now reading. I picked up my pen many times to write it, and many times I put it down again because I did not know what to write; and once, when I was baffled, with the paper in front of me, my pen behind my ear, my elbow propped on the writing table, and my chest resting in my hand, pondering what I would say, a friend of mine, a man who is witty and wise, unexpectedly came in and seeing me so perplexed asked the reason, and I hid nothing from him and said I was thinking about the prologue I had to write. *Vale.*
>
> —Miguel de Cervantes, *El ingenioso hidalgo Don Quijote de la Mancha*

The maddening, self-induced quibble of *how* and *where* to begin yet another written scholarly enterprise on Miguel de Cervantes catalyzes, feeds, and soothes my writer's block. The signposts "Idle Reader" and "*Vale*" that frame the epigraph from the prologue of part 1 of *El ingenioso hidalgo Don Quijote de la Mancha* (1605) call into question the ramifications of a reader's good will, disposition, and training—or lack thereof. As a literary critic, I forge a coarticulation between Cervantes and blackness, highlighting a Cervantine unsettling of *idleness* that indexes the backlash of what idle behavior, minds, and practices bypass, erase, and fail to absorb, comprehend, and sense during the consumptive process of reading.[1] This most certainly applies to the exercise and practice of scholarly criticism conducted by a public of readers (and authors) studying the so-called presences and representations of blackness. The closing "*Vale*" reports Cervantes's feisty demand for respect: a catty farewell, or warning, that forecasts what's in store for lazy readers. Not just a "farewell" in its own right, this closing iteration of Cervantes's authorial *Vale* implicates readers and critics alike. Following Cervantes, my intervention in this book urges its audience—or at least those who're hip to and receptive of such a task—to create an inverted sense of its idleness, to see different methodological shifts and theoretical outcomes at the threshold of Cervantes studies and critical black studies.

Cervantine Blackness embodies my unapologetic, unflinching, and unhinged black authorship that channels black culture, black expression, and black livingness in the oeuvre of Cervantes. In doing so, I do not take blackness as a uniform, self-coherent concept. It is capacious, complex, unsettled, spatial, and rich, while its utility is historical and rhetorical. To be clear, this book does not seek to prove, recover, nor reiterate the overused category of black agency. As a concept, my coinage of the term "Cervantine Blackness" charts new methodological and theoretical terrain and possibilities that problematize the way in which agency has stifled and truncated the analysis and examination of black Africans and their descendants in early modern studies, most notably in Spanish cultural and literary production. Instead, I urge herein, my dear, idle reader, that we must trouble the blind faith we lend to agency—and its coterminous analogues "presence" and "resistance"—as the primary heuristic for examining the lives of diasporic black people in early modernity.

This book will perturb some of its readership. As this prologue walks you through the architectural contours and polemical convictions of *Cervantine Blackness*, it is not my intention nor wish to dupe you, my dear reader, by departing from some of the chief claims made in my first book *Staging Habla de Negros: Radical Performances of the African Diaspora in Early Modern Spain*. A clarification for those readers whom this book will stir, quake, and move: I've matured, I've moved on, and I've evolved from theorizing about agency and terms analogous to it. This book reflects growth and rising competence.[2]

Cervantine Blackness disturbs and fucks up the insistent, paternalistic, knee-jerk reaction to redeem black people's agency by way of abject, dehumanized, and subordinated blackness. I'll polemically put it out there: *it's not all about agency*. The caché that agency—specifically as early modern literary scholars have instrumentalized it to study "presences" of enslaved and free black Africans, their ancestors, and their descendants—has garnered in recent years has caught considerable traction, ranging from a host of new publications and workshops to an inundation of panels at conferences far and wide. (It's even glaringly bereft and unethically remiss that *still*, at a 2022 MLA panel hosted in Washington, DC, titled "The Problem of Race in Cervantes," *visibly* black and brown scholars were absent from such an important discussion in the field of early modern Spanish studies.) Do optics matter? Does the examination of black agency qua critical race studies guarantee a field's longevity and relevance in the arguable wane in institutional interest, hiring practices, and study of topics related to the so-called Spanish Golden Age? If we are now, suddenly, doing "antiracist" and "decolonial" work in early modern studies writ large, what are the epistemological and phenomenological reasons behind such missteps?

The corrective to these missteps doesn't remedy itself by outing people or naming names. This is counterproductive and unnecessary. To name names distracts us from the ongoing interior work needed to correct, curb, and undo injustices of all sorts rampant in academic and nonacademic spaces. Contesting liberalism and the liberal individual's history, theorist Dorinne Kondo points out that "challenging the individual, the anthropology of the twentieth century critiques the personal as a category that is itself an artifact of language and culture, problematizing the subject/world division. The subject is inextricable from the structural."[3] To name names indulges, reifies, and participates in the highly problematic nature of self-individualized liberalism. This is not my point. *Cervantine Blackness* is not a classical, liberal book. While, in the backdrop of its conception and theoretical interventions, this book embraces Dylan Rodríguez's critique, "The Pitfalls of White Liberal Panic," *Cervantine Blackness* does not take interest in the business of exoneration. Instead of naming names, the work herein criticizes, within and beyond the bounds of agency, systems and schools of thought codified in early modern studies.

Another point of contention that may aggravate an already perturbed readership is the notion that Cervantes studies—as well as early modernists working outside of black studies—isn't the culprit or problem. This idle readership would proffer that it is black studies interlocutors who ought to rethink *their* presupposition about the history of blackness, the place of Spain in that history, and so on. The point I'm making in *Cervantine Blackness* is converse. The goal is to engage the structural and systemic ways in which Cervantine studies refuses to dialogue with non-Eurocentric modes of scholarly inquiry to talk about Cervantes, sub-Saharan Africa and its transoceanic diaspora, and the black people who populate his literary imagination. As far as I am concerned, tasking specialists of Cervantes and their students to decenter Eurocentrism and to take seriously the critical category of blackness—and not the other way around—derives from the ethical, ideological, and moral premises from which I am grounded and take seriously.

In what follows I argue that the payoff from the concerns raised and the topics treated in this book will resonate with a wide-ranging readership, one who will learn from the case of Cervantes and his predecessors and contemporaries. While *Cervantine Blackness* innovates and theorizes a new kind of early modern studies, I gently remind you, my dear reader, that this book isn't a pedagogical nor teacherly text. Time and time again black people are demanded to coddle, enlighten, and teach generic nonblack interlocutors about systematic oppression and its hydra-headed microaggressions. This problematic expectation also encumbers women as well as people from queer and trans communities. *Cervantine Blackness* is not this kind of project.[4]

Methodologically, *Cervantine Blackness* performs a close reading of Cervantes's writings and the implications of those works in the wake of his worldwide legacy. While Equatorial Guinean thinker and writer Francisco Zamora Loboch—in his *Cómo ser negro y no morir en Aravaca* (1994) and the poem "Estefanía," from the collection *Memoria de laberintos* (1999)—would categorize Miguel de Cervantes as an "antiracist," this book does not exalt Cervantes as such.[5] Nor does it marshal the now trendified and performative practice of applying concepts willy-nilly—at times just empty slogans and underdeveloped progressive ideals—to literally *everything*: antiracist, decolonial, global, and so on. The grievance I have with these terms is that each sloganizes culture, history, and ideology. They collapse the historicity and singularity of each movement for wholesome trendy gains and relevance. Each isn't transferrable. In my view these three terminological positionalities lack nuance and precision through flattening and misrepresenting unique historical, philosophical, and theoretical formations for different communities, lands, nations, polities, and sovereigns.[6] To think with Kara Keeling's astute insights made in *Queer Times, Black Futures*, each has taken shape as a part of the organization of capital into forms of "globalization" and "financialization" that various fields and subfields maneuvering under the rubric of early modern studies have facilitated. These three terms—"antiracist," "decolonial," and "global"—commensurate different forms of capital, representing financial derivatives that are themselves "computations of relative values, embodying social relations of competition, not just trust, power, promises and obligations."[7] This widespread Amazonification of concepts must cease and desist. Or, at a minimum, we must apply them with better critical nuance and conceptual precision.

Placing Cervantes in conversation with our current times and highlighting the relevance of his corpus to contemporary society, *Cervantine Blackness* dialogues directly with *What Would Cervantes Do? Navigating Post-truth with Spanish Baroque Literature*, coauthored by William Egginton and David Castillo. *Cervantine Blackness* also complements Ana Laguna's *Cervantes, the Golden Age, and the Battle for Cultural Identity in Twentieth-Century Spain*. While discussions of race relations, racial justice, and racialized discourses remain absent in both volumes, the pages you either hold in this book or scroll through on a screen enhance the erudite and timely contributions of Egginton, Castillo, and Laguna. Through my concept of "Cervantine Blackness," this project delves into the current understanding of Miguel de Cervantes's works by filling a void in Cervantine criticism that has remained woefully silent about the author's compelling literary construction and cultural codification of black Africans, sub-Saharan Africa, and the African diaspora.

To not fall into the trap of hypocrisy, I'm very cognizant of and intentional in my eschewing of dubbing *Cervantine Blackness* as *the* "first" book of its kind that analyzes blackness in Cervantes's writings. To do so and to make such a claim means participating in the politics of Columbusing and settler-colonialist beliefs that I critique throughout this prologue—mostly fiercely in the next section, titled "Against ~~Agency~~: The Scramble for Blackness." I tread carefully here in how I have envisioned the gaps this project seeks to fill. *Cervantine Blackness* does not recover any essentialisms nor essentialized meanings about racialized blackness. This book expresses no interest in recovering Miguel de Cervantes as an exemplary savior of black people and black suffering. My intervention here not only provides a critical response to the recent international explosion of content and interest in the so-called black African in early modern Spain—and, arguably, other disciplines that fall under the umbrella of early modern studies—but also problematizes the carnivorous exploration of and exploitation constituted in *the study of* black bodies, black characters, black content, and black histories in early modern Spanish cultural and literary criticism to date.

Against ~~Agency~~: The Scramble for Blackness

Cervantine Blackness explores a set of problems as demarcated by, or perhaps framed by, this prologue's title: "The Scramble for Blackness." This effort functions as both an intellectual concern and a cultural critique. A trendy uptick and expeditious interest in the study of blackness and black people have overrun early modern Spanish literary studies. I identify this peaked awareness, concern, and curiosity with a series of events: the 2019 publication of *Staging* Habla de Negros, the beginning of the pandemic lockdowns in the spring of 2020, and a spate of police killings in the United States, whose victims included Breonna Taylor (March 13, 2020), George Floyd (May 25, 2020), and Tony McCade (May 27, 2020) that launched a volume of protests unprecedented in US history. As philosopher Olúfẹ́mi Táíwò cogently explains in *Elite Capture: How the Powerful Took Over Identity Politics (and Everything Else)*, "The protests were not only large, but combative. Across the country, luxury mall and retail stores were sacked and pillaged. In Minneapolis, police fled the Third Precinct for their lives as rebels smashed windshields with projectiles and set the building on fire." Táíwò adds, "The protests were global in scope. This global solidarity undoubtedly owes itself to the steadfast international organizing work of Black Lives Matter chapters, the umbrella Movement for Black Lives, and a number of other organizations around the world working in partnership and solidarity with them. These problems are among the many legacies of our immediate past that shape our lives today."[8]

At this juncture Táíwò's *Elite Capture* jogs our memory of and understanding about how Black Lives Matter movements worldwide have mobilized what I call a savior-mode zeitgeist in recent and forthcoming scholarly publications in early modern Spanish studies that focus on the study of blacks and their racialized blackness. What undergirds this scramble for blackness in early modern literary criticism manifests in Táíwò's ideation of elite culture at "every scale" in the ivory tower.[9] Put simply: to center blackness through the prisms of agency, joy, resistance, and subversion, scholars working in the field of early modern Spanish studies—and its adjacent established and emergent fields and subfields across geographies and languages—have perpetrated elite capture. These singularly progressive and enlightened acts, disguised as noble intellectual efforts and pursuits, concretize a scramble for blackness that aims to conquer and extract the glitzy agency, joy, and presence of black people and their thematic blackness across continental Africa and the vast African diaspora. If we were to follow and track recent publication trends and their recent and forthcoming metrics, such publication output might leave us with the impression that scholars with little training in critical black studies and its foundational genealogies, histories, methods, or theories seek to produce "new" work that fails to honor—or even mention—earlier scholarship created by black scholars across class, gender, and sexuality.[10]

Fig. 1. Caricature of Cecil John Rhodes, 1892. Edward Linley Sambourne, "The Rhodes Colossus," *Punch*, December 10, 1892.

I analogize the scramble for blackness to the colonization, division, extraction, occupation, and invasion of the African continent by seven Western European powers between 1880 and 1914, most notably known as the "Scramble for Africa," sponsored by Otto von Bismark's Berlin Conference of 1884.[11] As illustrated in and politicized by figure 1, the scramble to further discover and extract black Africans' agency—or to propel the insistence that blacks instrumentalized their agency to resist and subvert antiblack racism, discrimination, and enslavement—as if one has struck theoretical gold has its limits and can lead us to a dead-end analysis. We cannot easily disentangle black agency from the fanciful abstraction that blackness becomes for many scholars. I connect and identify the problem of agency to T. J. Tallie's important reminder for us, in "On Black Autonomy and Responding to Abstract, Genteel Contempt," that some white scholars "see us [black people] only as extensions of their noble projects. They see objects of study. They see informants. They see things to be spoken over or for or abstracted."[12] The stakes of analogizing colonial processes of extraction with the scholarly pursuits of overemphasizing black agency demonstrate how perceivably benign, well-intentioned celebrations of that black agency

PROLOGUE 7

collude with a literary criticism and an intellectual history that attend to the longer historical arcs of racial capitalism.

Another way to read my frustration manifests in an astute Twitter post by geographer Katherine McKittrick: "Theorizing should not be a scramble to make (and therefore own) a concept. beginning a project with a sexy new concept risks undermining theoretical activity because the sexy concept ends up controlling and undermining our analytical creativity and limiting how and who we read. (theorizing is about writing, sharing, reading, fighting about ideas—concepts help us do this, but how concepts are entangled with other ideas and stories and conversations is really beautiful and exciting)."[13] *Cervantine Blackness* isn't a scramble for new trendy theoretical gains and ends, replete with the extractive logic of racial capitalism. In accord with McKittrick's perceptive charges, this book encourages us as critics and readers of Africans and African diasporic communities and their histories to not fall into the repeated myopic and seductive clutches of merely scrambling for messiah-like terms. The bandwagonism must end.

As early as 2003 and as recent as 2021, social historians have debated the elisions and implications foreclosed within the capital and jargon of enslaved persons' agency. In his essay "On Agency," Walter Johnson explicates my point as follows: "The term 'agency' smuggles a notion of the universality of a liberal notion of selfhood, with its emphasis on independence and choice, right into the middle of a conversation about slavery against which that supposedly natural (at least for white men) condition was originally defined." Johnson adds, "And out of this misleading entanglement of the categories of 'humanity' and (liberal) 'agency' has emerged a strange syllogism in which the bare fact (as opposed to the self-conscious assertion) of enslaved 'humanity' has come to be seen as 'resistance' to slavery."[14] Urging us to think about Africa as having its own trajectory and sovereignties rather than bestowing agency on Africans, Herman Bennett argues that we must assume Africa and Africans' existence from the very start. To illuminate my position even further, in dialogue with Bennett's powerful push back against John Thorton's insinuation of liberal causality and ill-defined African agency, he prods, "What are the implications of assigning Africans agency when Western humanism assumes as much with regard to philosophical Man? Does not the very act of bestowing agency foreclose its unquestionable universalism? Asked differently, does the gesture of granting agency not risk giving legitimacy to the very political-conceptual practice that exercised its existence among Africans in the first place?"[15]

Raising similar concerns, Marisa J. Fuentes cogently inverts the meaning of resistance, as it's linked to agency, in her indispensable work *Dispossessed Lives: Enslaved Women, Violence, and the Archive*. Fuentes rebukes "our search for subversive agency as the dominant way to understand enslaved humanity."[16] In its phenomenological dialectics—not necessarily one attributed to the master-slave dialectic from Georg Wilhelm Friedrich Hegel's "Lordship and Bondage" treatise from *Phenomenology of Spirit* (1807)—I propose we scholars of early modern studies aspire to conceive anew agency and its coterminous analogues by suspending them—holding them in tension, if you will—with the diametrically binarized tenets of black pessimism and black optimism. Wielding no connection to the categorically facetious racialized grouping and status of *tente en el aire* (upended or suspended in the air), which is visually depicted in the colonial Mexican *sistema de castas* (society or system of castes), my recommendation is to *suspend*—or perhaps puppeteer—the antinomies and complexities of black personhood through a critical engagement with talking about blackness in all of its capaciousness through what I like to call "the and *and* the with." Affirmation and negation must be comingled.

So how do we rethink black agency in the works of Cervantes and his contemporaries? The black feminist academic pornographer Mireille Miller-Young offers some counsel. She explodes the concept of agency "by moving away from reading of its equivalence with resistive (sexual [and racial]) freedom." She proposes, "We might instead read agency as a facet of complex personhood within larger embedded relations of subordination. Agency then might be seen as a dialectical capacity for pleasure and pain, exploration, and denial, or for progressive change as well as everyday survival."[17]

Taking a methodological cue from Kevin Quashie's theorization of "black aliveness" provides an additional framework for us to consider. In *Black Aliveness, or A Poetics of Being* Quashie reminds us that "antiblackness and white supremacy, as they live in and are enacted by any person in implicit or explicit or structural registers, both are sins against the human."[18] Thinking closely with Quashie, I too depart "from black pessimism" and want to use *Cervantine Blackness* in this intellectual and justice-oriented tradition by reflecting on new possibilities of theorizing the capacious category of early modern Iberian blackness within Cervantine criticism. Channeling my *Cervantine Blackness* paradigm through Quashie's "black aliveness" concept, this project embraces a critical imperative that implores its audience to "imagine a black world." I am a black thinker and writer who invokes and sees in Cervantes's texts a world where blackness exists in the tussle of being, in reverie, in terribleness, in exception, and in ordinariness.[19] To decentralize the primacy of agency's overuse, I propose, instead, we think in terms of the "phenomenology of blackness"—that is, when and where blackness is being imagined, defined, and performed and in what location, both figurative and literal.[20]

Meditation as Methodology I: On Form, Genre, and Style

My first book, *Staging* Habla de Negros: *Radical Performances of the African Diaspora in Early Modern Spain*, constitutes the well-behaved, obedient, traditional intellectual project. In a quixotic sense, its genealogy—or paternity test—started as a dissertation. In due course, depending somewhat on perfect Aristotelian *imitatio*, I reworked *Staging* Habla de Negros into a monograph that contains thematically structured chapters, a separate introduction, and a conclusion dubbed an "Afterword." Written with a clear, authorial voice, that book's two-pronged argument ebbs and flows in its own logical way. Much like other literary studies monographs, strange paternities and questionable genealogies influenced and informed how I examine—and perhaps still do to this day—primary sources and use secondary and theoretical materials to frame my discussion of literature. My inquisitorial-like confession draws from theorist Therí Alyce Pickens's sage counsel that the "picayune parameters" of a book project do not always require this formulation.[21]

Writing *Cervantine Blackness* has been profoundly cathartic and liberating. It is a theoretical work that belongs to black literary criticism. I identify this book, essayistic in form, as a manifesto or a provocation whose form, genre, and style is purposeful. It follows in the practice and tradition of black theorists such as Audre Lorde, Christina Sharpe, James Baldwin, Kevin Quashie, Marquis Bey, Saidiya Hartman, Toni Morrison, and W. E. B. Du Bois, among countless others. By no means am I a Baldwin, a Morrison, or a Sharpe! However, I am a student of theirs, and the way in which I've written this book—and *think* in this book—reflects their aesthetics, forms, styles, and traditions. The way in which I've crafted this project is not out of the ordinary. To date, a handful of extraordinary scholarly works that do not follow the neatly packaged—hegemonic, if you will—form, genre, and style of a so-called academic book do in fact exist and have excelled beyond measure. I list for you, my dear reader, several that come to mind: Herman Bennett's *African Kings and Black Slaves*; Marquis Bey's *Black Trans Feminism* and *Cistem Failure*; Tina M. Campt's *Listening to Images*; Saidiya Hartman's *Wayward*

Lives; Sharon Patricia Holland's *An Other: A Black Feminist Consideration of Animal Life*; Dorinne Kondo's *Worldmaking: Race, Performance, and the Work of Creativity*; Keguro Macharia's *Frottage*; Biko Mandela's *Black Life Matter*; Toni Morrison's *Playing in the Dark*; Jennifer Morgan's *Reckoning with Slavery*; Kevin Quashie's *Black Aliveness, or A Poetics of Being*; Alexander G. Weheliye's *Feenin' R&B Music and the Materiality of BlackFem Voices and Technology*; and Therí Alyce Pickens's *Black Madness :: Mad Blackness*. Again, there are many black and nonwhite thinkers who blur, mix, and remix conventional academic writing style with their vernaculars and stylistic constructions.[22]

While my use of alliteration in this book, for example, may dizzy some readers and may be uncharacteristic of book listings in early modern Iberian studies, *Cervantine Blackness* embraces the ways in which both critical black studies and critical theory have played with form, genre, and style. I'd like to remind those who aren't aware (or whose cognitive dissonance conveniently leads them astray): theory, too, is a *construction*, and it's not always *deconstructive*. In my justification of the stylistic choices carried out in this book, I reiterate that critical black studies creates and mobilizes theory in ways that function as method and vice versa. Critical black studies—and black feminist thought in particular—engages a methodological movement that interrogates the epistemology of knowledge production. As a black writing subject who has authored *Cervantine Blackness*, I hold onto the theory-method double bind as an apparatus for explicating the payoff and utility of my stylistic formulations.

For me this genealogy begins with literary theorist Barbara Christian, who precisely captures my motivations. Christian's pioneering essay "The Race for Theory," published in 1987, at the height of arguments about canons, exclusions, and theory, asserts unflinchingly, "My folk . . . have always been a race for theory."[23] For Christian theory does not exist distinct from the artistic production of black (women) writers; instead, theory constitutes and is constituted in the creative deployment of abstraction and eroticism in black arts. In Christian's conceptualization, black literary criticism—like black literature itself—is phenomenological and epistemological, an invitation to encounter being and becoming: "For me literature is a way of knowing that I am not hallucinating, that whatever I feel/know *is*." Following in the footsteps of black women theorists, this project treats new possibilities for writing and thinking in early modern studies that affirm and cohere the formulations, wisdom, and work of Barbara Christian, Audre Lorde, and Hortense J. Spillers.[24]

Meditation as Methodology II: Wax, Serpents, Images

Cervantine Blackness unfolds as a set of four meditations. The first, titled "Cervantine Blackness," unlocks the book's genesis by analyzing defaced statues in San Francisco's Golden Gate Park. The second meditation, "Granular Blackness and *Don Quixote*," concerns itself with the limits of agency and representation, asking if the literary imagination of blackness in *Don Quixote* irreconcilable. To address this question, I suggest that blackness in parts 1 and 2 of *Don Quixote* is granular, hence the coinage of my term "granular blackness." Such granularity allows us to sift through the ways in which Cervantes conditions, codifies, and structures blackness as alchemical, ephemeral, and phenomenological. The third meditation, "Rethinking Luis," historicizes and unpacks the sociocultural range of blackness exhibited by the old, black eunuch Luis from the story *El celoso extremeño* (1613). To achieve this, I distill and make meaning out of the intersecting phenomena that BDSM and pornography, music, queerness, and sound harness my study of blackness as a fecund space to think through the material consequences of Cervantes's construction of Luis. The final and fourth meditation, "Cervantes Unhinged," redirects our critical gaze from Cervantes to the celebrated Spanish writer María de Zayas y Sotomayor, who wrote during the late seventeenth century. In doing so I query how Cervantes's construction of racialized blackness changes or evolves in the works of high-born Spanish women like Zayas? This fourth rumination sheds light on Zayas's racially gendered construction of race relations, interracial intimacy, and the racialized embodiment of material culture at the turn of the eighteenth century. *Cervantine Blackness* ends with the epilogue "To Cervantes with Love," which comes full circle, speaking back to and troubling authorship, readership, and the grammar of black futures and freedom in Cervantine thought.

These meditations refer to, revise, augment, and sometimes may contradict one another. My preference for "meditations" over the conventional "chapter" nomenclature serves as an essayistic exercise that gets us to think about how we think when we think about blackness and Cervantes. Other synonyms we can apply to this formulation are "manifesto," "panse," or "provocation." As such, my meditations throughout this project resuscitate what Spanish philosopher José Ortega y Gasset would deem a "circumstance" or "the mute things which are all around us," with which we must reckon.[25] Concerning method and methodology, this section illumines how *Cervantine Blackness* employs its meditations to theorize on the meditation. To achieve this I delink meditation from contemplation and devotion.[26] While it's not my object of study to dissect and reassemble the sinew of long-standing and ongoing debates about the genre of devotional meditation from Saint Augustine to Saint Ignatius Loyola or René Descartes to Saint Teresa of Ávila, I am compelled, however, to push beyond the bounds of devotional *meditatio* by pursuing the epistemological and phenomenological underpinnings of meditation as a means to assess and reimagine how this book's meditations understand blackness's movement in Cervantes's literary imagination. Early modern Iberian studies has escaped this kind of thinking. In my view the field has insufficiently adopted, explored, and theorized about the machinations of epistemology (about the way we know) and phenomenology (about the structure of experience) regarding racialized blackness, race relations, and racial justice. Perhaps, in a sense, like Descartes's wax example from "Meditation Two" and the phenomenological (experiential, sensorial, situated) concerns and conclusions we learn from it, each meditation in *Cervantine Blackness* aims to remold and reimagine Cervantes's literary world of blackness as a black one that radiates a textuality for feeling and orienting.

Images and visual culture play important roles in this book. I use images to create an experience with the pages you may thumb through in a physical book or scroll up and down on a screen. Purposeful in their selection, these visuals frame and invite further theorization about the potential of what this book's meditations do, heighten, or incense in phenomenological terms for its audience. The most powerful of these images is one that graces this book's cover: Franciszek Starowieyski's *Teatr Dramatyczny, Sala Prób, Cervantes, Teatr Cudów* (Dramatic Theater, Marvelous Playbill, Cervantes, Theater of Miracles) from 1968 (see fig. 2).

What resonates most is the serpent and the two ouroboros figures that encircle an eye and the word "Cervantes" and another with a nail spike, or thumbtack, encircled by the accompanying Polish phrase "Teatr Cudów" (Theater of Miracles). The artist replaces the more recognizable ouroboros symbol of the serpent or dragon eating its own tail for humanoid hands that lock and bear Latin and Polish inscriptions. The left-sided ouroboros inverts a Latin phrase from Virgil's tenth eclogue *"Amor vincit omnia"* (Love conquers all) and depicts a second one that reads, *"Ubi tu Gaius, ubi ego Gaia"* (Where you are, there I am). The right-sided ouroboros states, *"Fides ad mortem"* (Faith unto death). Moving from the left ouroboros to the right ouroboros, four Polish phrases accompany these sentences in Latin. Here I offer English translations of the Polish script:

Fig. 2. Franciszek Starowieyski, *Teatr Dramatyczny, Sala Prób, Cervantes, Teatr Cudów*, 1968. Color offset lithograph, 83.1 × 58 cm. Yale University Art Gallery. Gift of George Hopper Fitch, B.A. 1932. 1973.60.10.

1. "*Baba z wozu koniom lżej*" (When the woman is off the cart, it's easier on the horses).

In Polish referring to a woman as *baba* is generally pejorative, though perhaps in the context of the image *baba* could be an antiquated or colloquial usage. What is more, symbolically, one may use this phrase to express happiness or pleasure from getting rid of something or someone.

2. "*Donna Elvira jest piękną Hiszpanką, ma wdzięk*" (Donna Elvira is a beautiful Spanish woman with charm).
3. "*Temperament & własne mieszkanko*" (Temperament and one's own little flat).
4. "*Stary mąż chrapie wciąż / O wyjdz na balkon dziewico, niczwazaj na wieczoru chłód*" (The old husband is constantly snoring / Oh, go out to the balcony, maiden, don't care about the evening).[27]

For all intents and purposes of this project, I'm especially drawn to the black serpent that stands out in Starowieyski's lithograph. Methodologically, my visual reading of this image reveals a potent linguistic register and symbol lodged between my pairing of "Cervantine" and "serpentine." To theorize further into this book's meditations, through my construction and unification of the Cervantine-serpentine homologue, I hope to tap into the ripe potential for linking aesthetics, art, and visual iconography into a broader understanding of *what* a meditation can perform and produce in this body of criticism.

With serpents outside of the West framed and positioned alongside and in continuum with West and Central African cosmologies, philosophies, and religious rites—as well as those that evolved and flourished in the Americas and the United States—I conjoin and conjure symbolic meaning into them. In Yorùbá *òrìṣà* (spelled *orixá* in the Portuguese contexts and *orisha* or *oricha* in Spanish contexts) iconography and religion, these serpents or snakes (called *ejo*, or *erè* or *òjòlá* for "python") would be recognized as divine, powerful, and sacred. The python, for example, held by one of the *òrìṣà* Olókun's wives, is said to represent another serpent god called Òṣùmàrè (the spirit of the sacred rainbow), who attends to and works closely with Yemọja and Ṣàngó. The python is also sacred to Erinlẹ̀ and Ọbàtálá. For the Fon of the Dahomey, Dã/Dan Ayido Hwedo is the rainbow serpent that represents the union of the archetypal masculine (Lisa) and feminine (Mawu) principles and powers that maintain a balanced world. This divine python is revered famously in the port of Ouidah in Benin. In Roberto Strongman's magnificent work *Queering Black Atlantic Religions*, we learn of serpentine embraces— and their metaphors—through the African diasporic Haitian Vodou *lwa* Dambala (the sacred earthly serpent) and Aida Wedo (the rainbow or serpent in the sky).[28] On both sides of the Atlantic, in the Kongo and its diasporic proliferation in Brazil, Cuba, and the US South, serpents of differing sizes and species embody divine guardianship, kinship, magic, and spiritual potency. For instance, in Cuba, since the onset of the colonial period but most notably during the long nineteenth century, priests of the Afro-Cuban, Central African–derived cosmologies and rites of Palo Mayombe (known as Tata Nkisi Malongo and Yayi Nkisi Malongo) have referred to serpents as *majá*, *mboma*, and *ñoca*.

Placed in conversation with Western constructions of serpents, in terms of the ouroboros and the serpentine content illustrated in Starowieyski's lithograph, I turn to serpent metaphors and iconography throughout *Cervantine Blackness* to tap into the ripe potential for linking aesthetics, art, and visual imagery into a broader understanding of *what* a meditation can do, perform, and produce in this book. Such a critical move calls attention to the cycles of destruction and recreation in the evolution of critical thought on Miguel de Cervantes.

Meditation as Methodology III: Black Worldmaking, Critical Fabulations

This book's meditations operate as an organizing compass that reflects my own vulnerable contemplation of conjoining Cervantes and blackness. To be honest with you, *Cervantine Blackness* embodies my scholarly vulnerability; it represents intellectual risks and political investments that at times scare me and take me out of my comfort zone. Blackness has always signaled vulnerability and risk—especially in the current state of the planet and the crises that afflict it. As such, to be vulnerable with Cervantes means to break through the frames, rubrics, and normative conventions that are imposed on us. My vulnerability remains predicated on what follows in the dissemination and reception of this book, like the release of Descartes's *Meditations*: the mark of controversy and polemics.

Cervantine Blackness is deliberately irreverent, rambunctious, and wayward. Taking methodological cues from Saidiya Hartman's *Wayward Lives, Beautiful Experiments: Intimate Histories of Riotous Black Girls, Troublesome Women, and Queer Radicals*, this project concerns itself with breaking open archival documentation—literary and otherwise—from Cervantes's and his contemporaries' worlds so that they might yield a richer picture of pre-Enlightenment Iberian black social life.[29] Through vulnerability and risks, I prefer to think of *Cervantine Blackness* as a fugitive text, marked by the errantry with which it identifies and that it catalogs. In this spirit, following Hartman, I read against the grain and press at the limits of the historical and literary archives associated with Cervantes and those in his writerly orbit. Waywardness in this book speculates about what might have been. As a method, the wild ideas reverberating in this book reimagine blackness through Cervantes's spirit of irony conveyed in writings—yet also his *pulcritud*, or neatly nuanced details—that simultaneously flicker before our eyes.

My privileging of the wayward in *Cervantine Blackness* thus allows me to consider how Cervantes narrated blackness not merely as a racial category of racialized colorism but, more interesting, in light of the cultural, ideological, linguistic, performative, spatial, and textual contours of such a critical fabulation and formulation. As I argue in meditation 2 on blackness in *El ingenioso hidalgo Don Quijote de la Mancha*, Cervantes gives us granular yet glasslike prisms beaming and refracting with content and (im)possibility to think about blackness. Concerning critical fabulation and speculation, the theoretical interventions of Saidiya Hartman, Donna Haraway, and Tavia Nyong'o activate my inclination to create new meaning out of the black lives and black diasporic worlds Cervantes assembles and imagines in his works.

Once activated, such critical fabulations empower me to fill in the blanks with interdisciplinary approaches and against-the-grain close readings desperately needed in early modern literary criticism. Drawing on my understanding of Cervantine scholarship and my own theorization of blackness in the early modern Iberian world, I suggest we make anew and shift our critiques in and of the author's narrative rendering of blackness. Narrative is *always* an act of selection, framing, editing, adjusting, and silencing, and Cervantes's writing of blackness—autobiographical, literary, historiographic, or otherwise—is not exempt from this recursive process. Ultimately, *Cervantine Blackness* positions Cervantes as a thinker who channels both the shortcomings and value of black Africans' aesthetic, cultural, historical, and political maneuverings in the Spain of his time. The book encapsulates a cultural, linguistic, and literary double bind that can no longer be ignored by scholars nor merely dismissed as insignificant or marginal.

I choose to nominalize Cervantes by adding the suffix "ine" to attend to the word as both description and category. My staged grammatical intervention in this book's title enables me to trouble the adjectival pronouncement and institutional(ized) recognition of its adjectival, genealogical, and institutional consolidation and footing (e.g., Instituto Cervantes, Casa Cervantes, and so on), most notably in relation to grammatically theorizing about blackness and vice versa. As a grammar and critical nomenclature for unpacking Cervantes's literary construction of sub-Saharan Africans and their diasporic worldmaking, my conceptualization of "Cervantine Blackness" provides a productive way for reading outside of the crevices and ridges of calcified narratives about black agency that have begun to stunt the field's evolution and foresight. I can then create, imagine, and pinpoint the formation of blackness that entails knowing and representing the cultural and literary history of the West, Europe's encounters with Africans, and the evolving account of racial becoming.

Additionally *Cervantine Blackness* understands "blackness" as geographic and spatial. This turn in my framing of blackness is heavily influenced by black geographers such as Katherine McKittrick, J. T. Roane, and Clyde Woods.[30] Likewise, the collection *The Black Geographic: Praxis, Resistance, Futurity*, edited by Camilla Hawthorne and Jovan Scott Lewis, has enriched my framing of early modern Iberian blackness within and outside of Cervantes studies. In its geographic and spatial capacities, I think of and sit with blackness as liquid, as nonlinear, a process. Drawing inspiration from new scholarship published in the Open Access journal *Liquid Blackness: Journal of Aesthetics and Black Studies*, I maintain in *Cervantine Blackness* that blackness in Cervantes operates as an ongoing process that manifests in black geographies and spaces. Like the Cervantine-serpentine homologue I introduced earlier, as well as my ideation behind the cover image, the serpentine reference metaphorizes the ways in which blackness undulates, traverses, and penetrates spaces, structures, and terrains that are integral to imagining how Cervantes and other writers from his time link blackness to broader themes of geology, land, and topography. The black geographies in Iberian early modernity have taken place in alleys, battlefields, brothels, castles, cathedrals, churches, convents, courtyards, docks, gardens, guilds, haylofts, hospitals, intersections of streets, jails, monasteries, palaces, plazas, ships, tile factories, universities, vineyards, and so on. In relation to Cervantes and his contemporaries, see table 1 to help pin down where black people show up.

I substantiate the claim that blackness is a process, liquid in its constitution, by exposing this book's many audiences to Cervantes's ability to portray sub-Saharan African blackness as active, fluid, and ongoing processes. With this in mind, we cannot disentangle blackness from geography and space. (And this is precisely why I maintain that clenching onto romanticized notions of agency, joy, presence, and recovery fall flat and stall in the

Table 1   Schematic of black characters

	Reference	Title	Geography/space
1	The black academician and manicongo figures	*Don Quijote de la Mancha*, part 1 (1605)	Providence of Ciudad Real, Castilla–La Mancha; castle or gravesite
2	Juan Latino	*Don Quijote de la Mancha*, part 1 (1605)	Granada; court, palace, or university setting
3	The unnamed housekeeper and her boyfriend	*Coloquio de los perros* (1613)	Sevilla; domestic space
4	The old eunuch Luis	*Celoso extremeño* (1613)	Sevilla; hayloft apartment
5	The enslaved girl Guiomar	*Celoso extremeño* (1613)	Sevilla; domestic space
6	Princess Micomicona (racially impersonated by Dorotea)	*Don Quijote de la Mancha*, part 1 (1605)	Castilla–La Mancha; continental Africa, fictionalized as "Guinea" and "Ethiopia"
7	Sancho Panza's reference to enslaving blacks	*Don Quijote de la Mancha*, part 1 (1605)	Castilla–La Mancha; fictionalization of colonial territories
8	Don Quixote's reference to black soldiers	*Don Quijote de la Mancha*, part 2 (1615)	Castilla–La Mancha; fictionalization of colonial territories
9	Guinea (West Africa) personified	*El rufián dichoso* (1615)	Span of continents and years

longevity and sustainability of their sophistication and theoretical potential.) As we see in this project, Cervantes's expansive literary archive catalogs and indexes blackness insofar as he channels and locates alternative forms of record keeping, measuring, and assigning value and nonproprietary modes of gathering. Energized by the pathbreaking interventions exemplified by the editors of the *Liquid Blackness* journal, my coinage and deployment of the term "Cervantine Blackness" gives a "variety of idiosyncratic, errant, and unruly indices to adopt improvisatory methods, which often prompt a measure of critical vulnerability: a willingness to be guided by objects of study and to learn from their rich complexity how to unspool" Cervantes's archive.[31]

Like a serpent, I crisscross and uncoil Cervantes's archive of blackness by way of meticulous and tedious detective work, an archaeological excavation of interwoven literary communities, histories, and influences of Iberian elites with whom Miguel de Cervantes interacted and brushed shoulders. Popping up unexpectedly in each meditation of this book, my Cervantine-serpentine method, interdisciplinary in its analysis, sheds light on the salient role Iberian elites had on Cervantes and his contemporaries. This was a society that Cervantes critiqued, satirized, and scorned—many of whom, in serpentine-like ways—made their wealth and solidified their fame and power by the trafficking in and selling of sub-Saharan Africans. At the opening of Cervantes's *El celoso extremeño* (1613), for instance, the narrator comments on the leisurely and slaker-like idleness of Seville's privileged class. Calculation, plotting, and strategy dictated their moves. Serving as counterpoints to some of the Cervantes's works presented in table 1, I list my findings from various archives in Seville, Spain:

1. Gaspar de Arguijo (1532–94) and his son, Juan (1567–1622), were influential and powerful merchants and *regidores* who made their fortunes from the African slave trade in the Canary Islands, Cape Verde, Honduras, and the Americas. A famed poet during Cervantes's time, Juan de Arguijo ran an intellectual literary circle out of his home. It is believed that Cervantes possibly attended these meetings. He mentions Juan de Arguijo in *Viaje del Parnaso* (II, vv. 352–57).
2. Francisco de Aldana (1537–78) was lauded by Cervantes as "El Divino" in the pastoral novel *La Galatea* (1585). In "Poema XXIV" Aldana affirms and boasts the potency of his enslaved Mandinga wet nurse's breast milk.
3. Miguel Cid (1550–1615) stipulated in his will in 1634 that he owned enslaved persons in his household, estimated at 15,000 *ducados*,

in addition to silverware and other pieces of furniture. Cervantes briefly mentions Cid in *Viaje del Parnaso* (II, vv. 46–48).

4. Felipe Godínez (1582–1659), dramaturge and author of *San Mateo en Etiopía* and *San Sebastián y la reina Esther*, left an indelible imprint on Cervantes, who recognizes his skill in *Viaje del Parnaso* (II, vv. 31–34).

In closing, *Cervantes Blackness* has allowed, compelled, and energized me to ground and recenter myself through cultural and literary criticism. Inspired by Biko Mandela Gray's method of "sitting-with," such a feeling in *Cervantine Blackness* has aspired to make the methodological commitment of sitting with—caring for, gathering, and tracking—Cervantes's and his contemporaries' engagement with blackness that may rock us to our core.[32] As I vibe with Langston Hughes, I invite you to wonder with me as I wander.

MEDITATION I

CERVANTINE BLACKNESS

Cervantine Blackness comes to life in tumultuous times, as I have reckoned with two global pandemics (antiblack violence and COVID-19), climate catastrophe, the aftermath of an attempted coup d'état of the US government by white domestic terrorists on January 6, 2021, and Vladimir Putin's war in the sovereign nation of Ukraine. Before the COVID-19 global pandemic, I had been living abroad in Granada, Spain, where I had finally convinced myself to *dare* to write a new book on the literary enterprise of Miguel de Cervantes and his depiction of sub-Saharan African blackness. (Initially, however, I had envisioned this project to amount only to a journal article.) I was living in the thick of genocide, pandemics, and wars, while simultaneously coping with their maddening and uncertain outcomes on our environment—evocative of the Four Horsemen of the Apocalypse from the Book of Revelation. Social unrest and organized protests had ignited across all corners of the globe. In the words of Malcolm X on December 1, 1963, "The chickens [have come] home to roost."[1] That same year of that wintery month, on December 20, 1963, James Baldwin prophetically reiterated in his essay "A Talk to Teachers," in the *Saturday Review*, "Let's begin by saying that we are living through a very dangerous time. Everyone in this room is in one way or another aware of that. We are in a revolutionary situation, no matter how unpopular that word has become in this country. The society in which we live is desperately minced . . . from within."[2] The genesis of the book you consume originates out of a revolutionary situation. For some, quiet as it's kept, the content and position of this book may be too bellicose and political. For some it may embody too much controversy and contain too many revolutionary ideas that might desperately mince or tug at the ideological sentiments of its audience. The polemical nature and political character of *Cervantine Blackness* doesn't entertain the sordid or the ugly. Instead, the work herein seeks to mobilize Cervantes in relation to how readers of various constituencies and generations relate our present era to early modernity.

That said, the origin story of *Cervantine Blackness* began on a cool summer day on June 19, 2020—historic and symbolic for many reasons, specifically because it commemorates the end of slavery in the United States—when a group of predominantly nonwhite protesters, exercising their right to unite and speak out against the murder of George Floyd, defaced several statues in San Francisco's Golden Gate Park, including the Miguel de Cervantes Memorial, sculpted by the Uruguayan-born American Joseph "Jo" Jacinto Mora (1876–1947).

Social media networks went viral. Journalists and public intellectuals from Spain and North America surely had their say on the controversy. In *ABC*, Spain's conservative-leaning newspaper, for example, more than two dozen articles devoted to the subject appeared since the act of vandalism. Cultural institutions such as the Royal Academy of History, the Cervantes Institute, and the Hispanic Institute have also done their bit, with the latter body launching an entire pro-Hispanic advertising campaign (with its hashtag *#RespectHispanicHeritage*), demanding the utmost respect for the Hispanic legacy in the United States. The Spanish government also joined the debate, with public complaints launched from the Spanish Embassy as well as the Ministry of Culture's José Manuel Rodríguez Uribes, who on Twitter referred to the attack as "incomprehensible," causing him much "pain and pity."[3] Rodríguez Uribes's tweet also caught the attention of the US ambassador to Mexico, Ken Salazar, who called the incident a regrettable "scandal" that could have been avoided if local- and state-level officials would have correctly intervened.[4]

As aestheticized in figure 3, our global society's cancel culture—most effectively expressed in the Spanish verb *tachar* (to cross out, to strike out), which was rendered visible through red spray paint and the appellative "bastard"—reared its head, demanding our societal critique of the legacies of Eurocentrism and Spanish colonialism in the wake of antiblackness and systematic inequality. While I do not wish to cancel or strike out Cervantes and his worldwide fandom and legacy, my purpose moving forward in linking the politically charged commentaries on the defaced statue with this book's

Fig. 3. Bronze bust of Cervantes, 2020. Golden Gate Park, San Francisco.

overarching concerns speaks to the ways in which the Western literary canon and its male authorship—and even more so literary titans like Cervantes and his contemporaries of the so-called Spanish Golden Age—have become memorialized and monumentalized in academic departments, popular culture, the arts, and so on.[5]

Uninspired by and dissatisfied with both conservative and progressive public responses to the so-called defiled bronze and stone monument of Cervantes, my academic coconspirator, Chad Leahy, and I deemed it necessary to intervene collaboratively on the topic. On July 3, 2020, we published an op-ed essay in the online venue *Ctxt: Contexto y acción*, titled "Cervantes y la materia de las vidas negras."[6] We opined that those previous conversations about the incident had failed to mention, let alone nuance, Cervantes's subversive critique and direct questioning of the sub-Saharan African experience in the broader Spanish imperial context. I urge my readers to recognize that, although rarely spoken of—a thematic lacuna that this book addresses and fills—there is no shortage of black histories and black lives with whom Cervantes contends. The cultural, embodied, and linguistic blackness of the writer's black subjects do, in fact, exist and matter, thus forcing us to reconsider in what sense their lives possess an inherent value within the author's literary corpus.

But let's not idolize Cervantes too much! Both popular and scholarly audiences have inherited the aestheticized reading practice of idolizing the literary bastion through the lasting consequences of German Romantic approaches to the novel. Anthony Close's classic *The Romantic Approach to "Don Quixote"* (1978) critiques and explains the construction of the romanticization of Cervantes with which I take issue. What gives me pause about such sentiments manifests in the cultural and intellectual idealisms and politics of Cervantes's magnitude, value, and worth. These sentiments code, color, and shade what's deemed *appropriate* and *inappropriate* as bodies of analysis. I argue that the woeful neglect of the inclusion of blackness falls into this category—and I would venture to include theoretical approaches and fields of critical inquiry such as queer studies and trans studies too.[7] In hopes of propelling forward Cervantes studies, Rebeca Rubio's essay "Cervantes racial: Humanidad, identidad, y libertad a la luz de un reparto diverso," for instance, jettisons romantic aesthetics and notions about Cervantes that have tendentiously overlooked the salient roles that color-blind casting, political activism, and racialized blackness have played in Spain's theater companies, such as the Festival de Almagro, Joven Compañía Nacional de Teatro Clásico, and Teatro de La Comedia de Madrid. Rubio's important work invites its readership to pay closer attention to the ways in which Spain's international festivals and its public theaters have started to tackle, albeit slowly, the ever-present themes of colonialism, marginalization, racism, and slavery in the entertainment industries.[8]

I view the tagging of the Cervantes statue in San Francisco, symbolically on a Juneteenth holiday, as an attempt to dismantle our personal and societal inheritances of colonialism, Eurocentrism, and white supremacist ideologies that potentially have less to do with Cervantes and more to do with antiblack oppression, racism, and violence. As Peio H. Riaño ascertains in his tour de force page-turning work *Decapitados: Una historia contra los monumentos a racistas, esclavistas, e invasores*, "Es hora de desmonumentalizar, de reconquistar los espacios públicos con la participación de la ciudadanía y de prescindir de los símbolos que mienten y agreden, que ocultan la historia. El monumento es un acto reflejo del poder, que se impone sin preguntar y es destruido sin pedir permiso" (It's time to demonumentalize, to reconquer public spaces with the participation of its citizens and to dispense with the symbols that lie and attack—that hide history. The monument is a reflexive act of power, which is imposed without asking and is destroyed without asking permission).⁹ In accord with Riaño's *Decapitados*, historian Ana Lucia Araujo's perspective article in the *Washington Post*, "Toppling Monuments Is a Global Movement. And It Works," extends a fruitful dialogue with previous claims made by Leahy and me as well as the overarching concerns explored in this book. Araujo's insights reveal how "historical research has greatly informed the work of black and Native American activists and their allies who demanded to contextualize or remove these monuments from public sight."[10] Indicative of Araujo's perceptive observations, *Cervantine Blackness* is in many ways, too, a plea that tries to invite into its vicinity all those who wish to oppose, undermine, counter, appose, destroy, abolish, or refuse the hegemonic constraints of power. It knows, like Malcolm X did in his later, wiser years, that "the only way we'll get freedom for ourselves is to identify ourselves with every oppressed people in the world."[11]

California Dreaming, California Love: The Entity Behind the Statue

If my opening remarks on blackness, monuments, and statues frame the genesis of *Cervantine Blackness*, then this section, the aptly titled and quasi-autobiographically inflected "California Dreaming, California Love," offers a second, twinned origin story about this project: California. Not coincidently, as I mirror my opening discussion of apocalyptic climate catastrophe, genocide, global unrest, protest, and revolution, I explore the cultural and sociopolitical catalysts that make the state of California a prime site for counterculture, which created a space for defacing and toppling statues in San Francisco's Golden Gate Park. To channel this Californication, I've got buzzing in my head the bars of 2Pac Shakur and Dr. Dre's 1995 megahit "California Love":

> Now let me welcome everybody to the wild, wild west
> A state that's untouchable like Elliot Ness
> The track hits ya' eardrum like a slug to ya' chest
> Pack a vest for your Jimmy in the city of sex
> We in that sunshine state where that bomb ass hemp be
> The state where ya never find a dance floor empty
> And pimps be on a mission for them greens
> Lean mean money-makin'-machines servin' fiends
> I been in the game for ten years makin' rap tunes

> Ever since honeys was wearin' Sassoon
> Now it's '95 and they clock me and watch me
> Diamonds shinin' lookin' like I robbed Liberace
> It's all good, from Diego to tha' Bay
> Your city is tha' bomb if your city makin' pay
> Throw up a finger if ya feel the same way
> Dre puttin' it down for
> Californ-I-a.[12]

I grew up in the nineties, so these funky and hypnotic verses riff off and vibe with my personal connection to and relationship with California. I was born in the City of Angels (aka Los Angeles), visited there and the Bay Area often as a teenager and young adult from Seattle, and returned to the river delta region of the Davis-Sacramento metropolitan area later as an adult. Perhaps confusing, distasteful, and jarring to some readers, the tenability and utility of these California-derived epigraphs—ripe with asymmetrical and illogical disquisition—musicalize the sonority of the popular culture and media that rivets the autobiographical personal accounts that have inspired and shaped this book.[13]

I drafted, wrote, and rewrote much of this meditation when I lived in Sacramento, California, from July 2021 to July 2022. Over this one-year span of time, I learned that to adequately attend to and grasp my self-derived queries—"Who is the Cervantes of the statue?"; "Why California?"; "What's so unique to the state's modern history that informs its early modern past?"—we must discuss and trace the public history of California and the moments of tensity that ensued on June 19, 2020, in San Francisco. As a point of departure for answering these questions, let's reflect on the writings of the fifth-generation Californian—born in Sacramento in 1934—Joan Didion. *Slouching Toward Bethlehem* (1968), her first collection of nonfiction, captures most vividly my ideation of the revolutionary angst and social unrest emblematic of the event inaugurating the defaced statues of Cervantes and other important figures of public California history. Didion reports what I identify as representative of the commotion and protest that had awakened in San Francisco's Golden Gate Park: "San Francisco was where the social hemorrhaging was showing up. San Francisco was where the missing children were gathering and calling themselves 'hippies.' When I first went to San Francisco in that cold late spring of 1967, I did not even know what I wanted to find out, and so I just stayed around awhile and made new friends."[14] Didion's use of "social hemorrhaging" suggests that what was going on in Haight-Ashbury demonstrated symptoms of some sort of national unraveling. In this regard, I venture to insist that Didion's terminology—one that clearly loathes, pathologizes, and sensationalizes the Beats, drug addicts, and "hippies"—creates a verbal montage of scenes from Haight-Ashbury that also references how some media outlets *and* conversative fans of Cervantes alike malign our society's counterculture and youth of the present time.

As I meditate on the defacing of the Cervantes statue in San Francisco—as a place and site geographically situated across its centuries-old conflictive and wrought histories (depending on whose version of history you privilege)—Didion's writing inspires me to further interrogate the implication of how this act of defacement was unique precisely because the accused perpetrators were primarily black and brown. As theorist Tiffany Lethabo King asserts in *The Black Shoals: Offshore Formations of Black and Native Studies*, "The Black actors of this form of symbolic violence created a cognitive dissonance for mainstream U.S. [as well as Latin American and Spanish] news audience[s] and their journalists."[15] Concerning the defacing of the statue and the worldwide rapid response it produced across the globe, critic and literary scholar Chad Leahy, in his forthcoming multitome volume of essays, *On the Uses and Abuses of Early Modern Spanish Culture*, urges us to reckon with *how* and *why* such sentiments have criminalized and denigrated the protesters.

In other public-facing venues, Chad Leahy and I have sustained this position by problematizing the ways in which the rapid global response to the defacing of the Cervantes statue has rhetorically positioned Cervantes's defamers as "vandals" or barbarians who lack reason. Such sentiment differs in no way from Joan Didion's vivid description and imagery of the "social hemorrhaging" that took place in the late 1960s in San Francisco's Haight-Ashbury. Protesters emerge as mere avatars of the so-called anti-Spanish pestilence denounced in conversative-leaning and extremist right-wing news outlets that label these black and brown actors as "vandals." In the comment sections that appear on several online sources that reported the story, commentators left a range of responses that evinced an inability to make the connection between black and brown death and black and brown rage with a graphic symptom of the Black Legend as well as a historical amnesia that refuses to recognize the exploits of the history of Spain, which ultimately have little to do with Cervantes. Along these lines, according to Spanish journalist David Alandete, "A hatred of Spain grows stronger in the United States."[16] And for Juan Manuel Cao, "Taking down our symbols is a way of discriminating against us."[17] Comments such as those reveal where the true priorities and ideological leanings of those who object to the "vandalism" of the Cervantes monument lay. The simple fact is that some are much more committed to the defense of Cervantes and Spain than to the destruction of the systems of oppression in whose interests Cervantes was sacrificed here. These last positions end up giving the protesters reason because for some authors it is very clear that Cervantes matters much more than black lives.

To echo Sanford Levinson in *Written in Stone: Public Monuments in Changing Societies*, "One might wonder if 'vandals' is quite the *mot juste* to describe those who might resist the celebration of Honecker on one of Berlin's main public venues. Just as one person's 'terrorist' is often another's 'freedom fighter,' so might one person's 'vandal' be another's 'cultural liberator.' As should be obvious, regimes in transition not only tear down monuments but build new ones."[18] The debate around who's justified in defacing the Cervantes statue tends to fail equally because it does not go far enough in considering all the possible implications of Cervantes's work to rethink social movements today. A return to Ana Lucia Araujo's powerful messages articulated in "Toppling Monuments Is a Global Movement" further elucidates and prescribes for use the importance of historical research that has greatly informed the work of black and Native American activists and their allies who demanded to contextualize or remove these monuments from public sight.[19]

Lethabo King offers a much more expansive, nuanced, and rigorous take on the "vandals" quip. Drawing from her analysis of the defacing of Columbus statues and settler colonialism in *The Black Shoals*, we can reconsider those who defaced the Cervantes statue as performers and actors who restaged the scenario of its erection and celebration. Such a restaging of the erecting ceremony "momentarily disrupts its temporal, spatial, and narrative power to disavow and unknow" the ongoing violence of conquest, Western hegemony, and Eurocentric ideals that defenders of the statue wish to maintain. I find it productive to explore how the act of defacing or bloodying—as visualized in figure 3 by the red spray paint delineating the Spanish verb *tachar*—the Cervantes statue in 2020, comparable to cases of defacing Columbus statues in 2015 and thereafter, might short-circuit the idea that conquest and the snobbery of privileging—*and romanticizing*—literary canons and national authors constitutes a past sin committed for the greater good. As Lethabo King explicates, "The presumably Black [and Brown] actors, or agents acting in the name of Black life, deface [Cervantes], as well as open up the possibility of contending with the ongoing violence of conquest [and the canon of Spanish literature]."[20] In a similar fashion, the agents and actors of social protest described by King align with literary critic and cultural historian of the long nineteenth century Xine Yao and her theorization of *disaffection* and the unfinished business of sentimentality. Yao's powerful work, *Disaffected*, gestures toward "the legacies of [feeling and unfeeling] for political recognition in the fantasies of justice in the present-day American culture of sentiment for racialized immigrants performing citizenship and the defiance of movements like Black Lives Matter. The black and brown activists, in their discontent, radicalized a critical dissatisfaction with white sentimentality: they quite frankly disregarded white feelings, white tears, and white fragility." Congruous to the disaffected ambivalence, critical dissatisfaction, and discontent fomented by social media critics and writers like Robert Jones Jr. (known as the "Son of Baldwin"), Yao illuminates for us how the descendants of the dispossessed and the enslaved couldn't have—nor would have—flinched nor batted an eye at defacing and toppling statues commemorating the white man: the rejection of the social contract of sympathy.[21]

To propel our analysis forward, let's consider, for instance, the public exorcism performed by San Francisco's archbishop Salvatore Cordileone. The purpose of Cordileone's exorcism sought to cleanse spiritually and restitute culturally the purported "sacred" lands where the statue of the eighteenth-century Spanish Franciscan friar Junípero Serra y Ferrer had been toppled days after the tagging of the Cervantes monument. In 2015 Pope Francis canonized Serra, who participated fully in the colonization, dispossession, and enslavement of the indigenous populations in what we now call the "Bay Area" of California.[22] Coterminous with the symbolic defacing of the Cervantes statue, Archbishop Cordileone proclaimed in his public exorcism that "evil has made itself present here." He pitched and proselytized to his supporters that the "act of sacrilege" instigated at the park was "an act of the Evil One." The priest ended his exorcism by stating that he felt "a great wound in [his] soul" from the "horrendous acts of blasphemy and the disparaging of the memory of Serra."[23]

Cordileone's episodic exorcism reenacts and repurposes Didion's "social hemorrhaging" concept. I read them both as sinister. The *Oxford English Dictionary*'s entry on "exorcism," and more effectively its definition of the verb "exorcize," instrumentalizes, invokes, and weaponizes the call to expel spaces of perceived "Evil Ones" and "presences." I see two competing exorcisms operating at once: Father Salvatore Cordileone's white supremacy as exorcism and disenfranchised and disposed communities (i.e., across intersecting lived experiences of access, class, gender, ethnicity, mental health, race, and sexuality) protesting (and defacing and toppling statues) as functioning as an exorcism against white supremacy. The topic of the exorcism of monuments, spaces, and statues—societal, spiritual, political—inculcates for us the urgent need to address the ways in which monuments, spaces, and statues speak back to us (during *and* after the perceived evil presence has been removed). As I've asked at the onset of this meditation about the entity (or Cervantes) behind the defaced statue, I remain fascinated with and struck by how art, music, and popular culture over the centuries have compelled us to examine entities carved out of and etched in stone. In 2007 the "Blink" episode from the British science fiction TV series *Doctor Who* invites us to explore the possibilities of statues possessing more life than the actual events and humans that interact with them. In the episode a time-traveling alien trapped in 1969 communicates with the character Sally Sparrow to prevent the Weeping Angels statues from taking control of the TARDIS. Sparrow and her best friend's brother, Larry Nightingale, must unravel a set of cryptic clues sent through time by the marooned doctor, left in DVD Easter eggs. What stands out are references to the petrified Weeping Angels as living beings that are "quantum locked" and "frozen into rock" but move when we (humans) blink. We're instructed, "Don't blink!"[24]

Let's ruminate some more on the symbolic power of statues who come alive before our eyes and speak to us. The play *El burlador de Sevilla* (*The Trickster of Seville*) and the commendatore scene from Mozart's opera *Don Giovanni*, K. 527, serve as two prime examples. In scene 3 of the opera, the brash, promiscuous noble (also known as Don Juan) wanders into a graveyard, where he is reunited with his servant, Leporello. Don Giovanni brags that he took advantage of his disguise to try to seduce one of Leporello's girlfriends. A voice comes from one of the graveyard's statues, warning Don Giovanni that "his laughter will not last beyond sunrise." It's a statue of a commendatore, bearing the eerie inscription, "Here am I waiting for revenge against the scoundrel who killed me." Leporello trembles, but Don Giovanni arrogantly taunts the ghost, inviting him to dinner (in the duet, "O statua gentillisima"). The phantom's arrival is announced with an ominous knock on the door. The commendatore offers Don Giovanni one last chance to repent. When Don Giovanni refuses, he is surrounded by demons and carried away to hell. A final ensemble contains the moral "Questo è il fin di chi fa mal, e de' perfidi la morte alla vita è sempre ugual" (Such is the end of the evildoer: the death of a sinner always reflects his life).[25]

The petrified have ghosts. Those specters lurk and make their presence known on grounds the living inhabit. As depicted in figures 3 and 4, each invites us to evaluate our dialogic engagement and performative interaction with stoned objects. Whether instantiated by an individual, a group of friends, or a

Fig. 4. Alexandre-Évariste Fragonard, *Don Giovanni Confronting the Stone Guest*, circa 1830–35. Oil on canvas, 41 × 32 cm. Musée des Beaux-Arts de Strasbourg.

united front, the art of defacing memorials and monuments—as well as the vocalized protest that reverberates around that aestheticized and performative act—communicates a larger symbolic intentionality and meaning for the call in and of itself. Keeping in mind the magisterial work of performance studies scholar Joseph Roach on effigies, in *Cities of the Dead: Circum-Atlantic Performance*, I cannot help but wonder who Cervantes would have dinner with. What would he have done in the turn of events that transpired on June 19, 2020? Could it be that once a monument or statue disappears, falls, or goes away, the conversation ceases? What now? Where do we go from there? In sum this section has tasked us with the burden of the ghostly remains of phantoms (a topic to which I'll return in the pages ahead). Phantoms—especially when they speak—reap what we sow in the living world as well as what has been sown across time, which is never linear in a hegemonic, Western sense. There are no easy, quick-fix, à la carte answers to any of the questions I've posed. Arriving at sincere answers coalesces in a joint effort within and outside of academe and public history. I implore my readers to revel in these analogues so that we can reconstruct our reception of not only the defaced Cervantes statue but all who were destined for a similar fate.

Serpentine Blackness and Its Liquid Potential

Black people, like me, aren't supposed to write about Cervantes. As evident in Toni Morrison's words, "It was the right thing to do, but she had to do it," I qualify this section's first sentence by taking inspiration from the borrowed line that Morrison uses to summarize Sethe's consequential action from *Beloved*: the attempt to kill her three young children rather than see them returned to the horrors of slavery, an unsanctioned sanctified act that succeeds with one child, the middle daughter. Morrison's chiasmus expresses the unresolved and unresolvable matter of ethics, the impossibility of Sethe being able to orient herself rightly in an antiblack world.[26] My opening assertion calls out and identifies the machinations of antiblackness operatives in the world of Cervantine studies. In this sense I agree with Francisco Zamora Loboch's assessment that Cervantes's writings execute antiracist principles. As such, in this context, I therefore believe that antiblackness has nothing at all to do with the historical and imagined effigies of Miguel de Cervantes. I don't consider him to be antiblack. I am of the conviction, however, that certain factions of Cervantes scholars—and their respective schools of thought—perpetuate antiblackness insofar as that blackness and the black people who embody it remain insignificant and nonrelational to them.

Speaking from personal experience, my opening claim—black people, like me, aren't supposed to write about Cervantes—not only acknowledges but combats the animus of racial affect and affective violence. What I'm communicating here has nothing to do with mere identity politics or a narcissistic lament. Ethically, to recapitulate a Morrisonian ethics, this is about rectifying and righting systematic practices of exclusion, elitism, gatekeeping, and antiblack racism. This bears no difference from the fed-up and incensed activists and actors who defaced and toppled monuments in San Francisco's Golden Gate Park. Another assessment of the issue, to cite philosopher and political theorist Joshua Myers in *Of Black Study*, "It is the gates that suffocate the life out of us. It is that gates that suppress our desires, assaults our capacities to evacuate the lies out of us. . . . The gates have enforced the logics of coloniality and state power. It is the settler and the police that guard these gates. Who then teach us their knowledges. Only they call themselves scholars."[27] Myers's insights activate my contention that black people, like me, aren't supposed to write about Cervantes in critical, impactful, and politically charged ways.

While the two previous sections unveil the genesis of *Cervantine Blackness*, this new section, intentionally placed and purposefully titled "Serpentine

Blackness and Its Liquid Potential," announces itself by simply putting it out there: it's about damn time early modernists working on Spain and its vast transoceanic empire situate Cervantes and blackness in conversation with each other in alternative ways. At this juncture I pick up where this book's prologue left off: an invitation to toggle imaginatively and theoretically between "Cervantine" and "blackness." Herein I substitute "Cervantine" with "serpentine." As such, I proceed with an important question that drives this project: Why has it taken so long, until the twenty-first century, for there to exist a book dedicated solely to a sustained critical examination of sub-Saharan African blackness in the works of Miguel de Cervantes? Surprisingly to date, in book form, no scholar has analyzed fully or illuminated sufficiently black being, culture, feeling, and life in the works of Cervantes and his contemporaries. I believe that it has taken so long because, as Jennifer L. Morgan so cogently illumines in *Reckoning with Slavery: Gender, Kinship, and Capitalism in the Early Black Atlantic*, "Writing the history of Black people, particularly in the early modern period, continues to be a struggle against the disciplining forces of knowledge production and the claim that Africa is a place without history." "The long-standing accusation that," she adds, "Africans have no legible past is older than Georg Wilhelm Friedrich Hegel and as contemporary as the hundreds of lives lost to the Mediterranean Sea as North African refugees desperately tried to enter Italy [and the Iberian Peninsula] in recent years."[28] To that end Bennett buttresses Morgan's illumination and my point by declaring that "Western theorists of power—philosophical, historical, sociological, cultural, and popular—have systematically eschewed any engagement with the transformation of the African into a colonized native or slave.... By ignoring slavery in their formulations of modern power, Western theorists display a profound methodologically conventionality on the subject configured around indifference and silence."[29]

What then happens when we recreate the existence and meaning of sub-Saharan African blackness (not antiblackness) in Cervantes's Spain through close readings that galvanize imaginative, radical, and transformative instantiations of an interdisciplinary examination of the capacious contours of racialized blackness during the so-called age of Cervantes and in present-day Cervantine literary criticism? This framework is not new, and I join the theoretical traditions of black feminists and queer people of color who understood their projects would reverberate beyond the strictures of traditional academic or institutional structures.[30]

Cervantine Blackness constitutes a body of literary criticism that extends Morrison's conviction that the white literary canon is always haunted by a black presence. This form of Morrisonian thought intersects with Ntozake Shange's remark that, "as black people, we exist metaphorically and literally as the underside, the underclass. We are the unconscious of the West world. If this is in fact true, then where do we go? Where are our dreams? Where is our pain? Where do we heal?"[31] The conceptual "white literary canon" and "underside [and] underclass" I identify here is that of Miguel de Cervantes and early modern Spanish literature more broadly. In the age of Cervantes and his contemporaries (Luis de Góngora, Lope de Vega, Francisco de Quevedo, Luis Quiñones de Benavente, and María de Zayas y Sotomayor, during the reigns of Felipe II, Felipe III, and Felipe IV), black Africans and their descendants (enslaved and free) ate, breathed, created, cried, danced, died, fenced, just made do, labored, laughed, lived, made love, planted, prayed, renounced, revolted, screamed, shouted, starved, studied, suffered, swam, traveled, wrote, and much more across the Iberian Peninsula and its colonial outposts and viceroyalties. We owe thanks to a wide array of sources, ranging from baptismal records, bills of sale, freedom documents, inquisition cases, testimonies, and wills from the sixteenth and seventeenth centuries to a slew of demographic sources that aggregate data from census reports that have pinned down African and African-diasporic communities. Most recently, for example, works such as *Trata atlántica y esclavitud en Sevilla (c.1500–1650)* and *The Iberian World, 1450–1820* calculate Seville's enslaved sub-Saharan population to have averaged 11 percent.[32] Data and numbers aside, my contemplation of the cycles of life and death that absorbed, claimed, and consumed both enslaved and free black communities remains central to any understanding of Cervantes's literary corpus and should not be permitted to hover at the margins of scholarly literary criticism.

The stakes of my refusal to not allow blackness to hover at the margins of Cervantine criticism align with legal scholar Jesús Rodríguez-Velasco's titanic theorization of the phenomenon *microliteraturas*. Rodríguez-Velasco compels me to see how

> *Microliteratura* es una forma de producción de la cultura escrita. También es su materialidad. Y es también un actividad por parte de quienes la producen. Una actividad febril, levemente enloquecida. El estudio de la microliteratura llama al estudio de objetos, de aspectos materiales, de círculos de trabajo y de formas de la creación de redes de comunicación. El estudio de las microliteraturas llama la atención sobre su actividad más prominente: *pensar con*. Pensar algo, lo que sea, en relación con aquello que se ofrece a la lectura

y a la crítica. Pensar con expresiones, conceptos, idea, imágenes, metáforas. Pensar con, no solamente interpretar.

[*Microliterature* is a form of the production of written culture. It is also your materiality. And it is also an activity on the part of those who produce it. A feverish activity, slightly mad. The study of microliterature calls for the study of objects, material aspects, work circles, and ways of creating communication networks. The study of microliteratures draws attention to its most prominent activity: thinking with. Think something, whatever, in relation to what is offered for reading and criticism. Thinking with expressions, concepts, ideas, images, metaphors. Think with, not just interpret.][33]

To construct his microliteraturas archive, Rodríguez-Velasco's insertion of the word *estudio*—perceptively conceptualized as the ethical and moral constitution of "study" or the "studying of"—characterizes and corroborates the scholarly activity and tenor of the various ways in which Cervantine studies and its adjacent early modern Spanish literary criticism more broadly have insufficiently dealt with blackness. In this regard my interventions in *Cervantine Blackness* cozily think with and sit with Rodríguez-Velasco's thoughts. In doing so, as I think with the gravitas of his microliteraturas terminology, I cannot help but emphasize the broader scholarly implications of how Cervantine studies in academe has siloed blackness in Cervantes's literary production, as if it were a corrupted microliteratura or an illegible gloss in and of itself.

Likewise, if Rodríguez-Velasco's paradigmatic influence conveys my sentiments about the epistemic and systemic maneuvering and machinations of isolating—or glossing over—the study of racialized diasporic blackness in Cervantes's oeuvre, then it also behooves us to link the critic's theory of microliteraturas to both established and new bodies of critical thought in critical black studies. Rodríguez-Velasco's microliteraturas framework constellates a cornucopia of theoretical possibilities. In concert with Elizabeth Alexander, Toni Morrison, and Ntozake Shange, for example, the goal of *Cervantine Blackness*, as a body of literary criticism and political commentary, aims to reveal how Cervantes's and his contemporaries' texts move beyond ethnoracial meanings of blackness. Once we resist the proclivity toward and seduction of situating Cervantes's and his contemporaries' constructions of blackness *only* within a fixed ethnoracial logic that presupposes the racialized blackness of black people as (w)holely abject, null, and static, can we then think with and *sit with* a Morrisonian politic of (re)building better-nuanced narratives about blackness—fictional or otherwise—by yanking the periphery and the margins to the center of our knowledge-making efforts.

In this book I want to put on the table a centering of blackness that *decenters* the primacy of antiblackness and black suffering that both general and scholarly readerships exalt and fetishize. My decentering of this kind of formulation of blackness—diasporic or otherwise—performs a snakelike dance that coils around, slithers across, and engulfs the sanctity of whiteness. In one sense this serpentine activity creates, for both blackness and Cervantine studies, the progress, rebirth, and rejuvenation of ideas and knowledge, like the ouroboros and the varieties of serpent gods and entities originating in West and Central Africa and proliferating in the Black Atlantic. Riffing off "Cervantine," my channeling of serpentine metaphors also problematizes the various ways in which academe—by way of hierarchies of epistemological formations and the schools of thought to which they cohere—eats itself and inhibits room for regeneration (see fig. 2). As I've proposed elsewhere, either in my public lectures, op-ed pieces, or scholarly publications, the centering and decentering of black people is a political act when it comes to early modern literary criticism.[34]

Beyond the dichotomous confluences of centering and decentering interventions and its stakes, I'm indebted to the critical thought and poesis of Elizabeth Alexander in *The Black Interior*. Following Alexander, I too am interested in black people's creativity as a technique for undergirding, with nuance, the artistic and interpretive exercise of centering blackness. As an inflection of Saidiya Hartman's critical fabulation and wayward reading practices, I highlight Alexander's call for us—black people, in particular—to imagine a racial future in the "black interior," where we are constrained to imagine, outside of the parameters of how we are seen by white people in the West. "The black interior," as Alexander puts it, "is not an inscrutable zone, nor colonial fantasy. Rather, [she] sees it as inner space in which black artists have found selves that go far, far beyond the limited expectations and definitions of what black is, isn't or should be."[35] As a kind of political intervention with high stakes—not the institutional relationship between state or state-sanctioned entities but rather the machinations and maneuverings of communities, constituencies, and individuals in relationship to power—*Cervantine Blackness* mobilizes and illuminates the complex history and culture of blackness produced during the age of Cervantes.

This is a reminder: my work throughout *Cervantine Blackness* recognizes black queer and black trans aesthetics, popular culture, and vernacular speech acts.

I'd like to privilege and showcase black queer and trans expressivity and language, extracted from Beyoncé's seventh studio album, *Renaissance*, and vocalized by the celebrity Ts Madison's sonic cameo in the album's track 2, titled "Cozy": "I'm dark brown, dark skin, light skin, beige Fluorescent beige, bitch, I'm black."[36] The importance behind this sonic induction resonates with the black (queer and trans) life and drama that I've envisioned for my Cervantineblackness paradigm. I remind you, my dear reader, that what I'm doing here is intentional, thereby seeking to free (up) stagnant assumptions about and understandings of diasporic blackness—most notably along the lines of color, space, and time—that both Beyoncé and Ts Madison communicate to us. In the comfort and juiciness of blackness and its queer and trans coziness, this track buzzes and jives well with theorist Jared Sexton's configuration of blackness. Listen to his take on the matter:

> As a matter of luminescence, black is a noncolor and white is the combined appearance of the entire visible spectrum. As a matter of pigmentation, though, white is the absence of color and black is the consummation of all colors. Thinking the world with black as the field and frame of reference not only decenters white as that mythic purity from which one deviates or falls short; it also opens a space of interrogation regarding the entire spectrum of color. Who or what is black? Who or what can inhabit it, embody it, understand it, enjoy it, or represent it? And who or what, if anything, is beyond it? With black, we can think about the production of color and noncolor as processes that are at once physio-optical and sociopolitical, as undoubtedly historical as they are historically irreducible, processes wherein we can question the material and symbolic consequences of the meanings ascribed not only to the various colors of the spectrum but also to the very idea of a color spectrum.

Liquid blackness, or the ideation of blackness as liquid, functions as a meaningful conceptual framework and theoretical strategy for analyzing blackness in Cervantes's works. Sexton reminds us that the experience of blackness—either chromatic, somatic, or temporal—is "at once scientific and philosophical [and] a matter of aesthetics and ethics, knowledge and disbelief, [and] fact and fantasy."[37] What is more, my application of liquid blackness also gestures my thinking about blackness toward Tavia Nyong'o's claim that "blackness is already queer," a topic that I'll take up in my analysis of the black eunuch Luis from Cervantes's *El celoso extremeño* (1613) in meditation 3. Like Nyong'o, I also clarify and insist that blackness is not queer "as an identity, role, or even community, but queer as a vector transecting the social diagram of the political, erotic, and racial given."[38] As such, in recognition of Cathy Cohen's pioneering essay "Punks, Bulldaggers, and Welfare Queens," queerness is also structural marginalization according to race, class, and ability that produces normative and deviant types of gender and sexuality.[39]

On Ghostly Remains, Hauntings, and Necromancy: I Am Not Your *Negro*

I'll let you in on a secret: Cervantes's figures in black and the spaces they inhabit have haunted me for many years. *Cervantine Blackness* extends Toni Morrison's conviction that the white literary canon is always haunted by a black spectral presence. As I reprise Morrison's charge in her landmark treatise *Playing in the Dark: Whiteness and the Literary Imagination*, the so-called white literary canon I identify here is that of Cervantes, his contemporaries, and early modern Spanish literary criticism. As a black writing subject and the author of this book, I begin to unpack my ideation of hauntings and ghosts by citing Avery F. Gordon's *Ghostly Matters: Haunting and the Sociological Imagination*. *Ghostly Matters* helps concretize and illuminate for us the ways in which Morrison "saw slavery living in the aftermath of its abolition [and how] she saw the anonymous, the phantom subjects of history, and imagined their talk, feelings, and habits, in all their concreteness and contradictions." Phenomenologically, the language and experiential modality of haunting, as I recapitulate Gordon's scholarship in *Ghostly Matters*, "describe those singular yet repetitive instances" when the "blind spot" of the underimagined and undertheorized specter of sub-Saharan African blackness "comes into view." "These specters or ghosts appear," Gordon explicates, "when the trouble they represent and symptomize is no longer being contained or repressed or blocked from view."[40] Since the first time I had ever encountered Cervantes's figures in black, as an undergraduate in the early 2000s, to having closely examined them with undergraduates and graduate students whom I've taught in recent years, Cervantes's assortment of references to blackness—aesthetic, cultural, embodied, geographic, imagined, linguistic, spatial—within and outside of the *Quixote*, have always enchanted me to expose the worlds in which they inhabit to colleagues, friends, strangers, and students alike. By filling this lacuna and performing this necessary task, *Cervantine Blackness* centers the overlooked, underexamined, underimagined, and undertheorized—yet queer and quixotic in how they flicker and flutter, disintegrating before our eyes—motley crew of black events, black people, black spaces, and black things in Cervantes's oeuvre.

Another critical edge, or valence, that grounds *Cervantine Blackness* returns to my signature and singular work on necromancy. The concept of necromancy has provided a pathway toward capturing and depicting Iberian blackness in all its fluidity and richness. As such, my understanding of blackness, as it stands before the Enlightenment (and those wrestling with that tradition), departs from *necro* prefixtures—such as necrocapitalism, Achille Mbembe's "necropolitics," or Orlando Patterson's "social death"—that privilege the business of death where civic and social norms remain in place outside the confines of law that allow forms of subjugation to occur, such as torture and other forms of destruction.[41] To quote the little white girl from Toni Morrison's *Beloved*, Amy Denver, "Anything dead coming back to life hurts." To be clear, I harbor no discord with any of these brilliant historical, literary, and theoretical formations. However, pain and pessimism aren't always one-sided, nor should they be simplified as such. In my view the business of death in which I partake belongs to necromancy. If, according to the *Oxford English Dictionary*, the word necromancy embodies "the art of predicting the future by supposed communication with the dead; (more generally) divination, sorcery, witchcraft, enchantment," then I, as the necromancer, aim to resurrect the memory of early modern Iberian blackness by placing Cervantine studies in dialogue with critical black studies.[42]

Opponents to and skeptics of the kind of necromantic work that I'm marshaling herein may analogize this approach and method to what we find in Deuteronomy 18: "No one shall be found among you who ... practices divination, or is a soothsayer, or an augur, or a sorcerer, or one who casts spells, or who consults ghosts or spirits, or who seeks oracles from the dead."[43] This applies as well to the Witch of Endor, whom, according to the Hebrew Bible in 1 Samuel, King Saul consulted to summon the spirit of the prophet Samuel.[44] Abhorrent or not, my necromantic exercise stands as an integral source to my framing and study of early modern Iberian blackness. As such, it empowers me to give voice to the varieties of West and Central African survivals alive and operative in the cultural and literary worlds of Cervantes and his contemporaries. Alive and rebellious in these early modern worlds, there exist—and existed—the execution, manifestation, and representation of West and Central African cosmographies, cosmologies, dances and songs, divination sciences, language and speech, and religious and spiritual practices that illuminate for us constellations of African and African diasporic epistemologies and phenomenologies that have been bureaucratically filtered, silenced, and regularized in archives and scholarly criticism across space and time.

I am not your *negro*. In closing my discussion on ghostly matters, hauntings, and necromancy, I'd like to revisit this book's prologue, "The Scramble for Blackness." In it I alert my readers to the trendy uptick and expeditious interest in the study of blackness and black people that have overrun the field of early modern Spanish literary studies. Polemically, I identify this peaked awareness, concern, and curiosity with the 2019 publication of my first book *Staging* Habla de Negros. Since its release I've come to realize that, in uncanny ways, the grievances expressed in the prologue cannot be disentangled from the ways in which I've served as the negro—or ghostwriter—for many.[45] Ranging from the unethical disregard of ethical citation politics to the appropriation of my fervent appeal to black agency and the celebration of black optimism, the unintentional ghostwriting in which I've dished out to a community of scholars—some of whom, perhaps, may be reading these lines—has challenged me, inspired me, and invigorated me to chart and dig for new pathways of sitting with early modern Iberian blackness. That first iteration of my scholarly self—through my intellectual preoccupation with protecting black agency, black presence, and black resistance—proved to be fungible and profitable for those whom it benefited. This new iteration of my scholarly self in *Cervantine Blackness*—a serpentine blackness in its X-ray vision, in its fugitivity, in its sloughing, and in its rebirth as an intellectual *despojo* (healing rite of cleansing or alleviation)—charts a new evolution of what I hold dear. No more (of my) fungible blackness is expended. No more apocrypha.[46] No more literary studies of apocryphal blackness. No more erasure. No more ghostwriting. I am not your *negro*.

Coda: *Cervantine Blackness* as an Antidote or a Meditation on the State of the Field

This coda picks up where the prologue left off: an invitation to imagine with me on this utterly wayward journey. *Cervantine Blackness*—as a book, conversation, paradigm, and theory—attends to the questions in its prologue and meditations: What is the matter of blackness in the oeuvre of Cervantes? How does the study of Cervantes make black life come alive? When the op-ed essay "Cervantes y la materia de las vidas negras" went viral on July 3, 2020, Chad Leahy and I had hoped to address the complicit role departments and programs in academe, such as the infamous Departments of Spanish and Portuguese or the more nebulous Departments of Modern Languages and Literatures, have instrumentalized and weaponized antiblack discourses, environments, ideologies, and sentiments. At that time, we had asked ourselves: How do these institutional structures and units simultaneously confront *and* collude with injustice of all sorts?

I prod, Where do we go from here? As I've already mentioned, surprisingly to date, no book-length study has examined the salient role sub-Saharan African blackness has played in the writings of Miguel de Cervantes. Yet, to the contrary, a significant number of scholars have given much attention to the cultural, literary, and historical lives of Iberian Muslims, Moriscos, North Africans, and Turks in the Cervantine corpus. Since the 1980s Caribbean, European, North American, and South Asian scholars of early modern English studies, most notably experts of William Shakespeare, have laid important groundwork for examining the tenability and utility of placing critical race and postcolonial readings of blackness in conversation with early modern English cultural and literary studies. I encourage my fellow early modern Hispanists and *cervantistas* to follow suit. Taking cues from Margaret Rich Greer's 2011 *PMLA* publication "Thine and Mine: The Spanish 'Golden Age' and Early Modern Studies," *Cervantine Blackness* aims to "[collaborate] across disciplines and national boundaries."[47] Reflecting on race studies in Shakespeare and the Spanish Inquisition in light of Cervantine scholarly criticism, William Childers in *Transnational Cervantes* cogently and legitimately contends, "Scholars working on early modern Europe . . . show disappointingly little interest in the cultural modes arising on the Iberian Peninsula in the late sixteenth and seventeenth centuries."[48] In accord with and inspired by Childers's compelling insights in his award-winning *Transnational Cervantes*, I insist that the field of early modern Spanish studies needs to reckon with sub-Saharan African blackness while examining Cervantes's textual production of it. To do so isn't a fool's errand or intellectually bereft or bankrupt of provincial simplicity. Such an intervention requires scholars and students of early modern studies writ large to think more creatively and perceptively outside of the erudite confines of the banal binarism of proving grotesque animalization and negrophobic victimhood *over* one's black agency or black joy. We must, I contend, hold in suspension and in tension these two dichotomous preferences for talking about racialized blackness.

I'll repeat what I've asserted earlier in this meditation: scholarly criticism among certain factions of Cervantine studies—and its adjectival, genealogical, and institutional consolidation and footing (e.g., Instituto Cervantes, Casa Cervantes)—remains to this day extremely traditional and resistant to forward-thinking approaches to the author's body of work. Another way to read the terrain: Cervantes, as presently idolized by some *cervantistas*, on both sides of the Atlantic (and arguably worldwide), stands as a literary bastion and icon whose image should not be forcibly misread and sullied by such scholarly pursuits with which I wrestle in this book. *Cervantine Blackness*, instead, braves the scholarly and popular lore that quickly stresses ideological contortions. This project dares to address and unpack the efficacy of Cervantes's handling of sub-Saharan African blackness, precisely because the critical analytic of blackness tends to have a penumbral presence in the field. Across scholarly generations, geographies, and factions, scholars of Cervantes often think of blackness as a decorative contribution rather than integral to Cervantes's oeuvre, especially for *Don Quixote*. But if, as Georgina Dopico suggests, "*Don Quixote* playfully and starkly reminds us that behind every book is a body, and with it, a madness, real and imagined, a genealogy, authentic and forged, a history, remembered or forgotten," then how could we not finally, for once, reconfigure blackness, in its categorical capaciousness, in terms of a book-body relation that calls African and African diasporic peoples into being as subjects or objects?[49]

As Julia Domínguez records in her erudite *Quixotic Memories: Cervantes and Memory in Early Modern Spain*, "Amazingly, Cervantes himself was able to remember and accurately cite an impressive number of sources for his [*Don Quixote*]: 104 mythological, legendary, and biblical characters; 131 characters from chivalric and pastoral novels; 227 historical personages; 21 celebrated animals; 93 books; and 261 geographical places."[50] I emphatically nudge, Then how could we not remember and (re)tell this black past and its black futures in Cervantes? But let's not be idle readers here about excavating the untapped reservoir of scholarly possibilities blackness provides in Cervantes's and his contemporaries' writings. *Cervantine Blackness* embraces the important charges put forth by Childers and Greer. In its interventions this book catalogs the complex, yet also contradictory, ways in which Cervantes wrote about black Africans, their descendants, and diasporic blackness during his time.

I opened this meditation by letting you into my world of the constellation of lived experiences that birthed *Cervantine Blackness*. The genesis of this book—its intervention, irreverence, and significance—comes out of worldwide crises in the formulation of what I've dubbed "tumultuous times." In the introduction to their special issue, "Black Temporality in Times of Crisis," in *South Atlantic Quarterly*, Habiba Ibrahim and Badia Ahad compel us to see "how experiences of times of crisis at any historical period are formative of Black life." They arrest us with the following questions: "How might various aspects of temporality contribute to what is knowable about Black life and moments of crisis? How does focusing on crisis reveal the constructedness of what is frequently taken to be natural and investable? How does crisis draw us toward the precarities, but also the possibilities, of Black life?"[51] I can tell you one thing: if the protests at San Francisco's Golden Gate Park hadn't have ensued, maybe, perhaps, I wouldn't have been driven to madly write the book you consume.

Quoting W. E. B. Du Bois's 1903 *Souls of Black Folk*, by interrogating the political power of the *now*, Ibrahim and Ahad remind us that the "previous century opened in a time of crisis." To explain the "now," the two critics explain that the "answer appears to point in two distinct directions: by returning to the Black historical past, and through the quotidian imperative to 'reclaim time.'"[52] The "Black historical past" with which this book preoccupies itself is the literary repertoire of Cervantes and that of his contemporaries. In closing I urge folks to please put things back in their place. Instead of crying out in agony over the injustices committed against a bronze statue—a monumentalized effigy of Cervantes—what would happen if we cast, for a moment, the one-armed man from Lepanto? Given a choice between defending the symbolic "life" of a defaced statue *or* that of the murdered bodies of George Floyd or Breonna Taylor, where would we want to locate ourselves? And what does the answer to these questions reveal about our values and our priorities? At the same time, what if we insisted on putting in place—at the center of the narrative—black being, culture, feeling, and life that for Cervantes himself clearly matter? *Cervantine Blackness* itself forces us to recognize the centrality of the matter of Africans and African diasporic lives across time. We most certainly can—and should—position Cervantes as an imperfect figure who, in a larger social justice–oriented critique and fight, imbued life-dealing forces into the cultures, lives, feelings, and experiences of the oppressed and the subjugated. Not romanticizing Cervantes too much, I invite you to imagine with me on this utterly wayward journey.

MEDITATION 2

GRANULAR BLACKNESS AND
DON QUIXOTE

This meditation treks the lore and terrain of *Don Quixote*, a site where blackness in all its capaciousness and instability flickers before our eyes. Blackness in *Don Quixote*, like the novel's protagonist, Alonso Quijano—who becomes the character Don Quixote—occupies spaces of fabulation, fiction, and theorization that merge as one. As we've learned from formidable thinkers such as Roger Chartier, Georgina Dopico, Michel Foucault, and Jennifer L. Morgan, books, bookmaking, and bookkeeping also represent bodies that become calcified as if they were exalted, etched, and transformed into stone.[1] (After all, Cervantes's *Don Quixote* reigns as one of the most translated books in the world and has been dubbed the first modern novel, among many other accolades.) For what it's worth, Cervantes's two-part masterpiece *El ingenioso hidalgo Don Quijote de la Mancha* (1605–15) stands as a textual monument in its own accord that engineers provocative critiques and depictions of the commodification, fungibility, and plasticity of sub-Saharan African blackness to be examined herein.

To sense how my paradigmatic imperative of *Cervantine Blackness* moves throughout parts 1 and 2 of *Don Quixote*, let's begin by delving into chapter 24, from part 2. In it we meet and confront Cervantes's commentary on new forms of antiblack racism and injustice, through Don Quixote's angry comparison of the fate of old soldiers to that of freed blacks. The text states, "No es bien que se haga con ellos lo que suelen hacer los que ahorran y dan libertad a sus negros cuando ya son viejos y no pueden servir, y echándolos de casa con título de libres, los hacen esclavos de la hambre, de quien no piensan ahorrarse sino con la muerte." ("It's not right that they be treated the way blacks are treated who are emancipated and freed when they are old and can no longer serve, and are thrown out of the house and called free men, making them slaves to hunger from which only death can liberate them.")[2] Cultural critic and literary scholar Miguel Martínez confirms this reading in his seminal work *Front Lines: Soldiers' Writing in the Early Modern Hispanic World* and his philological tour de force, *Vida y sucesos de la Monja Alférez*. Illustrating Cervantes's empathy for and sympathy with black soldiers, Martínez elucidates for us that "the parallelism reveals the stark abasement of the military profession throughout the sixteenth century, but it also discloses the constitutive social tensions of military discourses—Cervantes, the veteran, knew what he was talking about. The trope of the soldier as the empire's slave seemed appropriate to emphatically protest the barely tolerable levels of bodily violence, material deprivation, social marginalization, and personal disenfranchisement endured by soldiers."[3]

I would like to uncoil Martínez's astute reading of the "trope of the soldier as the empire's slave" a bit further. Cervantes's axiomatic twinning of "enslavement" and "soldier," across the Spanish Empire, coheres to the rhetorical figure of chiasmus. More than a statement of ambivalence or equivalence, this chiasmatic (black) slave-soldier double bind operates as Cervantes's rhetorical idiom of crossing or magic, where one thing gives into and becomes another. What I'm getting at here suggests that such chiastic literary imagery becomes reiterated by Cervantes's lived experience and enslaved status as a captive in Algiers and subsequently a veteran after the Battle of Lepanto, on October 7, 1571. As José R. Cartagena Calderón points out in a recent essay on disabled and veteran soldiers of war in seventeenth-century Spain, "Tinges of the autobiographical [are] underlying this episode."[4] Writing in his old age and speaking from the keen lived experience of captivity, bloodshed, and war, Cervantes speaks through the voice of an impassioned Don Quixote, who critiques the conditions of military service. As far as I'm concerned, it's crucial to frame Cervantes's lived experience as a soldier and a captive as analogues to other historical and literary references about black soldiers in early modern Iberia.

African horsemanship, for instance, exemplifies one kind of respected skill possessed by black soldiers. Black Africans across the diaspora not only found employment as soldiers in armies and as bodyguards but also, as Kate Lowe reports, served as captains in the 1520s and 1530s in the larger Mediterranean world.[5] One source of proof appears in the anonymous Flemish painting, *Chafariz d'el-Rei in the Alfama District* (1570–80). As I've explored elsewhere, the *Chafariz* portrait takes a snapshot of black life and its social history in Lisbon. In the lower right-hand side of the painting, we find a black horseman named João de Sá, the royal valet of King João III of Portugal. As depicted in the painting, João de Sá strides across the foreground of the painting on his luxuriously adorned horse, designating him as an aristocrat or noble. Sword in hand, he travels behind two black servants (holding halberds) who offer further protection. Sá's most overlooked detail is the red cross that adorns the left side of his cape. The cross corresponds with the insignia of the prestigious military Order of Santiago and identifies this otherwise anonymous figure as a knight.[6] As a knight, Sá achieved the status of noble, a rank reserved only for the highest rungs of society. The red cross on his cape publicly displays his nobility, purity of office and blood, Catholic devotion, and loyalty to the king.[7] As such, these aristocratic, chromatic, and somatic credentials situated him among the highest echelons of early modern Iberian society, thus epitomizing Christian ideals that positioned him to receive a noble title.[8] As argued by other scholars, most notably in the forthcoming article by historian Héctor Linares, João de Sá's position and rank as a noble destabilizes conventional interpretations that the diverse set of black figures represented in the *Chafariz* painting—and blacks Africans and their descendants more broadly in early modern Europe—embodied only abject, lowly categorizations.[9]

Other canonical literary examples of this sociocultural phenomenon become encoded by black swordsmen, black warriors, and the art and sport of fencing. Early textual evidence appears in the Spanish literary tradition of the seventeenth-century picaresque novel, for example, Francisco López de Úbeda's picaresque novel *La pícara Justina* (1605) and Francisco de Quevedo's *El buscón* (1626). In poetry Quevedo burlesques black and mixed-raced *mulato* swordsmen in his pimp poetry, known during the period as *jácaras* (deriving from the word *jaque*, or "pimp"). In theater the playwrights Andrés de Claramonte (in *El valiente negro en Flandes* [1620, 1638]) and Félix Lope de Vega (in *El santo negro Rosambuco* [ca. 1607] and *El prodigio de Etiopía* [1650]) dramatize fencing and martial skills as well as heroic military careers at various lengths and limits. Cervantes, writing both in prose fiction and scripts for theater, also represented fencers in the play *El rufián dichoso* (dated between 1580 and 1615) and the short story *Rinconete y Cortadillo* (1613).[10]

I open with these framings of black soldiers and their coterminous analogues to black swordsmen, black warriors, and fencers to ground and to equip this book's conceptualization of Cervantine Blackness in *Don Quixote*.

The narrativized enunciation of black soldiers and all its coefficients characterize *how* Cervantes talks about blackness in ephemeral and fleeting yet succinct ways. Unlike in other works by the author, blackness in *Don Quixote* is not sustained or unified. As such, I deem the behavior and movement of blackness in both parts of the novel as granular, hence my manufacturing of the term *granular blackness*. I characterize Cervantes's treatment of blackness as granular precisely because the author conditions, codifies, and structures blackness as alchemical, ephemeral, and historical. Cervantes granulates blackness. Throughout *Don Quixote* black events (slavery, freedom, racial mimicry), black people (Juan Latino, *manicongos*, soldiers), black things (*habla de negros*, coins, metals), and black geographies (Guinea, Ethiopia, Kongo) acquire a sand-like quality, whose particles flicker, sift, and shift, as if enclosed in an hourglass or falling freely from our hands. Granular blackness in *Don Quixote* refracts in content, context, and symbolism. Blackness's granularity will certainly escape any reader who does not read the text closely, methodically, or meticulously—even the most expert and seasoned connoisseur.

In its tracking and trekking of key moments of granular blackness, this meditation on *Don Quixote* then facilitates a paratextual analysis of granular blackness through an interdisciplinary mode of investigation that demands a theoretical application of black feminist historian Saidiya Hartman's "critical fabulation." If we remember correctly, as touched on earlier, Hartman's articulation of the wayward also ideates my understanding of critical fabulation. Following the illuminating insights of theorist Tavia Nyong'o, this essayistic case study—as well as the entire premise of this project—also gestures to the "speculative fabulation" proposed by feminist science theorist Donna Haraway.[11] Seeking and yearning for something else, something other, and something more, my literary criticism executed herein on *Don Quixote* looks to the ways the study of blackness can rearrange our perceptions of chronology, geography, time, temporality, and space. Inspired by Nyong'o's trailblazing work in *Afro-Fabulations: The Queer Drama of the Black Life*, my aim, moreover, is to speculate on how blackness moves through Cervantes's art of fiction. As Nyong'o firmly notes, "Fictions, a theory of fabulation can tell us, do not simply attach themselves to moments of idle fantasy, play, instruction, or other socially acceptable occasions of storytelling." "Fictions instead," he warns, "arise out of the indeterminacy and flux of living and dying, with life being perhaps the greatest fiction of all."[12] As touchstones for my thinking of granular blackness in Cervantes's quixotic fictions, Hartman's and Haraway's work in enacting and imagining a critical speculative poetics of fabulation allow for a transformative reading of both *Don Quixote* and blackness, a reading that ruthlessly throws into crisis the intransigent and ever-mutating antiblackness cloaked in the progressive politics that attempt to contain, misread, and mold Cervantes's construction of blackness throughout *Cervantine Blackness*.

Arms and Letters: Manicongos, Erudite Black Men

Black Africans living in continental Africa and making new lives across the diaspora emerge as historical subjects in *Don Quixote*. One method for displaying this plays out in the overarching commentary on the failures, tenability, use, and value of the arms and letters discourse that unfolds in *Don Quixote* 1.37–38. As addressed at the onset of this meditation, my attention given to black soldiers and their coterminous analogues to black swordsmen, black warriors, and fencers figures prominently in my analysis and theorization of granular blackness in *Don Quixote*. Let us consider, for instance, two poems that bookend *Don Quixote*, part 1, from 1605: the laudatory poem from "Urganda la desconocida" and the epitaph "El monicongo, académico de Argamasilla, a la sepultura de Don Quijote." I contend that Cervantes utilizes these two poetic paratexts to counter insidious controlling images of black men through a more expansive cultural and literary history of erudite African diasporic ambassadors, captains, emissaries, kings, princes, academicians, soldiers, and warriors. I bravely insert Juan Latino and rulers from the kingdom of Kongo (often referred to as manicongos) into the broader age of Cervantes.

Directing our attention to Juan Latino first, my intervention here seeks to disrupt his distorted image as the poet and educator who emerged through a process of canonization in caricature during the seventeenth century after his death, circa 1594. "Shortly after his death," as Elizabeth Wright explains, "a series of writers reimagined his upward mobility, teaching career, and interracial marriage in comic terms that reflect a solidifying colour prejudice against blacks, as well as anxieties about Granada's Muslim heritage."[13] Cervantes participates in this reimagined tradition of Juan Latino in the following way:

> Pues al cielo no le plu-
> que salieses tan ladi-
> como el negro Juan Lati-
> hablar latines rehu-

[Lest it the heavens it might discommmm
should you emerge so converrrrr
as the black Juan Latiiiii,
to speak Latins you must refuuu].[14]

For our interests these verses embody Cervantine Blackness with respect not only to Cervantes's poetic representation of Africanized Castilian (commonly referred to as *habla de negros*) but also to the legacies of erudite black men in early modern Spain. As I have mentioned in *Staging* Habla de Negros and elsewhere, poetic uses of habla-de-negros speech events were so common because of the diversity of Renaissance poetic forms, genres, subjects, and other material factors. When written down, habla-de-negros poems circulated in manuscript anthologies whose varied formats and contents reflect heterogeneous tastes, goals, and audiences. As illustrated by the previous quote, Cervantes also participates in the Renaissance Castilian cultural and literary traditions that spotlight habla-de-negros speech forms through the usage of "broken end" verses (*versos de cabo roto* in Spanish), in which he elides the unstressed last syllable of Castilian octosyllables. As Wright confirms, the voice of Juan Latino in the poem "speaks a broken Castilian." In *The Epic of Juan Latino*, Wright reminds us that "for most readers of the last four centuries, the first contact with Juan Latino has been the [previously cited] parodic poem that Cervantes inserted as a preface to his 1605 *Don Quijote*."[15] What catalyzes my reading of Cervantine Blackness in this context is the way in which Cervantes nestles his poetic reference to Juan Latino within the "Urganda la desconocida" textual frame of the "Versos preliminares" or "introductory poems." Subjunctive inflection characterizes Cervantes's preamble-like poetic verses, for they parody the author's creation of and intervention in his hoped-for and imagined advance praise for part 1 of *Don Quixote*. It is precisely because nobody would blurb or vouch for Cervantes's skill in the work at its inception—a snub, perhaps, for Cervantes—that he then likens such disrepute against him as a writer to what Juan Latino might've faced. With the chivalric romance *Amadís de Gaula* (1508), the figure of Urganda enchants as a sage sorceress. But what is more, she qualifies the adjectival and nominal wordplay of *desconocida(o)*, the "unknown" or the "outsider." Albeit reimagined through the burlesque of *versos de cabo roto* and literary tradition of chivalric romances (*los libros de caballerías*, in Spanish), through this laudatory poem and the trope of *desconocido*, I believe that Cervantes subversively promotes, recognizes, and ultimately dusts off Latino's overshadowed legacy and life as an erudite black man who once boasted a career as a poet and educator.[16]

I build on Wright's reading of Juan Latino by adding that Cervantes's poetic depiction of the poet's broken language, as rendered in the *versos de cabo roto*, operates as a racialized discourse of stuttering. In my view the trope of brokenness embodies an instantiation of the conjoined images of linguistic blackness that elicits speech impediments as a type of disability linked to newly arrived enslaved *bozal* Africans.[17] To put it plainly, Juan Latino, as an erudite Latin poet, stutters, in a poeticized habla-de-negros aesthetic, as if he were a primordial *bozal*—but certainly *not* in the same clichéd and contrived yet formulaic registers later instituted by Francisco de Quevedo in the 1631 *Libro de todas las cosas* and *Premática del tiempo* (1628–48). As I have argued elsewhere and wish to develop here, my call to link the literary representation of Africanized Iberian languages (not only Castilian but also Catalan and Portuguese) to speech impediments and stuttering owes its ideation to disability studies as a theoretical field. Scholar Michael Davidson, in *Distressing Language: Disability and the Poetics of Error*, captures the crux of my fascination. The perceived brokenness of Juan Latino's habla-de-negros speech events, as poeticized by Cervantes, aligns with the phrase *disability poetics* and its wide-ranging possibility of meanings. As an example of "distressing language," this unique Cervantine construction of habla de negros qua Juan Latino pushes me to consider more broadly the ways in which Africanized Iberian languages spoken throughout the Iberian Peninsula and the larger Mediterranean world become seen through the optic of disability, a visual schema where the totality of the social symbolic order is challenged by black "disarticulate" figures.[18]

The gaffs, delays, and verbal missteps of tongue-tied black folk—whether real-life West and Central Africans entering and exiting the Iberian Peninsula or a fictionalized Juan Latino—gift us as readers with new meaning about the affect, confusion, and duplicity of language and language varieties. In this regard I believe that Cervantes's Africanized broken-versification conduces us, ever so slightly, to draw out hidden meaning in language, the traces of social places, marginal spaces, and social ruptures. Borrowing from Davidson as well as from some of the leading authorities on crip studies, I contend that Cervantes—as well as some of the literary titans studied in my first book *Staging* Habla de Negros—registers acutely a crip speech through Africanized Castilian.[19]

A second noteworthy yet consistently overlooked and underimagined granular reference to blackness in the 1605 *Quixote* is the figure of the manicongo. In *Don Quixote* 1:52 the narrator informs us of "las palabras primeras que estaban escritas en el pergamino que se halló en la caja de plomo eran éstas" (the first words written on parchment discovered in the lead box were these):

> Los académicos de la Argamasilla, lugar de la Mancha, en vida
> y muerte del valeroso don Quijote de la Mancha,
> HOC SCRIPSERUNT
> "El Monicongo, académico de la Argamasilla, a la sepultura de don Quijote"
>
> [THEY WROTE THIS
> The Academicians of La Argamasilla, in La Mancha, on the Life
>   and Death of the Valiant Don Quixote de La Mancha
> El Monicongo, Academician of La Argamasilla, at the Tomb of Don Quixote].[20]

The word *manicongo* derives from the Kikongo-language title for kings, or *mani* (lords or princes), from the Kongo. The early history of the Kongo Kingdom was characterized by technological innovation and territorial expansion. Founded in the 1300s, according to oral history and archaeological evidence, the kingdom of Kongo was at the outset a highly centralized polity. Its political organization centered on the person of the king, who ruled with absolute power from his capital city over large territories through governors, or *mani*, he sent from his court to provincial capitals. In her two beautifully illustrated and conceptually arresting books, *Images on a Mission in Early Modern Kongo and Angola* and *The Art of Conversion: Christian Visual Culture in the Kingdom of Kongo*, art historian Cécile Fromont explains that "the regal function was not hereditary; rather, a group of qualified electors chose the new king from a pool of eligible candidates." "Kongo monarchs therefore," she adds, "depended heavily on a range of regalia, myths, and ritual apparatus to demonstrate their power and naturalize their rule."[21] As noted by John K. Thornton and Kristen Windmuller-Luna, "Early visitors were greatly impressed: in 1491, the Milanese ambassador in Lisbon described Kongo's houses as 'the best in all Guinea (Western Africa),' compar[ing] its capital to Evora, in Portugal, and not[ing] that it had 'the greatest justice' against adultery, theft, and treason."[22]

These sources about sub-Saharan African kings and lordship frame, on the one hand, and undergird, on the other hand, Cervantes's channeling of Portuguese cultural, literary, and social histories in *Don Quixote*. The literary business qua aesthetic-stylistic conventions of armed knights and chivalric narratives Cervantes parodied in the novel cannot be siphoned from how we imagine the literary treatment of manicongos in sixteenth- and seventeenth-century Iberian materials and texts. Indicative of a twinned Spanish competition and fascination with Portuguese maritime discoveries in narrative form, Cervantes inherited a variety of Castilian and Lusophone literary traditions about Africans kings and their subjects that seep into *Don Quixote*.[23] Significant inheritances come from Lope de Rueda's *Coloquio de Gila, Comedia, Eufemia*, and *Los engañados* and Simón Aguado's *Entremés de los negros* (1602).

Another clear and immediate example appears in *Jornada tercera* from Bartolomé de Torres Naharro's theatrical work *Comedia Trofea* (1517). In this play an interpreter introduces and showcases sub-Saharan African kings who pay tribute to the Portuguese monarch João III, "the Pious." The interpreter identifies four African kings as "Rey de Monicongo" (v. 1065), "Rey de Guinea (v. 1075), "Rey de Bemuí" (v. 1085), and "Rey de Çapa" (v. 1105). A century later, in 1618, Lope de Vega provides a new dramatization of African kings in act 1 of the play *El príncipe perfecto*. In his theatricalization of the black king "Rey Bemoy," or the king of Senegal, alongside other central concerns and themes, Lope de Vega crafts a theatrical space and world that correspond to the shift in diplomatic relations between Portugal and Spain under one monarch.[24] I'd like to remind my audience that, in historical terms, these theatrical cross-pollinations of putting African kings, diplomacy, and ambassadorial affairs on early modern Iberian and Italian (Roman) stages overlap with the life and social and political activity of João de Sá and the court of João III.

Written for the Roman papal court, Torres Naharro's *Comedia Trofea* addresses the theme of the Portuguese expeditions to the Atlantic and Pacific Oceans, showing the colonization process in a transoceanic context. Without a doubt *Comedia Trofea* broadens European colonialism and expansionism.[25] Performed in the midst of extensive courtly splendor, Torres Naharro's work performs a historicity (perhaps a veridiction too) of an embassy hosting 140 people that included a parade through the streets of Rome on March 12, 1514, in an extravagant procession of exotic fauna and wealth of the Indies, a white elephant named Hanno, two leopards, a panther, some parrots, turkeys, and rare Indian horses. It is a commissioned work that would be performed for the visit of the Portuguese ambassador to the Castel Sant'Angelo in Rome after the announcement that King João III had conquered the Maluku Islands (Moluccas), an archipelago in the eastern part of Indonesia. According to the philologist John Lihani, the work was performed between March 21 and April 25, 1514.[26] Arranged around the confrontation between the comic character Ptolemy—who has returned from hell to complain and inquire about the territories that King Manuel has conquered—Fame responds by naming the conquered places of twenty non-Christian kings. The two shepherds, Juan Tomillo and Caxcoluzio, transmit the news and other interesting events to the audience.

Comedia Trofea follows a *momo*, or *mojiganga*, structure, in which a parade of African kings pays tribute to the Portuguese monarch through an interpreter. The play serves as a means of spreading news (in its printed version) as well as celebrating a historical event in courtly terms (in its performative staging) designed for the public. The African kings, a Monicongo, a Mandinga, a Çapa, a Milindo, and an Aden, among many others, speak in their respective languages that an interpreter translates. Each of these distinct African kings—and their lands or polities—registers in the minds of both lettered and illiterate audiences an attainable, concrete, and vast black geographic mapping of sovereignty. Drawing from and in conversation with Herman Bennett's spellbinding *African Kings and Black Slaves: Sovereignty and Dispossession in the Early Modern Atlantic*, I view Torres Naharro's theatrical representation of African kings as a dramatic piece that wrestles with real and imagined geographic and spatial misrecognitions and readings of Africa that far exceed the world described by Ptolemy.

Before I continue my discussion of *Don Quixote*, I'd like to take a moment at this juncture, as an aside, to highlight signature moments that historicize, mark, and verify Cervantes's and his contemporaries' literary overlays with so-called real historical occurrences. As I've demonstrated elsewhere, the likelihood and possibility of the in-person arrival, existence, sight, and viewing of black African kings—royals and sovereigns—was not unlikely for early modern Iberians across all purported ethnic and racial lines. Iberian urban centers such as Lisbon and Seville boasted ethnically diverse black populations. Like the numerous African kings portrayed in *Comedia Trofea*, so too, in real-life historical terms, sub-Saharan Africans came from Angola and the Congo Basin; the Cape Verde Islands; the kingdom of Dahomey; the Senegambia region and its intricate aquatic networks of inlets, mangroves, and rivers; Mozambique; and neighboring Portuguese outposts in East Africa and Goa. And it is not at all coincidental that Miguel de Cervantes, in his chivalric adjustments in *Don Quixote*, either identifies or substitutes these places for fictional ones. In their philosophical colloquy in *Don Quixote* 1.18, about fantastical adventures and epic battles that purported to have had vanquished Islam and the religion's adherents, the characters Don Quixote and Sancho Panza name concrete squadrons of black—or black adjacent—peoples, geographies, kingdoms, and polities. I list three examples here:

1. Alifanfarón, as ruler of Taprobana, or Taprobane Island (Ταπροβανῆ, or Ταπροβάνη, in Ancient Greek): Ceylon or present-day Sri Lanka.
2. Garamantes (Γαράμαντες, in Ancient Greek) of Libya and the northern Sahara (500–700 BCE): Archaeological digs conducted in 2010 by Marta Mirazón Lahr excavated skeletons from Fezzan dating to the Roman era and found that these remains most closely matched Neolithic Sahelian samples, from Chad, Mali, and Niger. In her findings Lahr concluded that these remains were the Garamantes.
3. "Los etíopes, de horadados labios, y otras infinitas naciones, cuyos rostros conozco y veo [Pierced-lipped Ethiopians; and an infinite number of other nations, whose faces I recognize and see]."[27] I also associate this reference to the Nubian kingdoms of Makuria and Alodia (400s–late 1400s).

I encourage us all, as specialists and students of *Don Quixote*, not to fall into the trap of mistreating continental Africa as an anomalous abstraction devoid of potent meaning. The vast continent of Africa held more kingdoms than medieval Europeans imagined. As explicated in the beautifully curated and timely Getty Museum catalog *Balthazar: A Black African King in Medieval and Renaissance Art*, "The names of some of these polities match or resemble those of countries today, such as Mali and Congo (historically spelled Kongo), but the borders and ranges of influence shifted over time, as all such geographic divisions have done and continue to do. Although histories of Afro-European contact have traditionally focused on the three faiths of Judaism, Christianity, and Islam, Africa was home to many other religions and literate and oral traditions."[28] *Don Quixote* is a work that connects continents through trade and diplomacy. In doing so Cervantes reconstructs from medieval Iberian knowledge and sources a world that met Africa through travel, trade, and diplomacy. Regardless of where you align yourself ideologically, intellectually, or textually with *Don Quixote*, I maintain that it's intellectually lazy and irresponsible to dismiss and ignore the salient role sub-Saharan Africa plays in Cervantes's literary fictions and historical imagination. There lies deep meaning and symbolism in the character Don Quixote's descriptions of ancient references. This is how I ideate and imagine granular blackness in *Don Quixote*.

In their granularity I read the diverse sets of examples treated herein as important overlays to Cervantes's fictional reference to the manicongo in *Don Quixote*. Explanatory notes in scholarly editions (e.g., those of Castalia,

Cátedra, Cuesta, and Real Academia Española) skirt precision. These editions systematically flatten Cervantes's "El Monicongo," only to provide underwhelmingly scant information about the figure's cultural history and literary significance in Iberian early modernity. What is more, Edith Grossman's critically acclaimed English translation of *Don Quixote* irresponsibly translates "El Monicongo" as "Ignoramus."[29] I recognize that for Cervantes the poetic burlesque of his "El Monicongo" operates as a referent for perceived insignificant comical fictionality. But apocryphal or real, the historical and political statuses of these manicongos beg our critical engagement and historical rooting. What strikes me here is Cervantes's sophisticated recapitulation of reframing, retelling, and weaving a social history of a complex early modern Atlantic Iberian literary world order, in which he lived and inherited. Unlike the editorial notes that reduce manicongos to insignificant "black men from the Kongo," I task my readers to consider earlier stages of Portuguese expansion in the kingdom of Kongo and the rivers of Guinea that would have informed Cervantes's knowledge about and usage of the term.[30]

As depicted in figure 5, the significance of the escutcheon in António Godinho's 1548 Portuguese manuscript armorial—that formalized Afonso's story of accession in the typically European format of heraldry—speaks to the existence and plausibility of armed and erudite black men who wrote and dispatched letters that encompassed core visual elements. Many of these diplomatic correspondences appear in Padre António Brásio's encyclopedic, multitome *Monumenta missionaria africana*. Drawing on this corpus of literary-political saliences, Afonso keenly perceived the potential of his narrative and emblem—the vignette labeled "Rei de Manicongo" and a crest of five sword-carrying armored limbs—as tools to insert his rule and his realm in the historical and symbolic space of Christendom. I borrow again from Fromont's expert analysis: "The arms," wrote Afonso, "are for us [Kongo nobles] to carry on our shields, as the Christian Kings and Princes of [Europe] have the custom to do, as signs of whom and whence they are [and come] and so that by them they should be known by all. In word and image, Afonso of Kongo heralded himself as a Christian prince, companion in arms to Saint James, and one for whom the cross of Constantinople appeared."[31]

The fact that Godinho's *Coat of Arms of the Manicongo Kings* (1528–41) predates Cervantes's birth (the author would have been one year old in 1548) is beside the point. Throughout *El ingenioso hidalgo Don Quijote de la Mancha*, Cervantes nimbly cites, parodies, and references medieval and Renaissance Iberian codes, texts, and visual iconographies. I contend that the background, sources, and visual culture of the kingdom of Kongo uniquely

Fig. 5. António Godinho, *Coat of Arms of the Manicongo Kings*, 1548. Pigment and gold on parchment, 430 × 320 mm. Direção-geral dos Arquivos-Torre do Tombo, Lisbon, MS CF-164, fol. 7 (detail). Godinho, *Livro da nobreza e perfeiçam*.

inform Cervantes's textual reimagination of "El Monicongo" from *Don Quixote*. As sustained by Fromont and a consort of historians of the early modern Atlantic world, such as David Wheat, Erin Kathleen Rowe, Gabriel de Avilez Rocha, and Herman Bennett, "It is crucial to understand that the cross-cultural interactions between the kingdom of Kongo and Europeans were not ruled by colonialism or unfolding under dynamics of oppression and resistance. Instead, owing to the successful intervention of Afonso and his successors, the Kongo enjoyed a rare status among non-European polities in the early modern era, one defined by its independence and its standing as a Christian land."[32] Privileging this historical narrative and setting the fictionalized burlesques aside, Cervantes's "El Monicongo, The Academician of Argamasilla" could have and would have existed well before and during the publication of the 1605 *Quixote*. It is not—nor was it—impossible to correlate manicongos to erudite academicians, ambassadors, lords, and princes. As stipulated in this meditation's documentation, you'll find that there's an abundant bibliography and historiography that corroborates and documents the bureaucratic, collegiate, and daily lives of the so-called fictional and paratextual Academic Monicongo created by Cervantes. As far as I'm concerned, this exemplifies my ideation of granular blackness, an overlooked and underestimated constitution of blackness codified in Cervantes's larger rhetorical devices and literary techniques about chivalry, knights, and letterer-warrior men.

Sancho Panza: The Gluttonous Embodiment of Reckoning with Slavery

Let us get to the root of things. For a few centuries now, blackness has been big business, attracting attention and reaping raw profit not only in the West but increasingly in the world at large.[33] In *Don Quixote* 1.29 Cervantes illustrates this material world of sub-Saharan African blackness when Sancho Panza schemes a plan for trafficking black bodies:

> —¿Qué se me da a mí que mis vasallos sean negros? ¿Habrá más que cargar con ellos y traerlos a España, donde los podré vender, y adonde me los pagarán de contado, de cuyo dinero podré comprar algún título o algún oficio con que vivir descansado todos los días de mi vida? ¡No, sino dormíos, y no tengáis ingenio ni habilidad para disponer de las cosas y para vender treinta o diez mil vasallos en dácame esas pajas! ¡Par Dios que los he de volar, chico con grande, o como pudiere, y que, por negros que sean, los he de volver blancos o amarillos! ¡Llegaos, que me mamo el dedo!

> [What difference does it make to me if my vassals are blacks? All I have to do is put them on a ship and bring them to Spain, where I can sell them, and I'll be paid for them in cash, and with that money I'll be able to buy some title or office and live on that for the rest of my life. No flies on me! Who says I don't have the wit or ability to arrange things and sell thirty or ten thousand vassals in the wink of an eye? By God, I'll sell them all, large or small, it's all the same to me, and no matter how black they are, I'll turn them white (silver) and yellow (gold). Bring them on, then, I'm no fool!][34]

Peppered with his rambunctious, rustic dialect, Sancho's fantasy articulated in this passage imbued real-life implications for its audience. Employing the technical lexicon of merchants, Sancho utilizes Castilian terms such as *"comprar"* (to buy, to purchase), *"pagar de contado"* (to cash out), and *"vender"* (to sell) to pun on two levels: the first involves the metaphorical, alchemical magic of racialized language: transforming black bodies (persons, subjects) into silver and gold coins (metal, things), while the second references racial thinking along the lines of colonial metallurgy and the pigments (skin color) of enslaved persons. In the age of Cervantes, *esclavos blancos,* or "white slaves," generally consisted of Morisco communities who became abundant following the failure of the Alpujarras Rebellion of 1568–71, whereas *esclavos loros* referred to "yellow"-hued, darker-complexioned slaves of any ethnic or racial background.[35] But these so-called puns possess a cultural capital for both Sancho's and Cervantes's audience that run much deeper than the author's literary conceits. Sancho's punning signals the profoundly symbolic power that Cervantes invests in what I like to call his material world of blackness—or, better yet, following the insights of Kyla Wazana Tompkins, "a new materialist history of race (and an old materialist history of race if one might say that unironically)."[36] An example of racial thinking, this material world of blackness carries an all-too-familiar (auto)biographical imprint in Cervantes's cultural imagination and literary journey, as his grandfather owned *esclavos negros* and *esclavos blancos* and the author himself suffered five years of slavery in Algiers (1575–80).[37] The autobiographical imprint I trace here enables me to breathe an actual life into the above-cited passage's intersectional materiality, thereby showing the importance of recognizing the interplay of the author's familial pasts and his literary corpus.

This narrativized scene from *Don Quixote* 1.29 does much more than attend to and poke fun at Don Quixote's chivalric madness and Sancho Panza's gluttonous avarice. Yes, of course, Sancho contemplates the possibility of his slave-trading fantasy to crystallize a suspicion about Don Quixote marrying Princess Micomicona.[38] And although I'm at once compelled and expected to say at least *something* about Princess Micomicona, I profess that Cervantes's racially gendered treatment of Dorotea fulfills a sloppy dramatized performance—a costume, an imitation, a parody, or otherwise—of sub-Saharan African queenship, royalty, and sovereignty. If anything, Cervantes's Dorotea/Princess Micomicona concoction compounds and intersects his acute and measured engagement with book history, historiography, literary theory, and theater that originates from a vast textual archive and repertoire, where Africa and its inhabitants, imagined and real, either appear in or predate the first part of *Don Quixote,* from 1605. I'm specifically referencing the mythical Prester John of Ethiopia ("de las Indias," as Cervantes states in his prologue to part 1); the stargazer Baltasar from the thirteenth-century *Auto de los Reyes Magos*, a wide assortment of thirteenth-century sources from the learned king Alfonso X; the "Exemplum 32," from Juan Manuel's *El conde Lucanor* (1335); Joanot Martorell's *Tirant Lo Blanch* (1490); Garci Rodríguez de Montalvo's *Las sergas de Esplandián* (1510); and *Lazarillo de Tormes* (1554). It's also worth mentioning that Alonso Fernández de Avellaneda, in chapters 22–33 from *El Quijote apócrifo* (1612–13), retools the slave-trading interests of Sancho Panza and the Dorotea-Micomicona episode.[39] With this diverse set of texts in mind, concerning book history and literary theory as strategies for extracting meaning out of Dorotea's poorly conceived performative racial drag of a sub-Saharan African queen, I believe that Cervantes adds to and riffs off already-established historiographic and literary traditions that reflect intertextuality. Without necessarily reifying race qua blackness and whiteness in essentialist terms, intertextuality refers to the interpretation of texts in relation to other texts.

Cervantes's skill at novelistic intertextuality in this episode also assays a renarrativization of Sancho's fantasy as imperial governor and *negrero* (trafficker of black bodies). These *negreros*, whom Sancho aspires to emulate and to fashion himself after, resemble real-life aristocrats and merchants whom Cervantes despised: the slave-trading men of the wealthy Arguijo family as well as Godínez, who ran into trouble with the Inquisition, and Juan de Jáuregui, the son of *negreros*. Daniel Nemser efficaciously reminds us that "far from a theory of government, Sancho's slave-trading fantasy articulates an abdication of rule fueled by tangible greed [that] embodies a model of African slave trading modeled on Portuguese colonialism."[40] As Allison Margaret Bigelow points out in her exemplary book *Mining Language: Racial Thinking, Indigenous Knowledge, and Colonial Metallurgy in the Early Modern Iberian World*, "Materiality has informed literary, philosophical, and art historical studies of [metals], labor, race, and empire in the early modern era."[41]

Another way to look at it: this scene codifies the haptic materiality of blackness and its sensorial effects of racialized thinking. To grasp this episode's emotive and sensorial possibilities, catalyzed by Sancho's greed and wild imagination, the narrator informs us that "con esto [Sancho] andaba tan solícito y tan contento que se le olvidaba la pesadumbre de caminar a pie" (this made him so eager and happy that he forgot about his sorrow at having to walk).[42] Eric Clifford Graf, in his essay "El Greco's and Cervantes's Euclidean Theologies," frames this scene in light of the disappearance of Sancho's ass, which articulates Cervantes's "Apuleian criticism of Spanish imperialism and colonialism, the latter delineated most acutely by Sancho's dark plan to get rich by selling the black African citizens of Micomicón into slavery." "The critical zenith occurs," writes Graf, "when the squire stumbles on his brutal idea, and it's no accident that this is the only moment when he's happy in the absence of his ass."[43]

I would be remiss if I did not historicize Cervantes's granular reference to Sancho Panza's hunger for African gold qua fungible black African flesh. In his extensive and revelatory magnum opus, *A Fistful of Shells: West Africa from the Rise of the Slave Trade to the Age of Revolution,* Toby Green jogs the memory of those who possess a selective amnesia and cognitive dissonance regarding African gold and its modernity:

> Gold, therefore, mattered hugely both to Africans and to Europeans. But, when it comes to the gold trade, West African and European sources do not entirely match up. European expansion is often seen as the trigger for modern history. In the fifteenth century, the place of gold was central to the expansion project and the European image of Africa as the "golden country," as, indeed, the Catalan Atlas suggests, with its depiction of the gold nugget held by Mansa Musa front and center. In the 1490s, João II, King of Portugal, became known to Italian contemporaries as *il rei d'oro*, or the "Golden King," because of his access to West African gold markets.
>
> Where historical evidence from West Africa makes plain the place of long-distance trade in gold, in traditional European historical narratives it was the Portuguese "voyages of discovery" along the Atlantic African coast in the fifteenth century that first brought West African communities in contact with global influences. . . . When the Portuguese arrived on the West African coast in the 1440s, therefore, the societies that they found had emerged from many centuries of trade and cross-cultural exchange with North African traders, scholars, and craftspeople. The mixed urban cultures that had emerged in towns like Timbuktu, Kantora, Oualata and Goa were in many ways early harbingers of modernity.[44]

What Cervantes simultaneously captures and reveals in *Don Quixote*, through Sancho's obsession with African gold and enslaved black Africans, cannot be delinked from the material and societal transformations that sparked urban growth across West Africa and also in European cities such as Lisbon, London, and Seville—all of which grew rapidly along the rise of long-distance trade. In this Iberian-African history, Green further contextualizes for us, "As Akan gold miners in the forests of the Gold Coast dug deeper into their mineral seams, and the caravans brought ever more gold across the Sahara to the north, more money was washing around in the cities of Algiers, Cairo, and Tunis. This led to the transition from a credit economy to a bullion economy, which, with the growing valorization of coinage, set the terms for what would happen after the Spanish opening of silver mines in the New World." In his thematic exploration of gold—and, perhaps, in the critique of it—Cervantes brings into clearer view an interconnected material and social history of gold between Africans, Iberians, and the Mediterranean world.[45]

In a different context, as we may cast aside Sancho's missing donkey, I build on Chi-Ming Yang's Marxist approach to the study of silver and other metals to illuminate Sancho's fantastical sensory experience and his desire to alchemically alter sovereign black bodies into silver and gold, touching them, seeing them, weighing them, and hearing them as if they were converted into "aesthetic and affective value."[46] Sancho's sensorial affect and desire—euphoric, frenetic, frenzied—conveyed in the text, in my opinion, cannot be conceptually, historically, or ideologically dislocated from how we codify Cervantes's critique of capitalism qua slave trading as it relates to the institutions of captivity, colonialism, and slavery. A figurative accountant or bookkeeper (*contador*, in Castilian and Portuguese) of some sort, Sancho (and Don Quixote), far from cosmopolitan Europeans, concretize Cervantes's literary adaptation of Europeans who believed sub-Saharan Africans to occupy the same economic and symbolic register as gold and silver did; these Africans became a form of specie, a reliable coin, that rendered them into financial instruments. This economic information would have been documented in accounting books known as *peças* or *peças de escravos* at royal factories and trading posts at Arguim and at Ughoton in Benin and São Tomé in the Bight of Biafra. The Castelo de São Jorge da Mina in present-day Ghana (commonly known as "The Mine," or Elmina Castle) surely cannot be overlooked in the booking and processing of captive Africans.

This scene from *Don Quixote* 1.29 exposes us to Cervantes's sustained multilayered discontent with not solely Sancho's self-interested ruminations as a slave catcher but for all who embody this kind of ideology and inhumane work. Let's recall *Don Quixote* 1.4, for example, where Cervantes introduces us early on to his distaste for deception, injustice, and physical abuse against those who can't readily defend themselves. In this sally we meet a topless fifteenth-year-old boy named Andrés, who has been tied to an oak tree and mercilessly whipped with a leather strap by a strong and well-built peasant, whom we come to learn is a wealthy farmer named Juan Haldudo. After Haldudo nearly flayed the teenager like Saint Bartholomew, Cervantes sheds light on his unethical and immoral behavior through the defrauding of nine months' worth of wages owed to Andrés as well as the way in which he wickedly laughs at the weeping and distraught boy, who later runs off into the woods as Don Quixote leaves the scene riding atop Rocinante. While conventional readings of this episode may focus on its comical intent and ironic undertones, we mustn't permit the humor and comical relief imbued in Don Quixote's out-of-touch ridiculousness—as demonstrated by his inability to effectively protect and save Andrés—to serve as the conclusive driving interpretive force of our analysis.[47] The exchanges between Andrés and Don Quixote throughout chapter 4 reveal Cervantes's indictment of those who brutalize and steal wages from their laborers.[48] Although Don Quixote's intentions are noble, one could also call into question the waning efficacy of justice-keeping and justice-seeking knights—after whom Don Quixote has fashioned himself—who work to maintain order and right wrongs.

Oscillating between comical jest and critical commentary, Cervantes further rebukes the abuses and misuses of justice and power, as authorized and executed by the King's Law, in about two-thirds of chapter 22 from part 1 of *Don Quixote* in the episode of the galley slaves. Upon catching a glimpse of the chain gang, Sancho Panza remarks, "Ésta es cadena de galeotes, gente forzada del rey, que va a las galeras." ("This is a chain of galley slaves, people forced by the king to go to the galleys.") To this Don Quixote replies, "¿Cómo gente forzada . . . es posible que el rey haga fuerza a ninguna gente?" ("What do you mean, forced? Is it possible that the king forces anyone?")[49] As explained by Anthony Close in his essay "The Liberation of the Galley Slaves and the Ethos of *Don Quijote*," the question twists the legal sense of "gente forzada del rey," galley slaves, into a literal, emotive channel that fits the Quixotic preconception of the chained men as unfortunate victims of duress. Close adds that "Sancho scrupulously corrects this perversion of meaning: 'No digo eso, . . . sino que es gente que por sus delitos va condenada a servir al rey en las galeras, de por fuerza.'" ("I'm not saying that, . . . but these are people who, because of their crimes, have been condemned to serve the king in the galleys, by force").[50] Cervantes's emphasis on Don Quixote's underscoring remains striking: "Comoquiera que ello sea, esta gente, aunque los llevan, van de por fuerza, y no de su voluntad." ("For whatever reason, these people are being taken by force and not of their own free will.")[51]

As Cervantes was once was held captive in Algiers and incarcerated twenty years later in Seville, his galley-slaves episode—and the picaresque tradition it highlights through the fictional and historically referenced figure Ginés de Pasamonte and others like him—gestures at a crucial moment and turning point in the author's life.[52] This thematic content, constitutive of chapter 22 of *Don Quixote*, part 1, compels me to excavate the profound implications inscribed in Cervantes's social history of crime, incarceration, punishment, and slavery. I remind you, my dear reader, that Cervantes was booked and processed in the Royal Jail of Seville in 1597 and was later released in the first months of the following year. Located on Calle Sierpe (or Serpent Street), Seville's Royal Jail held, according to one of Cervantes's most esteemed and illustrious biographers, Jean Canavaggio, two thousand prisoners.[53] It is from the confines of this carceral institution—its penal time, its penal space, and its penal matter—where Cervantes, I propose, acquired firsthand experience for depicting the daily life, landscape, and underworld of seventeenth-century Seville as well as conceived the idea of writing *Don Quixote*. We mustn't downplay Cervantes's biography or the literary history that informs his creation of *Don Quixote* in relation to the aesthetics, culture, and knowledge produced within prison cells.

In the interest of propelling forward my analysis, I would like to frame Cervantes's lived experiences as a formerly enslaved captive and a prisoner as plausible evidence for his ability to ideate philosophical questions and provocative debates that germinate in the galley-slaves scene from *Don Quixote* 1.22. Creating, thinking, and writing from prison, Cervantes embodies what art historian and cultural critic Nicole R. Fleetwood calls "carceral aesthetics" in *Marking Time: Art in the Age of Mass Incarceration*. For Fleetwood, as she has drawn from the work of independent curators and public scholars such as Risa Puleo, carceral aesthetics is the production of art under the conditions of unfreedom; it involves the creative use of penal space, time, and matter. I want to be upfront and very clear that, while the aesthetic and theoretical foundation and underpinning of carceral aesthetics "builds on black radical thought and traditions that center the cultural production of people held in captivity," I maintain that my linkage of this term to Miguel de Cervantes still captures an artist-writer who held varying identifications that trouble our immediate unhinged assumptions about devaluation, dispossession, gender, race, and so forth. If we are to accept Cervantes's written depiction of the galley slaves as a kind of carceral aesthetics, then I cannot help but liken the text's signaling of "doce hombres a pie, ensartados como cuentas en una gran cadena de hierro, por los cuellos, y todos con esposas a las manos" ("twelve men on foot, strung together by their necks like beads on a great iron chain, and all of them wearing manacles") to the black men and women working on chain gangs during the Jim Crow era of US history.[54]

These ruminations on a Cervantine-inflected carceral aesthetics and carceral writing inspire me to channel the Nigerian-British singer Sade's song "Is It a Crime?" As I thread and weave meaning into the interlocking insidiousness of bondage, dispossession, enslavement, incarceration, and punishment that knot up, jumble, and then disentangle over the course of *Don Quixote*, I query, What constitutes and justifies "crime"? Why does Sancho Panza *feel* for the predicament of the galley slaves yet is so unfeeling in his ravenous eagerness to capture, enslave, ship off, and profit off fungible black flesh? Is it a crime to be black? Is it crime to feel for black people?

In the Spain of Cervantes's time, Old Christians (*cristianos viejos*, in Castilian) auctioned, trafficked, and owned enslaved black Africans, as did the Morisco populations, specifically Moriscos living in Granada before and at the onset of the Alpujarras Rebellion (1568–71). Cervantes invites us to contend with this history of slavery in the Iberian Peninsula and Mediterranean world—at least those who wish to acknowledge it and see it. As far as I'm concerned, the author furnishes a tangential intellectual and social history of the sub-Saharan African slave trade that tasks us as general readers and expert connoisseurs of *Don Quixote* to calibrate and nuance our misunderstanding of the geopolitics of black enslavement outside of the Atlantic world. While this subject may be potentially illegible for some readers' analytical and historical purviews, I'm interested in utilizing this tangential aside on the Morisco involvement in sub-Saharan African slave trading to generate a deeper close reading—if not, perhaps, also a meta meditation—of Sancho Panza's Old Christian lineage that he fictitiously fashions as a purported powerful elite to justify his claims to imperial governorship and slave trading. In one sense the overall arch of the so-called Morisco problem or question raised by Cervantes in his complete works—I'm thinking of Cenotia from *Persiles*, the Morisca woman from *El licenciado Vidriera* who poisons an apple to provoke the Glassed Graduate's madness, Cañizares from *El coloquio de los perros*, Ricote and Ana Félix from part 2 of *Don Quixote*—temper my reading of Sancho's ideological convictions as an Old Christian expressed in *Don Quixote* 1.29. In another sense Sancho's assertive claims to enslaving black Africans dialogues with the historical battles, dramas, and tensions between the Spanish Crown and Morisco communities during the reigns of Felipe II (r. 1556–98) and Felipe III (r. 1598–1621). As explained by a cadre of Spanish historians such as Fernando Bouza, Aurelia Martín Casares, Margarita

García Barranco, and Raúl González Arévalo, among others, historical evidence appears as follows:

> Desde comienzos del siglo XVI, la comunidad morisca se convirtió en un problema para la Corona, puesto que sobre ella recayó todo un abanico de sospechas y recelos que no hicieron sino empeorar su situación con los cristianos viejos. De manera progresiva fueron surgiendo una seria de normas y leyes encaminadas a regular y sancionar los comportamientos y modos de vida de los moriscos. Sin embargo, en general y hasta mediados de siglo, cristianos y moriscos compartieron un interés común: la posesión de esclavos negros; en el caso de los granadinos, la procedencia de sus esclavos era subsahariana. Frente a las sucesivas prohibiciones de la Corona, los moriscos defendieron a "capa y espada" su derecho a personas esclavizadas.
>
> [At the turn of the sixteenth century, the Morisco community became a problem for the Crown, since a whole range of suspicions and misgivings fell on them, which only made their situation worse with the Old Christians. Progressively, a series of norms and laws were emerging, aimed at regulating and sanctioning the behaviors and ways of life of the Moriscos. Generally speaking, however, until the middle of the century, Christians and Moriscos shared a common interest: the possession of black slaves. In the case of the *granadinos*, the origin of their slaves was sub-Saharan African. Faced with the successive prohibitions of the Crown, the Moriscos defended and fought hard for their right to keep their enslaved blacks.][55]

What is more, in his 1566 *Memorial en defensa de las costumbres moriscas*, Francisco Núñez Muley (ca. 1490–ca. 1568) negotiates with powerful church-state institutions such as the courts of Toledo, the Holy Office of the Inquisition, and the Synod of Bishops to barter for and justify the possession of enslaved blacks. As early as 1526 in the Junta de la Capilla Real, during Carlos I's stay in Granada and later in January and February, in meetings of the Synod of Guadix and Baza in 1554 Catholic authorities issued decrees to prohibit Moriscos from owning enslaved persons. And with more archival documentation, I'd like to underscore that "Ley XIV, título Segundo," from book 8 of the 1567 *Recopilación de leyes del Reino* declares, "Que los moriscos no compren esclavos negros, ni los tengan, ni de Berbería" (May no Morisco purchase black slaves nor own them, not even from the Barbary Coast).⁵⁶ With respect to the "ni de Berbería" clause, Aurelia Martín Casares explains:

> Los documentos que prohibían a los moriscos tener dependientes hacía únicamente alusión al color "negro" de los esclavos y no a su precedencia. Los moriscos aún tratándose de la élite ansiosa por integrarse, no poseerían musulmanes blancos. El hecho es que la mayoría de los propietarios de personas esclavizadas que he identificado como moriscos en los protocolos notariales a lo largo del siglo XVI suelen comerciar con personas esclavizadas procedentes de las colonias portugueses en el África subsahariana (Santo Tomé, Cabo Verde, Guinea y Congo). Debemos tener en cuenta que algunas personas esclavizadas calificadas de berberiscas eran, en realidad, de origen negroafricano y procedían de la trata transahariana, como Mubaricha que es de "negrería" pero se crió en Orán. Sin embargo, cabe la posibilidad de que más de sesenta años después de la toma de Granada, la élite conversa no tuviera reparos en comprar árabes berberiscos como esclavos y sin ánimo de libertarlos posteriormente. Quizá el deseo de ser reconocidos como parte integrante de las clases viejas privilegiadas les llevó a someter a antiguos correligionarios a esclavitud.

> [The documents that prohibited the Moriscos from having dependants only alluded to the "black" color of the slaves and not to their precedence. The Moriscos, even though they were the elite eager to integrate, would not have white Muslims. The fact is that most of the owners of enslaved persons that I have identified as Moriscos in the notarial protocols throughout the sixteenth century used to trade in enslaved persons from the Portuguese colonies in sub-Saharan Africa (Sao Tome, Cape Verde, Guinea, and Congo). We must take into account that some enslaved people described as Barbary were, in reality, of black African origin and came from the trans-Saharan trade, such as Mubaricha, who trafficked in enslaving blacks but grew up in Oran. However, it is possible that more than sixty years after the capture of Granada, the converted elite had no qualms about buying Barbary Arabs as slaves and with no intention of freeing them later. Perhaps the desire to be recognized as an integral part of the privileged older classes led them to subject former coreligionists to slavery.]⁵⁷

These crucial historical and legal details predate and build up to the chronicler Luis del Mármol Carvajal's *Historia de la rebelión y castigo de los moriscos del Reino de Granada* (1600) but also inform Núñez Muley's adjudication of his position in his *Memorial*:

> Tampoco hay inconveniente en los naturales tengan negros ¿Estas gentes no han de tener servicios? Decir que crece la nación morisca con ello es pasión de quien lo dice porque habiendo informado a su magestad en las cortes de Toledo que había más de veinte mil negros en este reino en poder de los naturales . . . y al presente no hay cien licencias para poderlos tener. Esto salió también de los clérigos, y ellos han sido después los abonadores de los que los tienen, y los que han sacado interés dello.

> [Neither is there any issue with the citizens owning blacks. Shouldn't these people have services? To say that the Morisco nation grows with this is the passion of whoever says it, for having informed His Majesty in the courts of Toledo that there were more than twenty thousand blacks in this kingdom in the power of the citizens . . . and presently there are not a hundred licenses available to be able to have them. This also came from the clerics, and they have later been the subscribers of those who own blacks and those who have drawn interest from it (them).][58]

Núñez Muley's argumentation had profound implications on literature, which created bountiful content for debating—and defending—the right to enslave and own blacks, as evidenced in Diego Ximénez de Enciso's play *Juan Latino* (1634–52).[59] I contend that one of the many messages that reverberate in Cervantes's creation of Sancho Panza in *Don Quixote* 1.29 troubles Spain's fraught internal circulation and network of ideas about sub-Saharan African slavery.

As I digress from my anecdotal discussion of Morisco and Old Christian involvement in African slavery, let's now return to and further untangle Cervantes's critique and exposition of Sancho's abysmal depths and tyrannical desires to enslave black Africans, alchemically transforming them into gold and silver. To fully grasp the magnitude of Cervantes's underlying discomfort with and scorn for bondage, captivity, and enslavement, we mustn't overlook the history of slavery's deep economic and ideological valences. Through his literary characterization of Sancho and its correlation to real history over the course of the sixteenth and seventeenth centuries, Cervantes simultaneously sheds light on and reckons with the business of slave-trading work. To put it quite bluntly, Cervantes builds meaning into the role of capitalism in African slavery. (An argument can also be built around Cervantes's own life when we think about the interconnected economies and politics of his captivity in Algiers, his *rescate* [ransom or rescue paid], and his bureaucratic document, *Información de Argel*.[60])

Don Quixote 1.29 demonstrates how Sancho's expressed greed for transforming black flesh into gold and silver participates in the constellation of early modern ideas related to civility, currency, population, and trade that formed the ideological foundation for the logics of race. I concur with historian Jennifer L. Morgan's infinite insights in *Reckoning with Slavery*, where she prods, "But questions remain as to how slavery might be understood not just as bound up with the emergence of capitalist economies but as constitutive of commerce, value, money, and the new cultural logics embedded therein." Taking cues from Morgan's incomparable analytical and methodological intervention, yet also keeping in mind the groundbreaking work of scholars such as Herman Bennett, Vincent Brown, Kim F. Hall, Stephanie Smallwood, and Hortense Spillers, my take on Sancho's avariciousness and covetousness in *Don Quixote*—and its relationship to capitalism and slavery—is that it needs to be understood as a kind of alchemy. Morgan corroborates my earlier close reading of and references to alchemy: "Slave traders had the notion that they could transform human beings into wealth, assigning them a value that rendered them exchangeable and distributable through transport and markets."[61]

Cervantes's *Don Quixote* represents a textual moment, one of many Iberian foundations, if you will, that provides a window into a set of changes underway both in Iberia and sub-Saharan Africa. I want my readers to conceive of and to see how Cervantes encodes in Sancho a suggestive signpost of the transformations in how money, wealth, and value were being conceived during the period across vast oceans. The conceptual relationship between gold, silver, and slaves played a crucial role in making entire populations part of a racial valuation that deemed them enslavable. As an ideation of alchemy, Cervantes's construction of Sancho Panza critiques and parodies Europeans who believed that gold, silver, and other minerals were a universally applicable and legible standard of value. What I find Cervantes probing throughout chapter 29 of part 1 of *Don Quixote*—most notably Sancho Panza and perhaps, to a lesser degree, Dorotea's racial impersonation of the sub-Saharan African princess Micomicona—is how European writers produced copious records in the wake of contact with Africans that reflected both mutual confusion and disdain but also a burgeoning interest in quantification and in understanding populations as distinct, quantifiable, and transferable.[62]

Taking into account the global Iberian ramification of gold and silver, as embedded within Sancho's internal colloquy on enslaving blacks and turning them into gold and silver, implores us to consider historian Michelle Murphy's term "phantasmagrams," which retools Karl Marx's notion of the phantasmagorical powers of the commodity. Murphy argues that "phantasmagrams" embody "quantitative practices that are enriched with affect . . . and hence have supernatural effects in surplus of their rational precepts."[63] I turn to African studies to problematize for my readers, on the one hand, and expose them to, on the other hand, Cervantes's paradoxical and unsettled fictionalized construction of Sancho Panza as a merchant, imperial governor, and *negrero*. By way of conclusion, we might say, perhaps, that Cervantes's representation of Sancho in *Don Quixote* 1.29 exemplifies coexistent cultural and social histories active in late fifteenth- and sixteenth-century Portuguese accounts indicating that cowries were in circulation as currency in the neighboring kingdom of Benin, east of Yorubaland. Archaeologist Akinwumi Ogundiran, in his essay "Of Small Things Remembered: Beads, Cowries, and Cultural Translations of the Atlantic Experience in Yorubaland," illuminates the larger significance of Atlantic African commerce that not only impacted African-Iberian relations but also spanned vast oceans, such as the Indian Ocean.[64] Read alongside Cervantes, Ogundiran's essay can productively complicate how we approach, handle, and understand not only sub-Saharan African slavery in *Don Quixote* but also the relationship between historical memory, origin myth, and cowrie money. As Ogundiran summarizes it, cowries were brought to the Ondo-Yorùbá area of southern Nigeria as a form of money by vultures. Ogundiran reports that these vultures could represent both European slave traders and African raiders: "Vultures feed mainly on carrion and they symbolize greedy and ruthless people who prey on others, but in the narrative they heralded the introduction of cowries."[65]

As I wrap up this section, my meditation compels me to wonder: Could Sancho represent a foil to a rogue alter ego of Cervantes? Did Cervantes reconfigure him as a corrupted embodiment of what's to evolve in future *indiano* characters—especially in the nineteenth century, as illustrated in Benito Pérez Galdós's novels such as *Fortunata y Jacinta: Dos historias de casadas* (1887), as well as those touched on in discourses confronted by scholars of the Global Hispanophone?[66] Does Sancho Panza operate as a foil to

Christopher Columbus and other conquistadors and colonial migrants and settlers? Did Cervantes also insert Sancho within a larger Las Casasian critique of barbarism, dispossession, and violence committed in the Spanish Caribbean and Spanish-speaking Americas? Another interrogative side of the coin is what if the Spanish Crown *would have* allowed Cervantes to have traveled to the Indies? Does the humanist-lexicographer Gonzalo Correas's proverb, "El que va a las Indias es loco, y el que no va es bobo" (The one who goes to the Indies is crazy, and the one who doesn't go is a fool) apply to the writer?[67] Could the fact that Cervantes wasn't granted permission to travel to the Spanish Indies shape his position on brutality, corruption, greed, and enslavement? Cervantes leaves us with an arsenal of possibilities to form hypothetical answers to the questions I've posed. If anything, such inquiries can further assist us in making richer meaning out of Sancho's corrupt, death-dealing, and sinister antics throughout *Don Quixote*—as well as those who, in turn, dish it back to him.

In a futuristic sense, as the ideation and theorization of "futures" implies capitalism, capitalistic expansion, and capitalistic urgency, I conclude this meditation by reflecting across time and beyond early modernity. The futuristic ghostly remains of Sancho Panza's avarice and gluttony manifest clearly in the active, verbalized etymology of his name: *ensanchar*. From the 1732 third volume of the *Diccionario de Autoridades* to its modernized evolution by the Real Academia Española, the verb *ensanchar* means to enlarge, expand, extend, or stretch.[68] Increasing the original magnitude, proportion, and size of persons, places, and things, I cannot help but associate and transpose Sancho Panza's antics, ideology, and sentiments that we've examined in this meditation onto the larger sociocultural implications of the geographic, territorial, and topological domestication, expansion, and growth of urbanized Ensanche districts located in Barcelona, the City of Bata (Equatorial Guinea), and Manila. Bloated and big-bellied, Sancho Panza's behavior and ideological work stand as seventeenth-century precursors to Spain's nineteenth- and early twentieth-century cultural histories that financed and trafficked in slave labor; the illegal smuggling of and trading in Africans, Asians, and Indigenous persons and non-European commodities; and wealth originating in Africa, Cuba, Puerto Rico, and the Spanish Pacific.[69] I plunge further into these matters in meditation 4, "Cervantes Unhinged." Into the belly of the beast, we go!

MEDITATION 3

RETHINKING LUIS

Everybody has something to say about Luis. As early as 1768, at the Drury Lane Theater in London, the prolific English singer-songwriter Charles Dibdin repurposed Cervantes's black protagonist Luis from the story *El celoso extremeño* (*The Jealous Extremaduran*, 1613) in his two-act comic opera called *The Padlock*. Irish librettist and playwright Isaac Bickerstaffe wrote the play's text. In her new book, *Voice, Slavery, and Race in Seventeenth-Century Florence*, musicologist Emily Wilbourne returns to Monica L. Miller's rich discussion of *The Padlock*, where they both underscore the idea that "Bickerstaffe's condensation of Cervantes's morality tale turns Luis, a complacent Negro eunuch, into Mungo (performed by a libretto by Charles Dibdin), [an enslaved blackface caricature from the West Indies] with an attitude."[1]

While I would not necessarily reduce Luis's role in the novella to mere complacency, the purported notion of the black eunuch as complacent has unfortunately dominated generations of scholarly interpretations of the figure. As early as 1982, in *Cervantes and the Humanist Vision: A Study of Four Exemplary Novels*, Alban K. Forcione damns Luis as an "ignorant," "pathetic," and "simple Negro."[2] Juan Bautista Avalle-Arce, in his essay "'El celoso extremeño,' de Cervantes," emphasizes the picturesque touch Cervantes lends to Luis in the story. More recently, Eduardo Ruiz, in two complementary studies—"Cervantes's *Celoso*: A Tale of Colonial Lack" and "Counter-Discursive and Erotic Agency: The Case of the Black Slaves in Miguel de Cervantes's 'El celoso extremeño'"—examines how Cervantes treats two enslaved black

Africans, Guiomar and Luis, who remain central to the story's plot and the significance of blackness in Spain's colonial experiment, particularly along historical and psychological lines.[3]

Drawing from the critical reception bestowed on Cervantes's *El celoso extremeño*, I too wish to have a say on the matter of Cervantes's handling of Luis. I frame this meditation around one general yet crucial question: Why Luis? Yes, of course, it goes without saying that the protagonist of the novella is Felipo de Carrizales, for it is the name of the man who has provided the material for our tale.[4] But to ask about Luis invigorates a different kind of reading of Cervantes's story. To ask about Luis enables me, in my literary imagination of wayward black worldmaking, to decenter Carrizales, thereby picking up where Cervantine criticism has lagged. To ask about Luis therefore challenges us as readers to center Luis's blackness—castrated, gendered, historical, queer, sonic, sexualized—which then authorizes us to quell the temptation of beginning our analysis of him at the peripheral limits of the narrator's story. Let me be clear: just because the very category of "black" functions as a racialized schema in Western discourses and social formations, such a reality does not mean that Luis's blackness must be relegated to a mere colonial imposition on empirically verifiable black beings that preexist this classification. To the contrary, this arrangement defies any sort of quasi comprehensibility, if it does so at all, outside the modern West.[5]

As I've discussed in the prologue and meditation 1, *Cervantine Blackness*—not only as a book but also as a paradigm—seeks to merge conversations within Cervantine studies and critical black studies somewhat uneasily without positioning either as emancipatory vis-à-vis the other. In doing so my close reading of *El celoso extremeño* awakens, disturbs, and illuminates plentiful moments from the story that highlight Luis's multivalent blackness, however artificial and fictionalized some may prefer to think of it. We need to rethink Luis. I turn to gerunds to rethink Luis. Catalyzed grammatically and progressively by the *-ing* gerundial form of the verb *rethink*, my sustained reflection on *rethinking* Luis shall unfold herein over three disquisitions: (1) his status as black eunuch in relation to Cervantes's Ottoman-inspired motif of the harem, (2) his love for music and the guitar, and (3) his queerness and queer bond with Loaysa. As such, my three ruminations on rethinking Luis offer new ways for us to disentangle the inner machination of how and where Cervantine Blackness—as a concept and theory that understands blackness through aliveness, becoming, liquidity, mobility, and spatiality—manifests and moves in *El celoso extremeño*. To achieve this I distill and make meaning out of the intersecting roles that BDSM and pornography, music, queerness, and sound play in Cervantes's construction of the old black eunuch and those adjacent to him.

Who's Luis?

If we follow his trail of clues, if we know what to look for—how to *sense* it—Cervantes casts right before our eyes Luis's black being, culture, feeling, life, and space. The narrator of *El celoso extremeño* informs us that he's an old black eunuch ("un negro viejo y eunuco"). He lives at the threshold, the interstice, of the *casapuerta*, a combined apartment-cum-stable, erected for him by the seventy-year-old Carrizales, to guard the house and the women inside ("En el portal de la calle, que en Sevilla llaman *casapuerta*, hizo una caballeriza para una mula, y encima della un pajar y apartamiento donde estuviese el que había de curar della").[6] *Casapuerta*. Hayloft. Apartment-cum-stable. Each of these words identify the space in which Luis lives. Taking cues from Saidiya Hartman's *Wayward Lives*, I treat Cervantes's construction of Luis's threshold—or the interstice of his *casapuerta*—as a "black interior," a place for thought and action, for study and vandalism, for love and trouble.[7] This black interior, from which I take inspiration, dialogues in historical and theoretical terms with geographer J. T. Roane's concept of "plotting the black commons."[8] Drawing from Roane's field-changing scholarship in *Dark Agoras: Insurgent Black Social Life and the Politics of Place* and "Plotting the Black Commons," I rethink Luis's interstitial hayloft apartment as a liminal zone. With cues from Roane's theoretical apparatus, the spatial liminality of the hayloft allows me to historicize the work of enslaved, free, and emancipated communities to create a distinctive and often furtive social architecture, rivaling, threatening, and challenging the infrastructures of abstraction, commodification, and social control developed by white elites before and after the formal abolition of slavery.[9]

An idea to ponder: given Carrizales's old age, could Luis have accompanied and traveled with the jealous man to the Spanish Americas—and elsewhere—when they were younger? The narrator clues us in on fragmented details: Luis is his name, he loves music and wine, and the Castilian he speaks isn't the Africanized *habla de negros* spoken by the enslaved black girl named Guiomar (who also inhabits the Carrizales household), nor by many of the real-life black residents of Seville. Luis has his own money too—as indicated by the text's use of the word *quilates* (carats)—for he can afford to hire and pay Loaysa for music lessons ("Harto mejor os lo pagara yo—dijo

Luis—a tener lugar de tomar lición" ["I'd pay you even better—said Luis—for a chance to take a lesson"]).[10] Luis actively and consciously participates in Loaysa's ruse by helping him gain access to Carrizales's forbidden property and space: his house and teenage wife, Leonora ("al parecer de edad trece o catorce años" ["apparently thirteen or fourteen years old"]).[11] We learn from Loaysa that Luis has a high-pitched treble voice, one possessed by *castrato* singers ("más que he oído decir que vos tenéis muy buena habilidad, y a lo que siento y puedo juzgar por el órgano de la voz, que es *atiplada*, debéis de cantar bien" ["I've heard that you have very good abilities, and from what I hear and can judge from the instrument of your voice, which is high-pitched, you must sing very well"]).[12] Working in the field of early modern Italian studies, musicologist Emily Wilbourne confirms my inclination to breathe life into the idea of Luis as a black castrato in Cervantes's story. Wilbourne reminds us that "the Black castrato voice is . . . made for music in a very literal sense."[13] Much more than an instrument—identified as an "órgano de la voz" (instrument of your voice) in Cervantes's text—we come to learn in the pages ahead how the interlocking categories and cultural logics of gender, queerness, race, and sex undergird the fortitude and power foreclosed in Luis's black castrato voice.

My critical fabulation and wayward curiosity about Cervantes's fictional Luis aligns with real-life, historical Luises who lived in seventeenth-century Seville. For example, in *capítulo* 2 of his poetic enterprise, *Viaje del Parnaso* (1614), Cervantes lauds the Judeo-converso dramaturge Felipe Godínez in the following strophe: "Este que tiene como mes de mayo / como florido ingenio, y que comienza ahora / a hacer de sus comedias nuevo ensayo / Godínez es" (This Godínez, whose flowery wit like the month of May now begins / to make anew rehearsal out of his plays).[14] Recognizing his merits, Cervantes and his connection to Godínez captivate and orient my retracing of an untapped reservoir of literary history I wish to recreate. Both archival records and performance history sources tell us that Cervantes's contemporary Godínez had an active role in sub-Saharan African slavery. According to a document dated in 1620, housed in Seville's Archivo de Protocolos, Godínez owned a twenty-one-year-old African-descended man—"de color mulato" (*mulato* complexioned)—named Christobal.[15] Godínez's sister, Felipa, transferred her ownership of Christobal over to her brother as a kind of "donation."[16] Within Godínez's household, Christobal carried out an assortment of domestic duties, ranging from cooking and maintaining the house to running local errands. Over time Godínez developed a close bond with Christobal, whom he took under his wing, making him his apprentice and instructing Christobal in the art of advertising theater shows in Seville's *corrales de comedias* (playhouses) as a *pregonero* (town crier).

As I've discussed in *Staging* Habla de Negros, *pregoneros* reported breaking news or the hot topics of the given day or week as well as announced bullfights and theater shows. Sometimes they sold candy, snacks, and other kinds of street foods for any passerby to purchase and consume. One literary example that corroborates historical "fact" appears in act 3 of Lope de Vega's play *El amante agradecido* (1618). In this scene two black men, named Francisco and Pedro, speaking in habla de negros, sell butter and a loaf of bread unique to Andalusia, called a *mollete*.[17] To enhance their skill as orators, pregoneros would sing or perform live music with instruments. To advertise theater shows, in some instances, black and African-descended pregoneros, like Christobal, played drums after having glued playbills onto public structures. Under the apprenticeship and surveillance of Godínez, Christobal and other pregoneros alike would have put up playbills advertising performances by the theater company of Juan Acacio y Diego Valcelejo. The Corral of Doña Elvira in Seville hosted his troupe during Corpus Christi festivities in 1619. As we might take seriously the long history of black music and black soundscapes across the African diaspora, pregoneros participated in what literary critic Christopher Freeburg terms "counterlife." Performing either adjacent to or within Seville's auction blocks and other densely populated urban spaces around the city, the artistic and sensorial work—or counterlife—of black pregoneros sheds lights on the profound instability and mystery anew in the relations between black social life, artistic expression, and oppressive institutions.[18]

Historical sources designate the first use and circulation of theater playbills as early as 1561. (And the archive is saturated with Luises, so it seems.) It is during this time and several decades later, in 1602—a decade before the publication of Cervantes's *Novelas ejemplares* in 1613—where we meet a historical, real-life mirror to Cervantes's Luis: an enslaved black man named Luis. Records located in Seville's Archivo de Protocolos indicate that this man belonged to Luis Téllez de Guzmán. Working in concert with the playwright Luis de Oviedo, these documents explain that the enslaved black man, Luis, worked under contract for three months, starting on October 19. Luis's owner, Téllez de Guzmán, received two *ducados* (twenty-two *reales*) from the playwright. And in exchange for Luis's labor putting up playbills and playing his drum, he would receive one *real* daily.[19]

Taking these historical anecdotes into consideration, I wonder, What are the bounds and limits of Luis's enslavement? How might we rethink his access, movement, or perhaps "freedom" within the novella? Is he really the fungible, gullible, and pathetic creature that a cadre of literary scholars have insisted on reinscribing in Cervantine studies? To be quite honest, I question one's faithful and literal reading of the fixity and the rigidity of Luis's purported status as "slave" in the text. Throughout the story the narrator and other characters either call Luis by his name or refer to him as *"el negro"* (the black man), but categories such as *bozal* (unacculturated, unassimilated, unseasoned) and *esclavo* (slave) are not used. In this context I read against the grain of the established codification and conditioning of Luis's enslavement. As we shall come to hear, learn, and see, I suggest, in my Barthes-inspired ruminations on Luis's singing voice, we should listen for the embodied, musicalized, sonorous matter and noise embedded within the black eunuch's voice.[20] It's curious that Cervantes's narrator does not explicitly reference Luis's assumed-to-be-enslaved status to readers until the very end of the story, whereas the Francisco Porras de la Cámara 1606 manuscript leaves out this detail. And one could even retort that the narrator's initial mentioning of the *caballeriza* (hayloft apartment, stable) signals Luis's putative enslavement. Such a conclusive assumption traffics in antiblackness—an antiblack world whose antiblackness expects blackness from black people.[21]

This meditation, as does this entire book, follows in the footsteps of Kevin Quashie's and Saidiya Hartman's methods of wayward reading practices that create black worlds. While it is correct to remind ourselves that Cervantes is *not* a black writer (nor any of his predecessors or contemporaries treated in this book for that matter), this kind of binarized white-over-black thinking distracts us from the ethos I aspire to create in *Cervantine Blackness*. This project's ethos embraces the luxuries of thinking with and through the materiality of texts—that is, I privilege them and see them in a black world, in whatever manifestation of black worldness those texts create.[22] Blackness (not antiblackness) in its totality subtends Cervantes's idiom of the caballeriza in relation to Luis. Enslaved or free, Luis and his blackness in *El celoso extremeño* draws deeper meaning from much larger cultural and literary histories that inform and influence the works of Cervantes, his predecessors, and his contemporaries. Tethered to the caballeriza idiom, I reiterate my provocation of and commitment to reading Luis's hayloft apartment as a black interior that reflects a large black world. By doing so I elude the discursive trap of the black historical past qua the caballeriza as a monolith of terror wrought by the structure of modernity.[23] Thus framing the caballeriza as a black interior manifests in a wide range of literary sources such as Rodrigo de Reinosa's "Gelofe, Mandinga" (1516–24), the anonymous picaresque novel *Lazarillo de Tormes* (1554), and María de Zayas y Sotomayor's short story "El prevenido engañado" (1637; in *Novelas amorosas y ejemplares*), among many other Iberian-language texts that allude to enslaved black Africans in stables. But considering my own close reflection and historical analysis of the term, we can no longer uncritically assume that the terminological cohabitation of "black" and "caballeriza" automatically designate slave status to sub-Saharan African and African-descended people. Could it be that the narrator leaves it up to us as readers to decide? I surmise this pertains to Cervantes's construction of Luis's freedom in the novella: his maneuverings and movement within the textual and spatial thresholds of *El celoso extremeño* and Carrizales's house.

As this meditation dares to reimagine Luis's multidimensional role in *El celoso extremeño*, my interventions herein serve as a counterpoint to James D. Fernández's "New World" analysis in his classic essay "The Bonds of Patrimony: Cervantes and the New World." I build out of Fernández's conclusion that "the appropriate argument is not that 'El celoso extremeño' is exclusively about colonialism *but rather that in early modern Spain it is impossible to disentangle the discourses of race and gender, the concerns of colonialism and humanism—the architecture of harem, convent, and island.*"[24] Focusing on Cervantes's Ottoman-inspired motif of the architecture of harems, I move beyond Fernández's closing remark by taking up Cory A. Reed's astute claim that Cervantes casts Luis as the "Kızlar Ağası," or "Chief Black Eunuch," to guard the house and the women and girls inside—a fact that we should not disconnect from the idea of the harem motif in *El celoso extremeño* as a skillfully constructed metaphorical system.[25] More recently, in her award-winning essay, "In the Name of Love: Cervantes's Play on Captivity in *La gran sultana*," Ana Laguna substantiates the noteworthy idea of Cervantine harems.[26] To that end my rethinking of Luis's centrality, personhood, and power in the novella hinges on our methodological close reading, historicizing, and framing of Luis in these robust terms.

Cervantes's narrator doesn't tell us when, where, or at what age Luis had his genitalia removed. Could it be that a surgeon performed a radical castration on Luis, whereby the procedures for the castration of eunuchs were that the testicles were cut out through incisions in the scrotum, crushed, or even dissolved in young children by friction and pressed in a hot bath?[27] We just don't know. Cervantes tells us nothing. But what we can discern from the information provided in the story is that the old black man is in fact a eunuch.

Epistemologically, the category of the black eunuch invites us to come to know and encounter those ways in which Luis's racially gendered position as eunuch in *El celoso* lends itself to a wider black epistemology of what we as readers can further attest to and glean from Luis's being, personhood, and sensibilities. My philosophical and theoretical interests and concerns pertain to what I perceive as the embodiment of Luis's gender-fluid, genderqueer, or nonbinary configurations in the story. As such, my close readings of *El celoso* derive from, and are indebted to, cultural studies, queer theory, race studies, and social history. In the groundbreaking and timely work of Abdulhamit Arvas, we learn that "'eunuch' was a distinct category in the [early modern] period—one that productively demonstrates the ways that gender and race were co-constituted. Eunuchs' bodies were re-formed, re-figured, and re-inscribed, and ultimately existed beyond the male-female binary." Arvas further explains that "eunuchs became an important part of the administrative apparatus of the Ottoman Empire in the fifteenth century as domestic servants within the gender-situated royal household, or harem." For our interests, by highlighting Ottoman eunuchs' responsibility for supervising the women in the harem, we learn from Arvas that eunuchs mediate "between the sultan and his family members, [guard] access to the interiors of the palace and to the sultan's private chambers as well as [oversee] the early training and education of princes."[28] Placed in dialogue with Arvas's insights, both Laguna's and Reed's meticulous work on eunuchs and Cervantine harems corroborates the early modern cultural and literary histories Arvas expounds in "Early Modern Eunuchs" and his forthcoming book *Abducted Boys: The Homoerotics of Race and Empire in Early Modernity*.[29]

In Cervantine criticism, Reed clarifies:

> *El celoso* is not a disquisition on harems *per se*. Cervantes does not use this space to expose or judge Ottoman society of its practices. In fact, that author never uses the word "harén" in this story, and the dubiously-synonymous "serallo" appears only once, long after Cervantes has already established the confines and prohibitions of Carrizales' house in the context of the old man's jealously. Yet in his methodical delineation of the formidable dwelling, compared initially to a secluded convent, Cervantes evokes the harem in a subtle but deliberate way. The harem (in both its traditional and colloquial connotations) not only inspires Cervantes' narration of the house's architectural composition, but also underscores thematically Leonara's situation of confinement. The word "harem" derives from the

Arabic *ḥarām* meaning that which is unlawful or socially taboo and existing in opposition to the term *ḥalāl*, or that which is permitted by law. The harem ... is therefore literally a forbidden zone.[30]

Alban K. Forcione, Jateen Lad, and Leslie P. Peirce also underscore the architectural and institutional elements of the harem as a "forbidden space" that represented "diagrams of power [where] eunuchs were its principal upholders."[31] Cervantes also provides such architectural and institutional features of the harem, derived from Islamic and Ottoman models. For instance, the mention of doors, walls, windows, and turnstiles as the only tangible elements of Carrizales's house recalls the emphasis given on gates and barriers in the contemporary relations of the imperial harem. As documented in European diplomatic and intellectual circles during the late sixteenth and early seventeenth centuries, first impressions of the Topkapı Palace in Constantinople reflect how Carrizales's house possesses architectural components such as locks, portals, and walls that replicate the sultan's Topkapı Palace.[32] From these European narratives of the sultan's palace, I argue that Cervantes dislocates the Ottoman harem for early modern Western audiences. Through such a Cervantine dislocation of place and space, we can trace, reconsider, and reimagine how Carrizales closed off windows and skylights to reflect an analogous construction in the harem. What is more, we can learn from these texts' discussion of black eunuchs who guard the female quarters and prevent the unauthorized from entering. Together these components constitute European aesthetic, cultural, and literary ideations of the imperial harem, drawn from conventional wisdom as well as direct scrutiny by those allowed inside Topkapı. As discussed in the respective works of Laguna and Reed, Cervantes employs these same elements to delineate his description of Carrizales's house in *El celoso extremeño*. Such elements enable Cervantes to then create a hayloft apartment for the black eunuch Luis to guard the front entrance that mimics the two-story barracks of Turkish black eunuchs who likewise guard the harem, situated between the interior of the women's residence and the gatehouse or stable area.[33]

I queried at an earlier stage: Who's Luis? Mise en abyme. Mise-en-page. These two terms: one denotes and inflicts self-reflection in a written work, and the other speaks to the composition, design, and layout of a text, illustration, or picture. Mise en abyme and mise-en-page frame my constellation of wayward thoughts about Luis. Graduating our analysis from the literary and the historical to the visual, I close this section with an anonymous painting

Fig. 6. *African Kızlar Ağası*, source unknown, 1682. Photo: Balfore Archive Images / Alamy Stock Photo.

from 1682: *African Kızlar Ağası*. I gently remind you, my dear reader, that this image also accompanies and frames this third meditation. To imagine, see, and sense *visually* Luis, let's illumine the potential visual economies of the *African Kızlar Ağası*, or "Chief Black Eunuch," illustrated in figure 6.

Frames within a frame show regal, dark skin juxtaposed against a creamy off-white turban, an elongated bundle of spherical orbs—polished diamonds or pearls, perhaps—resembling a bovine or equestrian tail (I'm signaling explicitly the Yorùbá *ìrùkẹ̀rẹ̀*), and a mini vase-shaped tear-drop earring. The image gives us only a profile picture of the Kızlar Ağası.[34] Spatially, the portrait frames this person as flat and two dimensional, potentially indicative of his cutoff genitalia. A symbolic substitution for the eunuch's removed genitals, the phallic staff he grasps functions as another kind of frame that breaks from the spherical, coiffured turban. Whatever the Kızlar Ağası protagonized in this painting may lack, it thus becomes realized and repurposed by the objects draping his body in this visual representation. I rely on this anonymous painting to summon a deeper curiosity into Cervantes's written depiction of Luis—as well as the historical Luises from whom he could've derived inspiration—in *El celoso extremeño*.

Luis's Throat, Phallic Corridors

Cervantes remixes the meaning of Luis's racially gendered and marked body as a eunuch. He achieves this remixing through the tropes of music, musical instruments, and music notes (e.g., printed sheet music, the keys on a harpsichord or keyboard, the sonic capacities of the voice). Cervantes demonstrates a unique set of knowledge about the varied constructions of neutered male bodies across the color lines of ethnicity and race. And, however comical, fictitious, hackneyed, or superficial his perceived representation of Luis's connection to guitar playing and singing may be for some, I maintain that the thematic content of music and musical instruments is not mutually exclusive from how Cervantes encodes Luis's embodied blackness as a eunuch in the novella, which we must historicize to see how Cervantine Blackness operates conceptually in this story. In the same vein, Agustín González de Amezúa y Mayo's insistence that everything in the tale—the house, the characters, the urban setting, the songs, and the action itself—are "copies" from the reality of the Seville of Cervantes's time; such copies attest to the author's marvelous powers of observation.[35]

The so-called copies Amezúa identifies function as what I like to call *quotidian imports* from early modern Iberian real life. Cervantes's quotidian import of Luis accounts for, tracks, and recognizes the cultural and social histories of African diasporic black life reverberating in *El celoso extremeño*.[36] As art historian and theorist Tina M. Campt aptly puts it, "The quotidian must be understood as a practice rather than an act/ion." Campt adds that the quotidian "is a practice honed by the dispossessed in the struggle to create possibility within the constraints of everyday life."[37] Through his music and voice, Luis performs a variety of refusals against Carrizales's firm clutch on those inhabiting his home. To illustrate the unfolding of the themes of music, musical instruments, songs, and dances in the story, I'd like to quote at length a conversation between Loaysa and Luis:

> —Yo—respondió Loaysa—soy un pobre estropeado de una pierna, que gano mi vida pidiendo por Dios a la buena gente; y juntamente con esto, enseño a tañer a algunos morenos y otra gente pobre, y ya tengo tres negros; esclavos de tres veinticuatros, a quien he enseñado de modo que pueden cantar y tañer en cualquier baile y en cualquier taberna, y me lo han pagado muy rebien.
> —Harto mejor os lo pagara yo—dijo Luis—a tener lugar de tomar lición; pero no es posible, a causa que mi amo, en saliendo

por la mañana, cierra la puerta de la calle, y cuando vuelve hace lo mismo, dejándome emparedado entre dos puertas.

—Por Dios, Luis—replicó Loaysa, que ya sabía el nombre del negro—, que si vos diésedes traza a que yo entrase algunas noches a daros lición, en menos de quince días os sacaría tan diestro en la guitarra que pudiésedes tañer sin vergüenza alguna en cualquiera esquina; porque os hago saber que tengo grandísima gracia en el enseñar, y más que he oído decir que vos tenéis muy buena habilidad, y a lo que siento y puedo juzgar por el órgano de la voz, que es atiplada, debéis de cantar muy bien.

—No canto mal—respondió el negro—; pero ¿qué aprovecha, pues no sé tonada alguna si no es la de *La estrella de Venus* y la de *Por un verde pardo*, y aquella que ahora se usa, que dice:

A los hierros de una reja
la turbada mano asida?

—Todas ésas son aire—dijo Loaysa—para las que yo os podría enseñar, porque sé todas las del moro Abindarráez, con las de su dama Jarifa, y todas las que se cantan de la historia del gran sofí Tomunibeyo, con las de la zarabanda a lo divino, que son tales, que hacen pasmar a los mismo portugueses; y esto enseño con tales modos y con tanta facilidad, que aunque no os deis prisa a aprender, apenas habréis comido tres o cuatro moyos de sal cuando ya os véis músico corriente y moliente en todo género de guitarra.

A esto suspiró el negro y dijo:
—¿Qué aprovecha todo eso, si no sé cómo meteros en casa?

["I," responded Loaysa, "am a poor one-legged cripple who earns his living begging for the love of God from good people; and along with that, I teach some dark-skinned slaves and other poor people to play; and I have three blacks, slaves of three councilmen, and I've taught them so they can sing and play at any dance and in any tavern, and they paid me very, very well for that."

"I'd pay you even better," said Luis, "for a chance to take a lesson, but that isn't possible because of my master; when he goes out in the morning, he locks the street door, and then does the same thing when he returns, leaving me walled in between two doors."

"For God's sake, Luis," replied Loaysa, who already knew the black man's name, "if you found a way to let me in for a few nights to give you a lesson, in less than two weeks, I'd make you so good on the guitar that you could play on any street corner with no embarrassment at all; because I'll tell you that I'm a really skillful teacher, and besides that, I've heard you have very good abilities, and from what I hear and can judge from the instrument of your voice, which is high-pitched, you must sing very well."

"I don't sing badly," responded the black, "but what good does it do me since I don't know any songs except 'The Start of Venus' and 'Through a Green Meadow,' and that one that's so popular now that goes:

'The troubled hand that clutches
at the iron prison bars?'"

"All of those are nothing but air," said Loaysa, "compared to the ones I could teach you, because I know all the songs about the Moor Abindarráez and his lady Jarifa, and all the songs about the history of the great Sofí Tomunibeyo, and the sacred ones in the style of the sarabande that are so good they astonish even the Portuguese. And I teach all this with so good a method and so much facility that, even if you're not in a hurry to learn, by the time you've eaten three or four heaps of salt you'll find yourself a run-of-the-mill musician in every manner and of guitar song."

At this the black sighed and said:

"What good is all this if I don't know how to get you inside the house?"][38]

In a tenor and style so unique to Cervantes's prose fiction, folklore bejewels this extensive conversation between Loaysa and Luis. The passage palpitates with quotidian flare, whereby we gain a sense of the popular songs and tunes of Cervantes's time. Through their ensuing homosocial bond, one that will intensify over the course of the story, we learn from this exchange that Luis plays the guitar so well that he gives instrument and vocal lessons to not just enslaved blacks but also impoverished people from diverse walks of life.

As the story evolves, it is through music that Loaysa enthralls, seduces, and woos not just Leonora but the other girls, women, *and* Luis inside Carrizales's house. What is more, this passage teaches us that those songs such as "La estrella de Venus," "Por un verde prado," "A los hierros de una reja," and the sequence of ballads of the so-called Moor Abindarráez and his "dama Jarifa" were in vogue during Cervantes's time. For what it's worth, these intertextual references lay the foundation for a broader and more expansive vision of interconnected Mediterranean, Iberian, and Ottoman worlds. To that effect Loaysa volleys a corollary of Sevillano quotidian dance, lyric, and musical cultures. Each element thus offers Luis a musical lexicon for thinking *beyond* the confines of his hayloft apartment. Luis's black interior constellates a space for thought and action, for study and creativity, for peering and spying. Bittersweet and ironic, it is through these ambient aural, musical, instrumental, and sonic urban landscapes that Loaysa implants seeds of fugitivity, refusal, and rupture into Luis's mind. A heuristic of frottage, or cross-cultural contact and intimacies, might also characterize how Islamic dance and sonic cultures cross-pollinate with Luis's embodied musical knowledge. Although not referenced in this quote—yet germane to the eroticized, voyeuristic peep-show scene in the novella, which I uncover in the next section—Loaysa's musical abilities and skills range from performing dances like the *zarabanda, Pésame dello,* and *seguidillas* to singing the *coplillas* from *Madre, la mi madre, guardas me ponéis* that famously filled the streets of Sevilla.[39] As I have not only demonstrated and analyzed extensively in chapter 1 from *Staging* Habla de Negros but have also proposed in other publications, black Africans in early modern Iberia and across the early African diaspora frequently addressed the institution of slavery and its attendant uncertainties and pressures with the most potent weapons at their disposal—not muscle and might but the materiality of clothing, food, hair, makeup, religion and spirituality, and song and dance.[40]

The dialogue between Loaysa and Luis also crystallizes Cervantes's brief history of sub-Saharan African race relations in a broader early modern Mediterranean context (e.g., Loaysa's references to black musicians and singers and enslaved blacks of council members, as well as his mentioning of the mythical Prester John).[41] More specifically, the theme of music and references to musical instruments featured therein ground Cervantes's keen awareness of the skilled occupations held by black Africans in early modern Spain and Portugal. Early modern European descriptions of West Africa and Ethiopia have stressed the role of music across African societies. Writing in the 1450s, the Venetian explorer and trafficker of enslaved Africans, Alvise Cadamosto, in *The Voyages of Cadamosto and Other Documents on Western Africa,* described Senegambian women's readiness "to sing and dance," pointing out for his readers that "their dances are very different from ours."[42]

Recapitulating Loaysa's playful evocation of "Preste Juan de las Indias"—as conceived by Cervantes to articulate Loaysa's promise to Luis that if he's able to penetrate Carrizales's house at night, he can then teach Luis better than Prester John of the Indies—a particularly illuminating piece of evidence, published in Francisco Álvares's *Do Preste Joam das Indias: Verdadera Informaçam das Terras do Preste Joam* (1540), lists musical instruments in use in Ethiopia in the 1520s. Álvares approximates African instruments, those from the legendary kingdom of Prester John, to ones he knows in Europe with the following names: cymbals, drums, flutes, tambourines, trumpets, and a single-stringed bowed lute traditionally from Ethiopia called a *chira-wata*, or masinko.[43] Describing other instruments, Álvares further comments, "There are trumpets, but not good ones; there are many kettledrums of copper which come from Cairo, and others of wood which have leather on both sides; there are tambourines like ours, and big cymbals which they sound. There are flutes and some instruments with chords, square like harps, which they call *David moçanquo* [masinqo], which means the harp of David. They play these to the Prester, and not well."[44] Cervantes's cultural and historical imports from sixteenth-century Portuguese travel writers reveal the fluid interconnectedness and rich intertextual approach the author utilizes to deploy not only Luis's blackness but also local and mythical formulations of blackness that move within and beyond Iberia and the Mediterranean.

The Portuguese context also informs the extensive conversation between Loaysa and Luis, which we cannot divorce from the real histories and real lives of black guitar players. As we can glimpse from the previously cited exchange, Cervantes explicitly conjoins the tropes of the guitar with Luis's black body. My take on Luis, as a black guitar player, seeks to rupture extant scholarly readings that see black guitar players' relationship to their instrument as only a stereotypical preference and proclivity.[45] I concur with musicologist Rogério Budasz's assessment that "regardless of the racist tone of most [literary works], black actors and musicians who were trained in the Iberian tradition could have explored the possibilities of combining the structures, rhythms and timbres of Iberian, Central African and Western African musical styles."[46] Black guitarists were not uncommon in the early modern period, as one might readily assume. These instrumentalists contributed to and participated in integral parts of daily life across the early modern Iberian world. One concrete example of a black musician well adapted to early modern Portuguese court culture and speaking Portuguese fluently— not the Africanized Portuguese commonly referred to as *fala de preto* or *fala da Guiné*—appears in Antonio Ribeiro Chiado's *Auto da natural invencão* (ca. 1580). In this dramatic work, performed around 1580 in the court of King João III of Portugal—when Felipe II assumed the Portuguese throne and was subsequently crowned Felipe I of Portugal—the black actor and guitar player challenges his purported subservient condition when asked to cede his chair to a visitor, but the black man revokes such an order when he performs and proves his talent and is acclaimed as a "Black Orpheus."

Cervantes explodes this Iberian tradition of black orphic references that predate his 1613 prose fiction repertoire of the *Novelas ejemplares*. In his exemplary novel *Rinconete y Cortadillo*, the swindlers Rinconete and Cortadillo marvel at Gananciosa's new palmetto broom because they had never seen one before. Taking note at their marvel, Maniferro says, "¿Admíranse de la escoba? Pues bien hacen, pues música más presta y más sin pesadumbre, ni más barata, no se ha inventado en el mundo; y en verdad que oí decir el otro día a un estudiante que ni el Negrofeo, que sacó a la Arauz del infierno." ("Are you surprised at the broom? Well, good for them, because no one in the world has invented music that is fast, less trouble, or cheaper; in fact, the other day I heard a student say that not even Negrorpheus who got Yuridis out of hell.")[47] The Sevillano soundscape that fills this scene—one where there are no musical instruments but one's body, rhythm, and soul—potently punctuates the organic, primordial, and raw materiality of music in Cervantes. The "instruments" identified are Escalanta's *chapín* (high-heel shoe), Gananciosa's palmetto broom, and Monipodio's thick shards of a broken clay roof tile or plate (carrying the counterpoint to the broom and shoe). Each item signals Spain's vast transoceanic reaches across the Iberian world. Just as much as this passage demonstrates Cervantes's renovation and revival of classical and mythological references in seventeenth-century Spain, it also punctuates a richly materialized circulation of global objects.[48] While not directly related to Marcel Camus's 1959 version filmed in Brazil, this cultural and literary tradition of Orpheus also manifested centuries later in the Afro-Brazilian context of Black Orpheus.[49]

Luis's throat. At this juncture I invite you to imagine with me Luis's castrated body and gender-queer voice through the embodiment and symbolic power of his throat. As defined by the *Oxford English Dictionary*, the "throat" is the location of the vocal organs and the place where speech or song originates.[50] As efficacious the *OED*'s entry is, I'd like to be more audacious with my usage of "throat." Luis's throat works as a substitution for his castration: his missing phallus. Luis's throat also cannot be delinked from how his voice reverberates throughout *El celoso extremeño*. Amanda Weidman tells us that "voice is both a sonic and material phenomenon and a powerful metaphor." Eroticized, racialized, and sexualized, Luis's throat encapsulates the material phenomenon of which Weidman speaks. The anthropologist further explicates that "the materiality of voice has to do with the sound itself as well as with the bodily process of producing and attending to voices."[51] What Luis's voice comes to signify in *El celoso extremeño* cannot be severed from the story's narrative descriptions. Another worthwhile way to reimagine Cervantes's construction of Luis's voice—and what I perceive his throat to accomplish, perform, and produce—manifests in the author's fascinating descriptor *atiplado* (high-pitched). As the tricksy Loaysa tells us, he can "hear and judge from the instrument [organ] of [Luis's] voice, which is *high-pitched*, [that Luis] can sing very well."[52] The high-pitched register with which Loaysa identifies Luis further marks the racially gendered embodiment of the black eunuch's castrated body. To an extent, the so-called high-pitched vocal range and quality by which Loaysa identifies Luis shed light on how Cervantes complicates, on the one hand, and inverts, on the other hand, the signification of a so-called masculine constitution of Luis's castrated black body. Cervantes's imagery of Luis's castrated black body thus signals to me the textured way in which the author obfuscates early modern Spanish literary constructions of black characters who sing songs and play instruments, as specifically codified through the verbs *cantar* (to flirt, to have sexual relations, to sing) and *tañer* (to caress; to fondle; to play, pluck, or strum a percussive or stringed instrument).

As such, Cervantes's written discourse on the castrated and high-pitched body of Luis allows me to trace and thread meaning into the messy entanglements foreclosed in the Spanish verbs *cantar* and *tañer*. As far as I'm concerned, these two verbs exacerbate and pervert early modern Iberian Atlantic and Mediterranean constitutions of how we, as present-day readers, might reformulate Luis's throat. One explicit text that I have in mind that performs such nasty work on the throat is an episode from the poem "Canta, Jorgico canta"—attributed to the Cantabrian poet Rodrigo de Reinosa—which renders pornographic tropings of the *argolla* (collar, necklace, shackle; v. 116) and *hierro* (v. 115) wrapped around the neck and foot of a black servant named Jorgico. From *argolla* and *hierro*, we can extract a racially gendered economy operating at the level of a lewd, twisted, and unequal interracial love affair that could potentially go the wrong way between Jorgico and the white Lady of the household (identified in the text as "La Señora"). What many scholars have failed to comment on plays out in the poem's evident portrayal of a domestic slave economy that ultimately relies heavily on the transformative poetic efficacy of the repetitive and sexually charged word *garganta* (throat). The poem speaks for itself:

La Señora:
Canta, Jorge, por tu vida,
¿porqué m'has aborrecida?
Agora que m'as vencida?
¿qué es la causa que te espanta?
No queré cantá.
No me espanta tu figura
que mi pena me asegura;
mas no es mia la ventura
ni merezco gloria tanta.
No queré cantá.
Jorge, no seas grossero,
pues que ves quánto te quiero;
con puro amor verdadero
en mí tu vista se planta.
No queré cantá.
Jorgico:
En el tiempo que he servido
nunca me avéys conocido;
de cantar sin ser querido
tengo seca la garganta.
No queré cantá.
La Señora:
Yo creo qu'estás sin seso
o qu'estás de amor compreso;
tienes mi coraçón preso
desd'el culo a la garganta.
No queré cantá.
Jorge, si vienes aýna,
matarête he una gallina
y sorberás la cozina
que te ablande la garganta.
No queré cantá.
Jorge, antes de acostar
te daré bien a cenar
de un capón que tengo assar

con un razimo de planta.
No queré cantá.
Jorgico, con tu canción,
detrás aquel pavellón
matarm'ás la comezón
cubiertos con una manta.
—*No queré cantá.*
Jorge, de que ayas cantado,
si de mí fueres pagado,
quedaré a tu mandato
con una voluntad tanta.
—*Ya queré cantá.*
Canta, Jorge, por tu fe,
y luego te quitaré
el hierro que traes al pie
y la argolla a la garganta.
—*No queré cantá.*
Si plazer q[ui]eres hazerme
y a tu servicio tenerme,
esto quieras concederme
pues es tu nobleza tanta,
—*No queré cantá.*

[**The Lady:**
For your life depends on it, sing (play), Jorge.
Do I disgust you?
Now that you've overcome me,
What scares you away (from me)?
—*What? You don't wanna play?*
Your body doesn't frighten me,
for my itch reassures me.
But the pleasure isn't mine
nor do I deserve such glory.
—*What? You don't wanna play?*
Don't be so rude, Jorge.
You see how much I want (love) you.
With true, unflinching love,
you can't take your eyes off me.
—*What? You don't wanna play?*

Jorgico:
In the time that I've served
you've never known me.
Singing without being loved
My throat is dry.
—*What? You don't wanna play?*
The Lady:
I believe you've gone crazy
Or, maybe, you're just head over heels.
You've got my heart jumping and open
From my asshole to my throat.
—*What? You don't wanna play?*
If you come by soon, Jorge,
I'll cook you up a hen
and you'll swallow up the kitchen,
so that you loosen up your throat.
—*What? You don't wanna play?*
Before you go to bed, Jorge,
I'll give you something good to eat
From a capon I must roast
with a stalk of bananas.
—*What? You don't wanna play?*
Jorgico, with your song
Behind that pavilion
You'll kill by death of unreachable itch, insatiable itch
Concealed by a blanket.
—*What? You don't wanna play?*
Jorge, since singing
If you were to have been paid by me,
I'll be at your service
so eager and ready.
—*Now he wants to play.*
In the name of your faith: sing Jorge,
And later on I'll remove
the iron chain bound to your foot
and the collar clutching your throat.
—*What? You don't wanna play?*
If you wish to pleasure me
and have me service you,

> it is your highest glory
> that you grant this wish.
> —What? You don't wanna play?][53]

Horniness. Itchiness. A horny itch. Reinosa exhibits ideations of race play that amount to coquettish vulgarity. To be clear, some would prefer to read the dialogue between Jorgico and the Lady as a rhetorical articulation of the sensuality of the voice, given its deep source in the center of the body (i.e., throat). While the bodies and body parts circulating throughout *Coplas de como una dama ruega a un negro* obviously do not belong to Luis in *El celoso extremeño*, I reject conventional interpretations that might foreclose and seek to obfuscate and occlude the interracial relationship between Jorgico and the Lady; such a claim to sensuality limits the suggestive and rigorous potential operative within the poetic discourse. It goes without saying that the passage's X-rated references, symbolisms, and wordplay make us skittish, calling us to recoil and clutch our pearls. Whether indicative of habla de negros or any other Iberian speech variant, Jorgico's marked language in the repeated refrain, "No queré cantá" (What? You don't wanna play?!), highlights the act of speaking the unspeakable.

Race play. If the so-called gesture of speaking the unspeakable—a black male servant *refusing* and perhaps *resisting* the carnal appetite and temptation of an aristocratic white woman's sexual advances—presents itself as race play, then I suggest we extend the theoretical aperture of racial pornographics through race play to consider how the unspeakable, violent pleasures exhibited in Jorgico's and the Lady's conversation enact race play. As theorized by Ariane Cruz in *The Color of Kink: Black Women, BDSM, and Pornography*, race play is a BDSM practice that explicitly plays with race. I use Cruz's definition to release the poem's kinky and racial pornographics codified in expletive throats that are interlinked by metal objects such as collars, necklaces, and shackles. Cruz further clarifies that "BDSM always already performs a kind of practice and theory of racial iconography. It channels moments of racialized excitement, signals instances of surprising pleasures in racialization, and illuminates hyperbolic performances of race that poke fun at the very project of race."[54] BDSM, as a new heuristic to analyze early modern Iberian literary works, opens our eyes to the ways in which these verses, attributed to Rodrigo de Reinosa, elucidate the dynamics of racialized shame, sadism, humiliation, and pleasure that undergird the genre of humor in performative poetry. As an example of a race-play pornographic text, this poem reveals how Jorgico and the Lady's intense, interracial aggression brings into sharp relief the kinky narrative of black-white intimacy that scripts early modern Iberian poetic narratives about the subjugated role between enslaved black men and aristocratic white women—a topic to which we will return in the next and final meditation, on María de Zayas y Sotomayor. What is more, this poetic work might be erotohistoriography's limit case: sadomasochistic role-play between black people and white people. I extend my interpretation and usage of role-play to the use of props and costuming that suggest specific social forms of power. Regardless of how one views sadomasochism, it is inescapably true that the body in sadomasochistic ritual becomes a means of invoking history—personal pasts, collective suffering, and quotidian forms of injustice—in an idiom of pleasure. Reinosa displays a potent poetic scene of interracial sadomasochism. As Saidiya Hartman argues of black physicality in *Scenes of Subjection*, the very ravished, wounded, discontinuous, fragmented, subjected body that anchors the scene of white subjectification holds out more possibility of restitution than the invocation of an illusory wholeness or the desired return to an originality plentitude.[55]

My analyses of throats—Luis's or otherwise—ultimately enable us to rethink the limits and bounds of his purported racialized masculinity, interracial intimacy, and erotic life tied to racism.[56] My sustained interest in Luis's "high-pitched" voice boomerangs back to Abdulhamit Arvas's meticulous investigation of the somatic traits that codify eunuchs as distinguishable according to large, beardless faces, high-pitched voices, and distinctive facial features and stature. As I explore in the following section, Luis's racially gendered and marked (amputated) body compels me to dig deeper into the significance of his cunning, existence, and movement in Carrizales's partitioned house.

Peek-a-Boo Peep Show, Queering Luis

There's a charged air and energy that permeates Carrizales's house. Moreover, a magnetic pulse charges the air around Loaysa and Luis. My fixation on the ambient and radiating thickness of nonbinary and nonnormative being in *El celoso extremeño* requires me, in this closing section, to rethink Luis through the queerness of his triply marked body as black, castrated, and fluid. Quiet as they are kept, and in disregard of what we're socialized to ignore, queerness and queer genealogies do in fact manifest in Cervantes's novella. Queer at heart and germane to central questions raised by Zeb Tortorici in his prize-winning book, *Sins Against Nature: Sex and Archives in Colonial New*

Spain, I follow in the historian's footsteps by asking how scholars might *queer* Cervantes's representation of Luis in *El celoso*. Drawing from Tortorici's self-reflexive work, my closing remarks herein aim to focus on what is strange, odd, funny, not-quite-right, and improper.[57] Reminiscent of the culture of BDSM, eroticism, kink, pornography, and race play discussed in the previous pages, Abdulhamit Arvas's insightful work makes a case for queering Luis. In doing so Arvas compels us to recognize the queerness of eunuchs' ambiguity insofar as it enabled them to oscillate between various spaces and power positions.[58] Roland Betancourt's interdisciplinary work in *Byzantine Intersectionality: Sexuality, Gender and Race in the Middle Ages*, for that matter, teaches us that eunuchs "served . . . as embodiments of genderqueer figures; nonbinary and gender-fluid in their bodies, roles, perception, and passing."[59]

This section performs a close reading of the sexually charged and voyeuristic peep show scene within *El celoso extremeño*, the very one where Luis uses the light from a candlestick to put on display Loaysa's young, fit body so that Guiomar (a Portuguese black girl who speaks habla de negros), Marialonso (a perceivably butch duenna), and the other enslaved and free Morisca women present can feast on his flesh through a peephole in a turnstile. To sense the queerness of the scene, I cite the narrator's description at length:

> Lo primero que hicieron fue barrenar el torno para ver al músico, el cual no estaba ya en hábitos de pobre, sino con unos calzones grandes de tafetán leonado, a la marineresca; un jubón de lo mismo con trencillas de oro, y una montera de raso de la misma color, con cuello proveído en las alforjas, imaginando que se había de ver en ocasión que le conviniese mudar de traje.
>
> Era mozo y de gentil disposición y buen parecer; y como había tanto tiempo que todas tenían hecha la vista a mirar al viejo de su amo, parecióles que miraban a un ángel. Poníase una al agujero para verle, y luego otra; y por que le pudiesen ver mejor, *andaba el negro paseándole el cuerpo de arriba abajo con el torzal de cera encendido*. Y después que todas le hubieron visto, hasta las negras bozales, tomó Loaysa la guitarra, y cantó aquella noche tan extremadamente, que las acabó de dejar suspensas y atónitas a todas, así la vieja como a las mozas, y todas rogaron a Luis diese orden y traza como el señor su maestro entrase allá dentro, para oírle y verle de más cerca y no tan por brújula como por el agujero, y sin el sobresalto de estar tan apartadas de su señor, que podía cogerlas de sobresalto y con el hurto en las manos, lo cual ni sucedería ansí si le tuviesen escondido adentro.

[The first thing they did was drill a hole in the revolving door to see the musician, who no longer was in a poor man's clothes but wore large breeches of tawny silk, wide in the nautical fashion, a doublet of the same fabric with gold braid, and a hunting hat of gold satin, and a starched collar with long lace inserts, all of which he had placed in his bags, supposing the occasion might arise when it would be advantageous for him to change his clothes.

He was young, charming, and good-looking; and since all of them had seen no man but their old master for so long, it seemed to them that they were looking at an angel. One peered through the hole to see him, and then another; and to allow them to see better, the black kept moving the twist of the lit wax up and down the young man's body. And when all of them had seen him, even the dim-witted black girls, Loaysa picked up the guitar and sang so perfectly that he left them all dumbfounded and amazed, the old woman as well as the girls, and they asked Luis to tell his teacher how to get inside so they could hear and see him up close, not just through a peephole, and without the fear of being so distant from their master that he could take them by surprise to catch them red-handed; which would not happen if they had the musician hidden inside.][60]

These passages invert the white male gaze. While Loaysa indeed has his own agenda that involves penetrating Carrizales's house and getting ahold of Leonora, the multiethnic, multigenerational, and multiracial consort of women spectators on the other side of the peephole—Luis included, considering his proximity to Loaysa's body—drive and organize the power relations in the scene. Their contribution to the story's development destabilizes gendered expectation and gender norms. In *A Taste for Brown Sugar: Black Women in Pornography*, Mireille Miller-Young explains that "the concept of the gaze, for many feminist scholars, serves as a paradigm for asymmetrical power relations: the domination of the slave by the master, the colonized by the colonizer, and woman by man."[61] But the theorist goes on further to elucidate that "since the 1970s many scholars have challenged gaze theory, arguing that the spectator/spectacle relationship is not merely one of social control, but is full of contradictions and reversals."[62]

Cervantes ropes us in as voyeurs. Multiple vantage points of acts of voyeurism are at a work. In this moment Luis executes his job faithfully (and commanding that of the candle as well): illuminating Loaysa's angelic body, one that's antagonistic and antithetical to the geriatric Carrizales. On a cautionary note, I'm not applying the terms *voyeurs* and *voyeurism* haphazardly and recklessly to arouse you with terminological gimmicks latent with cheesy shock value. Voyeuristic, or gawker-like, fetishes, practices, and sensibilities were not uncommon during the period in which Cervantes and Zayas lived. For example, it's productive to link voyeurs and voyeurism to inquisitorial modes of confession, spying, the tattletale and the nosey busybody, and the highly performative nature of the public auto-de-fé. Surely, auction blocks where those looking to procure enslaved persons satiated their voyeuristic appetites through the haptic regimes of smell and touch.

Not so distant from these historical configurations of voyeurs and voyeurism, we have the neglected example of *Los mirones*, a short-skit play that has long been attributed to Cervantes. In recent years theater critics John Beusterien and Alexander Samson have started retracing this work's connection to Alonso Jerónimo de Salas Barbadillo (1580–1635). Translating the text as *The Gawkers*, Beusterien and Samson render audible and legible for present-day readers and theatergoers—most notably under Carlota Gaviño's direction of the theater company Grumelot at the Festival de Almagro in Spain—the role voyeurs and voyeuristic acts play in the age of Cervantes.[63] As the prolific historian Nicole von Germeten notes, "The voyeur diagnosis has a complex history, in the sense that it can encompass too much and too little." Like Germeten, I hope "to resolve any potential controversy over my use of the term by defining *voyeurism* . . . as 'best applied to situations where people seek out and/or experience pleasure, gratification, and/or excitement, usually through observation of something that is typically hidden.'"[64]

Moved by Miller-Young's astute insights and trailblazing theories, what I am suggesting here is that Cervantes constructs a competing gaze that shifts the relationship of power, whereby the racially gendered, marginalized characters in the novella appropriate, deflect, and refuse a dominant gaze. Instead, Loaysa's fresh, young male body is on display. The climax of the encounter with Loaysa happens when the duenna Señora Marialonso "asiéndole de los greguescos, le metió dentro, y luego todas las demás se le pusieron a la redonda" ("grasps [Loaysa's] breeches, pulls him inside, and then all the others surrounded him").[65] But Cervantes doesn't stop here! The narrator continues, "En esto llegó toda la caterva junta, y el músico en el medio, alumbrándolos el negro y Guiomar la negra" ("At this point the entire crowd arrived together, with the musician in the middle and Luis the black man and Guiomar the black girl lighting their way").[66] Substituting Luis's role as inspector of Loaysa's body, Marialonso thus takes charge when she took una vela y comenzó a mirar de arriba abajo al bueno del músico, y una decía: "¡Ay, qué copete que tiene tan lindo y tan rizado!" Otra: "¡Ay, qué blancura de dientes! ¡Mal año para piñones mondados que más blancos ni más lindos sean!" Otra: "¡Ay, qué ojos tan grandes y tan rasgados! Y por siglo de mi madre que son verdes, que no parecen sino que son de esmeraldas!" Ésta alababa la boca, aquélla los pies, y todas juntas hicieron dél una menuda anatomía y pepitoria.

[a candle and began to look at the good musician from top to bottom, and one of the maids said, "Oh, what a nice forelock he has, so curly!" And another: "Oh, what white teeth! Too bad for trimmed pine nuts that are not whiter or prettier!" And another: "Oh, what big eyes, and so wide open! And by my mother's life, they're green, and they look just like emeralds!" One praised his mouth, another his feet, and all together they made a slow detailed examination of his anatomy and extremities.][67]

So what do we make of Luis's role in this overt cisgendered female gaze that appraises Loaysa's body? Placed on duty to surveil the premises for Carrizales—to ensure he doesn't wake up from his deep, opioid-induced slumber—the black girl named Guiomar assertively protests in her habla-de-negros speech that "all the white bitches have the fun" (¡Yo, negra, quedo; blancas, van: Dios perdone a todas!).[68] My reading of the room is that Guiomar, too, queerly and voyeuristically participates—passively or intentionally—in the eroticized, scopophilic moment where Loaysa stands in the middle. Cervantes inverts the role of cis (queer) men, where women and girls across age and generational divides appraise, judge, and sexualize Loaysa's normative cis male body. In many ways this bodily appraisal of Loaysa's assumed-to-be cis heteronormative male body—inaugurated and instituted by a candlestick and its flame—harkens back to sixteenth- and seventeenth-century Seville's bustling auction blocks, brothels, slave markets, and unloading docks. Seville's Merchant Exchange House (Casa Lonja) or the city's cathedral steps (*las gradas*) arrests my train of thought. The erotic (fore)play performed at the peephole—partitioned by Luis's hayloft apartment—aided by candlelight, powerfully demonstrates Cervantes's ability to invert and trouble the interconnected social histories of class, gender, race, and sex. Time waits for no one. Punctuated and nonmethodical, the candle illuminating Loaysa's body through the peephole melts with its wax splattering onto the floor—or running like molten lava onto a finger, or two. On both sides of that peephole palpitates and perspires an erotic life of desire. Things are done in secrecy—behind and *within* closed doors.[69]

I have always been struck by the homosocial, queer bond between Loaysa and Luis. Critics have also noticed their intimate proximity. In *Del teatro a la novela: El ritual del disfraz en las* Novelas ejemplares *de Cervantes*, Eduardo Olid Guerrero highlights how Loaysa "attracts and seduces" Luis with his guitar and music.[70] Alban K. Forcione also confirms similar interactions between the two in his 1982 classic *Cervantes and the Humanist Vision*. What strikes me as odd remains how and why scholars have acknowledged, on the one hand, yet have evaded, on the other hand, the explicit *naming*—calling out the social interaction and proximity for what it is—of the textual potential apparent in Loaysa's and Luis's interracial and same-gendered bond to each other throughout the novella. I cannot help but to explore the productive possibility of queering Luis in these terms, along the lines of the same-gender relations between white men and black men. Expanding on our understanding of how queerness ebbs and flows in *El celoso extremeño*, I gravitate toward Roland Betancourt's important work on Byzantium, eunuchs, and institutionalized spaces, where homosocial, homoerotic, and same-gender intimacy had room to maneuver in certain cordoned-off, private, or homosocial spaces, even if they manifested differently than in our own time.[71]

Quoting Eve Sedgwick's classic definition of "queer," Betancourt reiterates that queerness for Sedgwick moves as an "open mesh of possibilities, gaps, overlaps, dissonances and resonances, lapses and excess of meaning when the constituent elements of anyone's gender, of anyone's sexuality aren't made (or *can't be* made) to signify monolithically."[72] On queerness I privilege Robert Reid-Pharr's framing of the term: "If there's one thing that marks us as queer, a category that is somehow different, if not altogether distinct, from the heterosexual, then it is undoubtedly our relationships to the body, particularly the expansive ways in which we utilize and combine vaginas, penises, breasts, buttocks, hands, arms, feet, stomachs, mouths and tongues in our expressions of not only intimacy, love, and lust, but also and importantly shame, contempt, despair, and hate."[73] The diversity of textual material from *El celoso extremeño* that captures Luis's and Loaysa's connection and proximity to each other, through music, song, and dance, implore us to rethink Luis, through modes, spaces, and temporalities of queerness, in terms of vulnerability. Vincent Woodard in *The Delectable Negro* compels us to think about how "a master would often choose a 'favorite' male slave as the object of his cultivated delight. Black men in such contexts had to negotiate feelings of affection, hatred, shame, sexual degradation, and arousal toward white men [and women]."[74] When I *queer* Luis, I cannot help but to associate his queerness (beyond sexual acts and sexual desire) to the development of his relationship with Loaysa over the course of the story. Calling for a new kind of early modern studies, thinking across space and time, I end with the following query: How, when, and where do we uncover historical configurations of transoceanic Iberian Luises—yes, plural—that pop up across continents and oceans? Archives across a vast transoceanic Iberian world, before and during the age of Cervantes, house the movements, stories, and voices of many Luises: some castrated, others not, and some sustaining their West and Central African cosmologies and spiritualities, traditions of kinship, same-sex intimacy, and gender nonconformity.

MEDITATION 4

CERVANTES UNHINGED

This final meditation redirects our critical gaze from Miguel de Cervantes to María de Zayas y Sotomayor. In doing so I am concerned with the ways in which Cervantes's portrayal of racialized blackness changes in the works of his contemporary María de Zayas. As readers of Zayas, how do we negotiate and reconcile her historical and literary constructions of sub-Saharan African blackness? After all, she partakes in the writing of sub-Saharan African slavery situated in domestic spaces—gardens, kitchens, stables, royal palaces—and I mobilize in this fourth provocation new ways of analyzing the pressing matter of white women's written treatment of enslaved black people and their descendants, coupled with the perceived clear and present dangers they unleash in Spanish baroque society. To be clear the so-called clear and present dangers of African slavery to which I refer manifest in a term such as "frottage," as defined by Keguro Macharia in the book *Frottage: Frictions of Intimacy Across the Black Diaspora*. In the context of slave holds and slavery's maw, frottage, as conceptualized by Macharia, identifies several kinds of rubbings that take place: "bodies against each other; bodies against the ship; writing implements against ledgers; and the rubbing in the slave holds against the writing in the ledgers." In light of the prose fiction of María de Zayas, I repurpose Macharia's powerful theorization of frottage by departing from the image of the slave ship and going to the literary world of Zayas. Her literary world, composed of short stories that gesture toward elements of frottage, operate as metonymical slave ledgers that "record weight and monetary value instead of names, religious affiliations, geohistorical origins, or philosophical orientations."[1] Through frottage I illuminate a relation of proximity in Zayas's writings that feature interracial unions between blacks and whites and that highlight the racially gendered construction of interracial intimacy located in elite Spanish baroque domestic spaces. From frottage I am then able to establish and thread meaning into *intimacy* as my chief theoretical framework.

Let us first unearth intimacy's philological roots expounded in dictionaries. The lexicographer Sebastián de Covarrubias Horozco in his 1611 *Tesoro* tells us that the transitive verb *intimar*, or "to intimate," means "notificar jurídicamente por auto y fe" (to legally notify by order and faith). In its nominal form, *intimidad*, or "intimacy," according the *Diccionario de Autoridades*, embodies "confianza amistosa, o amistad estrecha de corazón" (friendly trust or close-hearted friendship).[2] The *Oxford English Dictionary* builds on these two Spanish sources in its definition of "intimacy" as "closeness of observation, knowledge, or the like"; "close in acquaintance or association"; and "closely connected by friendship or personal knowledge; characterized by familiarity with a person or a thing."[3] What these dictionary entries obscure from us then becomes elucidated in the theoretical repertoire of critical theory and cultural studies. For Lauren Berlant intimacy "involves an aspiration for a narrative about something shared, a story about oneself and others that will turn out in a particular way."[4] In *Monstrous Intimacies*, Christina Sharpe's designation of the concept captures the innermost part, at the very core of subjectivity and private to a (sexual or other) relationship. Polemically so, intimacy is always about desire—and perhaps specifically about what Ann Laura Stoler calls the "education of desire"—and the structures that organize and constitute the relationships between past and present and possible futures.[5] With this constellation of ideas in mind, as illustrated by this meditation's title—"Cervantes Unhinged"—I name, on the one hand, and trouble, on the other hand, Zayas's treatment of interracial race relations. The payoff of this approach thus sheds light on Zayas's discomfort with and distaste for intimate interracial bonds between blacks and whites across social class. These are indeed bonds that have been commensurate with, and deeply implicated in, capitalism, colonialism, empire, and slavery. Borrowing from Lisa Lowe's formulation of the "intimacies of four continents," my examination of intimacy in this meditation joins Lowe and a prolific assortment of theorists such as Ann Laura Stoler, Amy Kaplan, Laura Wexler, Antoinette Burton, Philippa Levine, Peggy Pascoe, Nayan Shah, Jennifer L. Palmer, and others whose groundbreaking interventions have demonstrated that the intimacies of desire, sexuality, marriage, and family are inseparable from the imperial projects of conquest, slavery, labor, and government.[6]

As early as 2000, Marina S. Brownlee in *The Cultural Labyrinth of María de Zayas* suggests that Zayas's work has the purpose of exposing gender, class, and race relations in seventeenth-century Spain. I contend that Zayas's narrativized codification of blackness—exemplary or otherwise—*unhinges* Cervantes's more complex, ironic, measured, and quixotic handling of sub-Saharan African blackness. Another way to read my ideation of "unhinged" manifests in Nieves Romero-Díaz's push for seeing the "post-Cervantine novella as a discourse that negotiates the contradictions through which a new urban middle nobility sought to define its own social and ideological model."[7]

Writing on the frameworks of eroticism, pornography, and violence in Zayas's oeuvre, Margaret E. Boyle reminds us that

> readers already familiar with Zayas will find themselves contending with many of the same questions [betrayal, murder, rape, and torture] that arise from her other work[s], noting the expressive range of female voices, the lively and sometimes anxious attention to corporality, and the uneasy presence of horrific violence and illicit desire. On the one hand, the reader plays voyeuristic witness to numerous scenes of violence inscribed on women's displayed bodies. On the other, these stories ask readers to become *desengañado* [undeceived], thus participating in a dense didacticism, where scenes of violence against women impart ethical concerns onto its readers. Part of the allure of the novellas has to do with the fact that they are a direct invitation into a private and exclusive world.

Boyle's insights temper my examination of blackness. Indirectly, Boyle teaches us that the story of sub-Saharan African blackness in Zayas intersects with other salient themes more readily studied. While some scholars may treat the black people populating Zayas's works as decorative and peripheral, my contribution herein builds on the solid foundation of criticism concerning the author and her writing that has been produced in the past thirty years. Lisa Vollendorf, for example, has argued persuasively that these novellas' exhaustive accounts of psychological and physical violence "give voice to women's suffering by privileging the feminine perspective and displaying the dismembered body in order to remember it again."[8] Together,

Boyle and Vollendorf gift us with an important puzzle piece integral to unpacking the representation of blackness and interracial intimacy in Zayas: psychological anguish and suffering.

To propel Zayas criticism forward, I insist that the field of early modern Spanish cultural and literary studies not only cites but processes the work of black women historians like Stephanie E. Jones-Rogers. Let us take, for instance, Jones-Rogers's critically acclaimed magnum opus, *They Were Her Property: White Women as Slave Owners in the American South*. Before I proceed and my critical approach to María de Zayas is maligned as presentist, I want to be clear that I am *not* claiming Zayas enslaved or owned black people. In the words of Keisha N. Blain and other black women historians, we know that there's no such thing as objective history.[9] To be clear there is no extant biographical evidence to prove Zayas owned enslaved black people. However, privileging historical sources on enslaved black African communities across Spain—halfway through the eighteenth century, roughly six thousand enslaved Africans and their descendants inhabited Madrid—cautions me not to discredit nor discount the subjunctive possibility of Zayas and her family's intimate knowledge of and proximity to enslaved African-descended people, especially given her elite status in Spanish baroque society and the subject matter of her novellas.[10] To that effect, in the interest of this meditation's conceptual and theoretical concerns, the register of intimacy that I'm signaling here within the history of slavery in Spain—and the literary construction of it—corroborates Sharpe's theoretical formation of intimacy as "spatial and temporal" insofar as it prompts us to think through "the configurations of relations that arise out of domination and that continue to structure relations across race, sex, ethnicity, and nation."[11]

Methodologically, Jones-Rogers's work allows me to pin down and probe the role that early modern Spanish white women authors have played, slave owning or not, in the cultural, historical, and literary enterprise of sub-Saharan African slavery. Thanks to her insights and theoretical unpacking of archival sources, Jones-Rogers's work has shaped my critical approach to Zayas as well as the questions I deem important in underscoring white women's fundamental relationship to slavery as a relation of property, a relation that was both compounded and intensified by exercising life and death power over enslaved women and men. This was a relation, redacted by the quill—in bills of sale, literature, ordinances, testimonies, wills, and the like—that positioned them as enforcers of the slave system.[12] As such, this relation had profound psychological consequences on the psyches of those white women who knew their white husbands and white sons savored black women's flesh, a predilection that then resulted reproductively in mixed-raced persons of African descent. (I'm thinking of the scenes of subjection described in Harriet Jacobs's *Incidents in the Life of a Slave Girl*. I'm also remembering those white women slave owners who weaponized the violent modernity of sadomasochistic torture—of iron cages and iron masks—that attempted to hide and erase the faces of black women from white men who saw them as beautiful.)[13]

Like Zayas and her contemporaries, white women's mental anguish and psychological torment then became transferred by the quill—dressed in black ink—onto white paper in their stories. Much later, in the eighteenth and nineteenth centuries, we can see evidence of white women, like María Cristina de Borbón, for example, trafficking in and profiting from not only West and Central African chattel slavery but also transoceanic slave trades active across the Indian and Pacific Oceans as well as the South China Sea. The important works of Dannelle Gutarra Cordero, in *She Is Weeping: An Intellectual History of Racialized Slavery in the Atlantic World*, and Erin Austin Dwyer's *Mastering Emotions: Feelings, Power, and Slavery in the United States* offers cross-hemispheric analyses of the history of emotional policing that govern racialized bodies. I turn to this register of the emotional politics of slavery, as fashioned by enslaved people and slaveholders, to tap into the ways in which emotions such as disgust, happiness, love, terror, and trust functioned as economic and social capital for slaveholders and enslaved black people alike.

Optically and visually, the artistic depiction and representation of white women being cared for by black girls and women can conjure and illumine for us the intricate recesses of interracial intimacies across age, class, generation, and sex. Figures 7 through 9, spanning the long sixteenth to twentieth centuries, invite us to assess and gauge white women's ongoing relationship to black women and black girls as proxies for property. These images reveal how intimacy transforms gender roles and racial status. They constellate a tapestry—the artwork of Cristóvão de Moráis, Francisco de Goya y Lucientes, and Ricard Canals—that pictorializes white girls' and white women's intimate relations to African slavery in their households. My commentary and intervention here is not an art historical one. However, I utilize these three distinct paintings to simply get my audience to think about the optics and visual implications of how European painters depicted girls' and women's connections to and participation in capitalism, servitude, and slavery across space and time.

In what ensues in this meditation, I unearth Zayas's racially gendered construction of interracial intimacy, material culture, and race relations in her two-part collection of novellas *Novelas amorosas y ejemplares* (*Exemplary*

Fig. 7. Cristóvão de Moráis, *Portrait of Joanna of Austria*, 1551 or 1552. Oil on canvas, 99 × 81.5 cm. Royal Museums of Fine Arts of Belgium.

Fig. 8. Francisco de Goya y Lucientes, *The Duchess of Alba with María de la Luz on Her Arms*, 1794–95. Wash, Indian ink on laid paper, 171 × 99 mm. Museo Nacional del Prado. Photo: Album / Alamy Stock Photo.

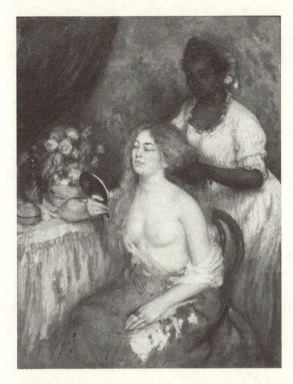

Fig. 9. Ricard Canals, *La toilette*, circa 1903. Oil on canvas, 1470 × 1135 mm. Museo Nacional de Arte de Cataluña, 003807-000.

Tales of Love; 1637) and *Desengaños amorosos* (*Tales of Disillusion*; 1647). The two texts up for discussion are "El prevenido engañado" ("Forewarned but Not Forearmed") and "Tarde llega el desengaño" ("Too Late Deceived"). Serving as case studies, these two works will shed light on the ways in which Zayas unhinges Cervantes's handling of blackness. Such a dislocation and dislodging from Cervantes's ethos, ethics, and style, I contend, reveals Zayas's sinister messages about not only blackness but also the incompatibility of intimate interracial race relations and unions in the domestic sphere.

Antonio's Scars and the Drama of White Women Who Lust After Black Men

The first black person we meet in Zayas's collection of short stories shows up in "El prevenido engañado" from *Novelas amorosas y ejemplares* (1637). Narrated on night 2 by Don Alonso, arguably the most misogynist of the two-part collection's male narrators, this story takes place in Seville and tackles the messy conjoined themes of racialized blackness, fragile masculinities, and interracial intimacy. At the novella's onset, Don Alonso informs us that the protagonist, Don Fadrique, a rich young gentleman in Granada, goes to Seville and falls in love with a widow, Beatriz, who says that in honor of her dead husband, she won't marry for three years.[14] Margaret Rich Greer's concise plot summary further explains that "after courting her for some time, Don Fadrique gets inside the house one night and sees her going to the stables to care for a dying black man, Antonio, whose lover she has been. Antonio dies and she then sends Fadrique a note saying that she will marry him immediately. He sends her a note suggesting she mourn her black lover another year, leaves for Madrid, and Beatriz marries another suitor."[15]

In "El prevenido engañado," as narrated by Don Alonso, Antonio's airtime in the text is minimal but sears the minds of those paying attention. We learn that Antonio, enslaved and infirm, resides in the horse stables attached to doña Beatriz's residence. Remarkably, considering Don Alonso's disapproval of Antonio, as illustrated by Don Fadrique's feelings and apparent stalker-like behavior, the ill black man does not speak in the linguistically marked register of habla de negros. Regarding Africanized Castilian, Zayas surely would have known about the literary enterprise of habla-de-negros speech events. Her close friend, Ana Caro de Mallén, in fact, uses habla de negros in the theatrical work "Loa sacramental que se representó en las fiestas del Corpus de Sevilla" (1639).[16]

"El prevenido engañado" denigrates and uglifies Antonio. Zayas disguises a grammar of antiblackness through the character Don Alonso's narrative voice:

> Grande fue el valor de don Fadrique en tal caso, porque así como llegó cerca y descubrió todo lo que dentro del aposento se hacía, vio a su dama en una ocasión tan terrible para él que no sé cómo tuvo paciencia para sufrirla. Es el caso que en una cama que estaba en esta parte que he dicho, estaba echado un negro tan atezado que parecía hecho de un bocací su rostro. Parecía en la edad de hasta veintiocho o treinta años, mas tan feo y abominable que no sé si fue la pasión o si era la verdad, le pareció que el demonio no podía serlo tanto. Parecía asimismo en su desflaquecido semblante que le faltaba poco para acabar la vida, porque tenía el pecho medio levantado, con lo que parecía más abominable.
>
> [Great was don Fadrique's valor in such an event, because as soon as he came close and discovered everything within in the little room,

he saw his lady in such a terrible circumstance for him that I do not know how he had the patience to endure it. In a bed that was in the place I have said lay a black man so scorched that his face seemed made of *bocací*. He appeared to be up to twenty-eight or thirty years old, but so ugly and abominable that I do not know if it was his death-bed suffering or if it was the way he really was, it seemed to him that the devil could not be so (ugly). It also seemed from his emaciated appearance that his life was not long from ending, because his chest was half raised, with which he appeared more abominable.]"[17]

As reported by Don Alonso's aseptic and cold description of Antonio, we learn that Don Fadrique medicalizes, in his own pseudoclinical gaze, Antonio's physical condition and state. Fadrique's purported "valor," according to the narrator, signals his hubristic victimization as codified by his masculinist entitlement and patriarchal role. The material object "*bocací*" and the adjective "scorched" contribute to this narrativized method, just as the identification of Antonio's approximate age—roughly twenty-eight or thirty years-old—alongside his "emaciated appearance" and "half raised" chest conjure images of him as an infernal agent of disease and a disseminator of contagion. A framework of medicalized blackness can help us as readers render more legible meaning into the bocací descriptor.[18] For me "bocací" names, signals, traces, and underscores Antonio's sub-Saharan African origins. What captivates my close reading of Antonio, in the pages ahead, compels me to dissect the material, haptic, and sensorial qualities of Antonio's face and skin. Does Zayas's text describe smallpox or syphilis scars? Are they ritual scarifications? Misdiagnosed acne scars or keloids? I offer no concrete answers, for all I do is imagine and speculate on the literary materialism constituted by Zayas. I contend that the bocací does not appear nor operate in the text as mere coincidence. Zayas aestheticizes the heft of Antonio's black African baroqueness—one that is grotesquely exaggerated and irregularly misshapen—through antithesis and perversion: his emblematic bocací-like, scorched black face is nothing like the buckram, or stiff cotton (or leather), conventionally associated with the (white) fabric and the white woman caressing him.

As I've codified, defined, and substantiated my conceptualization of the African baroque in my 2018 essay "Sor Juana's Black Atlantic," I encourage my readers to remember the longue durée of baroque aesthetics and corporeal excess that predate Zayas's oeuvre. I propose that we can trace an earlier cultural enterprise and literary history of racialized black and nonwhite peoples that are not at all mutually exclusive from Zayas's writings. The figure of Adamastor, from Luís Vaz de Camões's epic poem *Os Lusíadas* (1572), evidences my proposition. For instance, experts writing on Camões and early modern Portuguese maritime expansion, such as Vincent Barletta, Josiah Blackmore, and Giuseppe Marcocci, have analyzed and historicized the important ways in which Camões and his contemporaries poeticized Iberian confrontations with mythological and mythologized "monsters," like the racialized personification of the sea giant Adamastor, whose body parts and facial features are begrimed and racially exaggerated in *Os Lusíadas*.[19] I wish not to lazily dismiss Zayas's bocací description of Antonio's face by leaving it to hover at the margins of critical commentary.

If we are to align and thus read artistry and meaning into Antonio's face (emblematic of facial scarification or cicatrization), then figures 10 and 11 assist us in delving into African and diasporic archives that treat the ritual historiography and visual economy of cicatrization. In his extraordinary essay "Scarification and the Loss of History in the African Diaspora," Paul E. Lovejoy

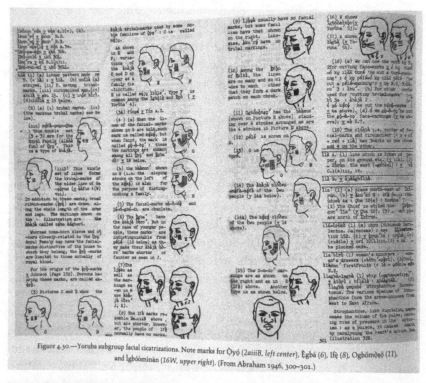

Fig. 10. Yorùbá subgroup facial cicatrizations, 1958. Abraham, *Dictionary of Modern Yoruba*, 300.

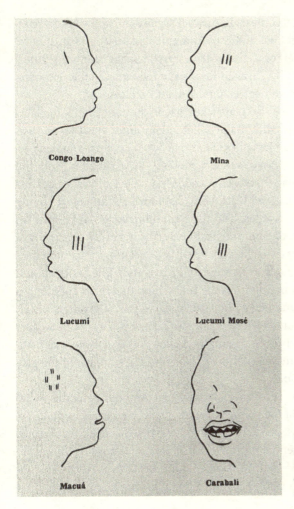

Fig. 11. Facial cicatrizations noted among Africans arriving in Cuba during the nineteenth century, 1969. D. Brown, *Santería Enthroned*, 203.

informs us that "the characteristics of ethnicity as conceived of and applied to Africans were often visual, distinctions marked by scarification, tattooing, piercing of ears and lips, hair styles, dress, jewelry, and cosmetics." On scarification, Lovejoy explains that the "use of scarification as markers of social identity varied." "In most cases, it seems," he adds, "scarification was a sign of free status, and sometimes incorporation into a family, if an enslaved child was given such markings, as among the Yoruba. Ritual scarification had meaning in local contexts in Africa, particularly West Africa, that was no longer functional in the Americas [and Europe]."[20] Zayas's narrativized construction of Antonio's face fits squarely within Lovejoy's claim that ritual scarification loses its meaning outside of local contexts in Africa. I argue that Zayas's bocací referent underscores the fraught possibility of Antonio's face serving as an archival indexing of a—or *his*—West or Central African past that has been substituted, suppressed, and forgotten by Zayas in favor of branding and other cicatrizations of slavery deriving from neglect, punishment, and torture.

Antonio's cicatrized face also plays a key role in the surveillance of blackness in early modern Spanish literature. Potentially antithetical to—or perhaps representative of Aimé Césaire's claim that "we have been branded by a Cartesian philosophy" in *Discourse on Colonialism*—slave branding with hot iron, Antonio's cicatrized face becomes encoded in Frantz Fanon's "epidermal racial schema" that the enslaved black body fashioned as "an object among other objects."[21] Zayas, Cervantes, and their contemporaries alike confirm and reflect Fanon's theory of epidermalization and its historical specificity of branding as a practice put to use to ascribe certain meanings to certain bodies as a unit of tradeable goods, runaways, and survivors.[22] The historical and literary sources abound, ranging from the Inquisition trial record of Eleno/a de Céspedes to the four branded white female slaves from Cervantes's *El celoso extremeño* and the character Isabel Fajardo/Zelima in Zayas's *Desengaño Primero* known as "La esclava de su amante." Lope de Vega also problematically toys with the metallurgic economy of iron and slave brands in the play *Los melindres de Belisa* (1608).

Traditionally, scholars also have claimed that Antonio embodies what Don Fadrique does not, for the young gallant is madly enamored by doña Beatriz's idealized whiteness, an ideological and racialized conceit that frames and juxtaposes, in a sequential narrative sense, Beatriz *against* Antonio's abject blackness. As framed by Don Alonso, doña Beatriz's sartorial and somatic whiteness enthralls Don Fadrique in the following manner:

> Traía la dama sobre la camisa un faldellín de vuelta de tabí encarnado, cuya plata y guarnición parecían estrellas, sin traer sobre sí otra cosa más que un rebociño del mismo tabí, aforrado en felpa azul, puesta tan al desgaire que dejaba ver en la blancura de la camisa los bordados de hilo de pita (en que es Sevilla más extremada que otra ninguna tierra de España) sus dorados cabellos cogidos en una redecilla de seda azul y plata, aunque por algunas partes descompuestos, para componer con ellos la belleza de su rostro; en su garganta dos hilos de gruesas perlas, conformes a otras muchas vueltas que llevaba en sus hermosas muñecas, cuya blancura se veía sin embarazo, por ser la manga de la camisa suelta a modo de manga de fraile.

[The lady wore over her chemise an overskirt of red reverse tabby, whose silver and trimming looked like stars, not wearing anything else but a shawl of the same tabby, lined in blue felt, so carelessly worn that it left visible the embroidery of pita thread (for which Seville is more renowned than any other Spanish land) in the white of the chemise, her golden hair caught in a little net of blue and silver silk, but disordered in some places, to adorn the beauty of her face; at her throat two strings of pearls, like many other rounds of them that she wore at her lovely wrists, whose whiteness was easily visible, the sleeves of her chemise being loose in the style of friar's sleeves.][23]

This passage details the economic capital of Beatriz's sartorial and somatic whiteness. As emphasized by Beatriz's golden hair and white skin as well as the garments, fabrics, and pearls that adorn her appendages, Zayas highlights both Don Alonso's and Don Fadrique's eroticized yet scrutinous male gazes. In keeping with the scholarly work of Yolanda Gamboa and José Antonio Maravall, Zayas's narrator also frames, on the one hand, and manipulates, on the other hand, a racially gendered male gaze that further co-opts the audience to play voyeuristic witness to Beatriz's foreshadowed proclivity for black male flesh.[24]

Antonio's dramatic refusal of Beatriz has garnered scholarly attention in the past decades. The narrator shares with us that "abrió el negro los ojos, y mirando a su ama, con voz debilitada y flaca le dijo, apartándolo con las manos el rostro que tenía junto con el suyo" ("the black man opened his eyes, and looking at his mistress, pushing away with his hands the face she had next to his, with a thin and weakened voice").[25] As the scene develops, Antonio complains about Beatriz's vicious, raptorial appetite that has brought him to his untimely demise:

¿Qué quieres de mí, señora? ¡Déjame ya, por Dios! ¿Qué es esto, que aun estando yo acabando la vida me persigues? No basta que tu viciosa condición me tiene como estoy, sino que quieres que, cuando ya estoy en el fin de mi vida, acuda a cumplir tus viciosos apetitos. Cásate, señora, cásate, y déjame ya a mí que ni te quiero ver, ni comer lo que me das; morir quiero, pues ya no estoy para otra cosa.

Y diciendo esto, se volvió del otro lado, sin querer responder más a doña Beatriz, aunque más tierna y amorosamente le llamaba, o fuese que se murió luego, o no quisiese hacer case de sus lágrimas y palabras. Doña Beatriz cansada ya, se volvió a su cuarto, la más llorosa y triste del mundo.

[What do you want of me, madam? Leave me now, for God's sake! What is this, that even as my life is ending you pursue me? Is it not enough that your dissolute nature has me as I am, but that you want me, when I am at the end of my life, to come to carry out your depraved appetites? Get married, madam, get married, and leave me now, for I neither want to see you nor eat what you give me; I want to die, for now I am in no condition for anything else.

And saying this, he turned to the other side, not wanting to respond further to doña Beatriz, however tenderly and lovingly she called to him. Or it could be that he died then, or that he did not want to pay attention to her tears and words. Doña Beatriz, now tired, returned to her room, the most tearful and sad (woman) in the world.][26]

Antonio performs the role of Beatriz's delectable *negro*. He exists for her consumption and pleasure. Zayas degrades the interracial intimacy between Antonio and Beatriz as monstrous, an abomination that foregrounds and signals the fraught history of cannibalism in the history of slavery and the slave trade.[27] Since Juan Goytisolo's *Disidencias* and more recent critical reception bestowed on this notorious scene since 2018, scholars like Eduardo Ruiz have noted that doña Beatriz "fully challenges the canonical representation of the standard Spanish lady: she rejects the pretensions of the *caballero* Don Fadrique for the physical love of a black slave lying sick in her stables."[28] He adds that "these misogynist admonitions against vice and sin advanced by a black man contribute to making the image of a Spanish lady lying with an African slave more palatable for contemporary taste, and they also shield the writer against censure."[29] As Marina S. Brownlee points out:

[The] sexual coercion [that] Beatriz exerts is distasteful, to say the least. The fact that it comes as a result of class power—she is the master, he the slave (and a black)—compounds the transgression, and Fadrique is understandably repulsed by this disclosure of her behavior. What is important extradiegetically is Zayas's ability to represent the diversity of female response; a widow who is not simply having an illicit affair, but one where she derives the kind of pleasure resulting from the power that men frequently exert over the maids who work in their households. It is an example of female sexual excess, and it is an interracial one. In this episode ... female fantasy—and even facilitation—of transgressive desire is potentially as diverse for women as it is for men.[30]

What also strikes me as resourceful textual content surely lies in Zayas's handling of interracial intimacy that frowns on miscegenation across class and racial lines.

The interaction between Antonio and Beatriz proves much more complex than mere "jungle fever," should we wink flirtatiously at Spike Lee's 1991 romantic US drama film *Jungle Fever*—or, for that matter, remind ourselves of Arthur Little's *Shakespeare Jungle Fever: National-Imperial Re-visions of Race, Rape, and Sacrifice* and John Beusterien's *An Eye on Race: Perspectives from Theater in Imperial Spain*. Moving beyond an essentialist and narrowly conceived rubric of jungle fever, I would like to complicate the Antonio-Beatriz episode as emblematic of a freighted interracial intimacy that underwrites a kind of frottage—or friction of intimacy—unfolding across early modern Spain and the vast reaches of its transoceanic empire. The narrative intensity of this scene is powerful and provocative. In Antonio's stable his begrimed, emaciated, and festered face rubs against Beatriz's plush, radiant, and white visage. Antonio's and Beatriz's skin, selves, and bodies wither away from speaking, pressing, rubbing, and touching, as both bodies reap what is sown from the institution of slavery's maw. This relation of proximity, so eloquently described by Keguro Macharia, captures for me the aesthetic and the libidinal in Zayas's work.[31]

Zayas highlights the precarity and weakness of elite (white) men. Don Fadrique (or Don Alonso) cannot fathom doña Beatriz's attraction to and affection for a perceived monstrous enslaved and deathly ill black man. Figure 12 best illustrates my claim here. The miscegenated frottage witnessed by Don Fadrique abhors him and disgusts those who harbor his misogynist and negrophobic sentiments. Macharia's theorization of frottage highlights "a multiplicity of sense-apprehensions, including recognition, disorientation, compassion, pity, disgust, condescension, lust, titillation, arousal, and exhaustion."[32] As mediated by Zayas, Don Alonso's narrative voice and Don Fadrique's reaction approximates as much as possible Macharia's theory of frottage. In sum this scene between Antonio and Beatriz—and those

Fig. 12. Eric Fraser, illustration of "El prevenido, engañado," 1963. Sturrock, *Shameful Revenge and Other Stories*, 83.

listening, observing, and judging, like Don Alonso and Don Fadrique—codifies a sensorium of disgust and irritation.[33]

At this juncture I'd like to pause my analysis of María de Zayas and direct our attention to Cervantes's portrayal of black love and intimacy in his exemplary novel *El coloquio de los perros*. In this novella the dog, Berganza, disrupts the expression of black love and intimacy when he mauls an enslaved black woman who resided in the household as she passed him in the night. The dog hated that the woman would feed her lover better than their master would feed the dogs. In this scene Cervantes tasks his readers to assess the ethical and moral dimensions of the enslavement, labor, and value of black Africans:

Berganza: Un caballero conozco yo que se alababa que, a ruegos de un sacristán, había cortado de papel treinta y dos florones para poner un monumento sobre paños negros, y destas cortaduras hizo tanto caudal, que así llevaba a sus amigos a verlas como si los llevara a ver las banderas y despojos de enemigos que sobre la sepultura de sus padres y abuelos estaban puestas. Este mercader, pues, tenía dos hijos, el uno de doce y el otro de hasta catorce años, los cuales estudiaban gramática en el estudio de la Compañía de Jesús; iban con autoridad, con ayo y con pajes, que les llevaban los libros y aquel que llabam *vademecum*. El verlos ir con tanto aparato, en sillas si hacía sol, en coche si llovía, me hizo considerar y reparar en la mucha llaneza con que su padre iba a la Lonja a negociar sus negocios, porque no llevaba otro criado que un negro, y algunas veces se desmandaba a ir en un machuelo aun no bien aderezado.

Cipión: Has de saber, Berganza, que es costumbre y condición de los mercaderes de Sevilla, y aun de las otras ciudades, mostrar su autoridad y riqueza, no en sus personas, sino en las de sus hijos; porque los mercaderes son mayores en su sombra que en sí mismos. Y como ellos por maravilla atienden a otra cosa que a sus tratos y contratos, trátanse modestamente; y como la ambición y la riqueza muere por manifestarse, revienta por sus hijos, y así los tratan y autorizan como si fuesen hijos de algún príncipe; y algunos hay que les procuran títulos y ponerles en el pecho la marca que tanto distingue la gente principal de la plebeya.

Berganza: Ambición es, pero ambición generosa, la de aquel que pretende mejorar su estado sin prejuicio de tercero.

[**Berganza**: I know a gentleman who prided himself on the fact that, implored by a sacristan, he cut thirty-two paper rosettes that were attached to black cloths and placed on a monument, and he attributed so much importance to this that he took his friends to see them as if he were taking them to see the banners and spoils of enemies on the tomb of his parents and grandparents. This merchant, then, had two sons, one twelve and the other almost fourteen, who were studying grammar in the school of the Company of Jesus. They went to school with a great deal of show, with a tutor and with pages who carried their books and what is called a *vademécum*. Seeing them go so ostentatiously, in canopied seats if the weather was sunny, in a carriage if it was raining, made me consider and remark on the simplicity with which their father went to the exchange to tend to his affairs, because the only servant he took was a black, and sometimes he even rode on an unadorned old mule.

Cipión: You should know, Berganza, that it is the custom and condition of the merchants in Sevilla, and even in other cities, to show their authority and wealth not in their own persons but in those of their children; because merchants are greater in their shadows than in themselves. And if they make an exception and attend to something other than their deals and contracts, they do so modestly; and since ambition and wealth long to show themselves, they explode in their children, and so they treat them and empower them as if they were the children of some prince. And there are some who obtain titles for them and place on their bosoms the sign that distinguishes eminent people from plebeians.

Berganza: It is ambition, but a generous ambition, of someone who attempts to improve his status without harming another.][34]

Superficially, this exchange between Berganza and Cipión renders visible a pseudoethnographic realism of the kind of labor, or work, performed by some enslaved black men. If we read the passage carefully, in all its folkloric references, irony, and nuances, Cervantes exposes us to the varieties of slave labor performed by enslaved blacks within and outside of Seville and its city walls. What stands out even more in this lengthy excerpt is Berganza's disapproval of and disbelief in the "freedom" with which the black man, who accompanies the wealthy merchant, moves within a classist and racially restrictive space. In this passage Cervantes recreates a late sixteenth- and early seventeenth-century Seville, whose main urban arteries and alleyways teemed with enslaved and free black people. As I've discussed in this book's previous meditations, this was the Seville dominated by powerful and wealthy merchants, *negreros*, and slaveowners such as Gaspar de Arguijo, his brother Juan Bautista de Arguijo, and his friend Esteban Pérez. Berganza's comments, I contend, cannot be disentangled from this broader social history that influenced Cervantes. Told to us through the experiences of two dogs, Berganza and Cipión, this quote references what I'd venture to call a black geography of Seville, a landmark, a space, and a terrain where sub-Saharan Africans and their descendants were not only auctioned off at the infamous Gradas of the Cathedral of Seville—or the Lonja—but also conducted their own personals affairs and ran errands for their masters and mistresses. In this 1613 novella, Cervantes depicts a quotidian life in Seville that was never realized—nor could have been realized—in the figment of Sancho Panza's imagination as imperial governor and trafficker of black flesh. Cervantes collapses historical realisms and literary fictions of capitalism, slavery, and subjection that foreshadow Berganza's antiblack sentiments and violent behavior that crystallize toward the end of the story.

During the third episode of the *Coloquio*, with his third master, Berganza unleashes his terror on the enslaved black woman who inhabits the same house where he resides. The dog justifies his hatred of her since she tried to poison him on one occasion, out of spite. Berganza bitterly recounts, "Con todo esto, aunque me quitaron el comer, no me pudieron quitar el ladrar. Pero la negra, por acabarme de una vez, me trujo una esponja frita con manteca; conocí la maldad; vi que era peor que comer zarazas, porque a quien la come se le hincha el estómago y no sale dél sin llevarse tras sí la vida." ("With it all, though they took away my food, they couldn't take away my bark. But to finish me off once and for all, she brought me a sponge fried in lard; I recognized the evil act; I saw it was worse than eating poison paste, because if you eat it your stomach swells and there's no way out except to die.")[35] Beyond his contempt for her, analogizing the black woman's dark skin to deviance, lust, thievery, and sin, Berganza brutally attacks and bites her. In another deep conversation between Berganza and Cipión, Cervantes exposes the contradictions of our perceived expectations of the so-called exemplarity of animals. The hypocrisy manifests through Berganza's racial bias hurled at the black woman and her partner:

> **Berganza:** Quiero creerte; y digo que, no contenta mi fortuna de haberme quitado de mis estudios y de la vida que en ellos pasaba, tan regocijada y compuesta, y haberme puesto atraillado tras de una puerta, y de haber trocado la liberalidad de los estudiantes en la mezquindad de la negra, ordenó de sobresaltarme en lo que ya por quietud y descanso tenía. Mira, Cipión, ten por cierto y averiguado, como yo lo tengo, que al desdichado las desdichadas le buscan y le hallan, aunque se esconda en los últimos rincones de la tierra. Dígolo porque la negra de casa estaba enamorada de un negro, asimismo eslavo de casa, el cual negro dormía en el zaguán, que es entre la puerta de la calle y la de en medio, detrás de la cual yo estaba, y no se podían juntar sino de noche, y para esto habían hurtado o contrahecho las llaves; y así, las más de las noches bajaba la negra, y, tapándome la boca con algún pedazo de carne o queso, abría al negro, con quien se daba buen tiempo, facilitándome mi silencio,

y a costa de muchas cosas que la negra hurtaba. Algunos días me estragaron la conciencia las dádivas de la negra, pareciéndome que sin ellas se me apretarían las ijadas y daría de mastín en galgo. Pero, en efeto, llevado de mi buen natural, quise responder a lo que a mi amo debía, pues tiraba sus gajes y comía su pan, como lo deben hacer no sólo los perros honrados, a quien se les da renombre de agradecidos, sino todos aquellos que sirven.

Cipión: Esto sí, Berganza, quiero que pase por filosofía, porque son razones que consisten en buena verdad y en buen entendimiento; y adelante y no hagas soga, por no decir cola, de tu historia.

Berganza: Primero te quiero rogar me digas, si es que lo sabes, qué quiere decir *filosofía*; que, aunque yo la nombro, no sé lo que es; sólo me doy a entender que es cosa buena.

Cipión: Con brevedad te la diré. Este nombre se compone de dos nombres griegos, que son *filos* y *sofía*; *filos* quiere decir amor, y *sofía*, la ciencia; así que *filosofía* significa amor de la ciencia, y *filósofo*, amador de la ciencia.

Berganza: Mucho sabes, Cipión. ¿Quién diablos te enseñó a ti nombres griegos?

Cipión: Verdaderamente, Berganza, que eres simple, pues desto haces caso; porque éstas son cosas que las saben los niños de la escuela, y también hay quien presuma saber la lengua griega sin saberla, como la latina ignorándola.

Berganza: Eso es lo que yo digo, y quisiera que a estos tales los pusieran en una prensa, y a fuerza de vueltas les sacaran el jugo de lo que saben, porque no anduviesen engañando el mundo con el oropel de sus gregüescos rotos y sus latines falsos, como hacen los portugueses con los negros de Guinea.

[**Berganza**: I want to believe you; and I say that my fate, not content with removing me from my studies and the life I led pursuing them, so joyous and composed, and trying me behind a door, and exchanging the generosity of the students for the stinginess of the black woman, ordered that I be disturbed in what by then I already considered tranquility and peace. Look, Cipión, you can consider it true and proven, as I do, that misfortunes search out and find the unfortunate man even if he hides in the farthest corners of the world. I saw this because the black woman was in love with a black man who was also a slave in the house; and this black man slept in the portico between the street door and the one in the middle, behind the one where I was, and they couldn't be together except at night, and for this they had stolen or copied the keys, and so, most nights the black woman came down, and covering my mouth with a piece of meat or cheese, opened the door to the black man, with whom she spent a long time, facilitated by my silence, and at the cost of many things she stole. Some days her gifts clouded my conscience, making me think that without them my flanks would grow thin, and I would look more like a greyhound than a mastiff. But in fact, led by my better nature, I wanted to be responsible for what I owed my master, since I received benefits from him and ate his bread, which is what should be done not only by honorable dogs, given their reputation for gratitude, but also by all who serve.

Cipión: This, Berganza, is what I want to be taken as philosophy, because these are words made up of good truth and good understanding; continue your story, and speak plainly, not going round in circles.

Berganza: First I beg you to tell me, if you know, what philosophy means; because even though I say it, I don't know what it is. I simply assume it's something good.

Cipión: I shall tell you briefly. This word is composed of two Greek nouns, and they are *philos* and *sophia*; *philos* means love and *sophia* means knowledge; and so philosophy means love of knowledge, and a philosopher is a lover of knowledge.

Berganza: You know a great deal, Cipión. Who the devil taught you Greek nouns?

Cipión: Really, Berganza, you're a simpleton, because you take notice of this; these are things that schoolchildren know, and there are also those who presume to know Greek and don't know it, just like Latin and those who are ignorant of it.

Berganza: That's what I say, and I'd like those people to be placed in a press, and by turning the handle the juice of what they know would be squeezed out of them, as the Portuguese do with the blacks of Guinea, and then they wouldn't go around deceiving everybody with the glitter of their false Greekisms and Latinisms.][36]

So much for the adage: *a dog is a man's best friend!* Present-day readers might pick up on the hypocrisy and irony of such a term in this saying. The author rehearses and threads a long cultural history and literary narrative about dogs brutalizing black bodies and tearing into black flesh—enslaved or not. Berganza embodies what I like to think of as a post-Quixote iteration of slave catchers, quite different from Sancho Panza but all the same in (t)his kind of inhumane work and evil thinking. In this scene Cervantes stages a hackneyed story and traditional critique about domestic slavery—note the clever way in which the author winks back at doors, vestibules, keys, and, most important, Luis, from *El celoso extremeño* (recall meditation 3)—where we must ask ourselves who is really "domesticated" here. What infringements and tensions become intensified under the rubric of domestication and enslavement? In response to Cipión's précis—a snippy quip about philosophy—it becomes crystal clear that Berganza harbors hate and ill-will toward black people. How odious does Berganza's *philosophy* need to be to convey antiblack ideologies and feelings when he exclaims that he'd "like those people to be placed in a press, and by turning the handle the juice of what they know would be squeezed out of them, as the Portuguese do with the blacks of Guinea, and then they wouldn't go around deceiving everybody with the glitter of their false Greekisms and Latinisms."

Indicative of an institutionally sanctioned policing body, Cervantes's construction of Berganza's attitude, thoughts, and words throughout *Coloquio de los perros* signals a broader culture and history of terrorizing black people in imperial Spain. I analogize Berganza, although an animal, to the human *perreros* and their band of dogs who hunted and punished enslaved blacks. Cervantes builds on a larger literary history and practice of canines who brutalize, police, and surveil black people. As I've discussed elsewhere, Luis de Góngora y Argote's *letrilla* "En la fiesta del Santísimo Sacramento" (1609) showcases a pairing between black people and canines. Lines 19 through 23 of the carol poeticize this human-animal relation though the voice of a black woman named Juana:

Juana	Vamo a la sagraria, prima,
	veremo la procesiona,
	que aunque negra, sa persona
	que la perrera me estima
[Juana	Let's go to the tabernacle, cousin,
	There we'll see the procession.
	Even though I'm black I am a person,
	and the keeper of hounds admires me][37]

In my translation of the habla-de-negros construction of *la perrera* to *perrero* (keeper of hounds or dogcatcher), I'd like to draw your attention to the way in which lines 21 and 22 reveal the delicate relationship between Juana's racially gendered personhood and womanhood and the dogcatcher's esteem for her as a person. Seventeenth-century Spanish writers often bridged broader social and religious lived realities between black women and the policing bodies and orders of the *perrero* and his dogs. Predating Cervantes's *Coloquio de los perros*, Góngora's 1609 poem opts out of using violent language—such as *galguineagra* and *perra*—to vilify the two black women protagonists, Clara and Juana. Instead, Juana negotiates the antinomies of abjection and personhood through her recognition of the *perrero*'s admiration. Góngora's referencing of the *perrero*—as mediated through his connection to dogs and the Cathedral of Córdoba—highlights the unique way in which Cervantes's contemporary forges sympathetic imagination through the animal.

Bracketing Góngora and my discussion of him, I'd like to add that Cervantes explodes the nefarious deeds of dogcatchers by zeroing in on the way in which Berganza brags to Cipión—and the audience—about having mauled the black woman in the house who, as she passed him in the night, would visit her boyfriend. If his words couldn't bite more and pack a punch, Berganza calls her a bitch—"yo volví a la pelea con mi perra"—and likens her skin to that of a sheep.[38] In the *Coloquio* Cervantes simultaneously interrogates and suspends the ethical and moral implications concerning not only antiblackness and the policing of enslaved blacks but also the valid question of "who's the animal, or the dog"? In *Canines in Cervantes and Velázquez*, John Beusterien adds to my conviction here when he notes, "By highlighting [Berganza's] violence and arrogance, Cervantes suggests that Berganza may not be a saintly model, but a negative one. Indeed, Berganza's animalization of the black woman makes the reader question the moral logic behind an antiblack animus that animalizes humans and, indeed, the role that the animal has in how humans define themselves as human."[39] Building on the pathbreaking work of John Beusterien and Adrienne L. Martín,[40] who have made magnificent contributions to animal studies approaches in Cervantes, I conjecture that Cervantes calls into question—and ultimately leaves on the table for us as readers to reconcile—what black feminist theorists, like Sharon Patricia Holland and Zakiyyah Iman Jackson, have richly examined in their work. Taking cues from Holland's *An Other: A Black Feminist Consideration of Animal Life* and Jackson's *Becoming Human: Matter and Meaning in an Antiblack World*, for example, I, as a scholar of critical black studies, want to "map a relationship among hum:animal:blackness that doesn't always already see animal life as something to descend *into* or as descent itself." My reading of Berganza, in sum, centers ethical commitments over ontological concerns about how black people ethically related with animals. To achieve this type of reading practice, I embrace and emphasize Jackson's nudge that "we as readers must challenge animalizing discourse that is primarily directed at people of African descent, and animalizing discourse that reproduces the abject abstraction of 'the animal' more generally because such an abstraction is not an empirical reality but a metaphysical technology of biopolitics and necropolitics applied to life arbitrarily."[41]

"Too Late Undeceived": Black Woman as Object of Culture

The second black person to appear in Zayas's two-part collection is an unnamed black woman—generically dubbed as "Negra"—from *Desengaño Cuarto*, also known as "Tarde llega el desengaño" ("Too Late Undeceived"), from *Desengaños amorosos* (1647). In this work the narrator, Filis, ruminates on male-female relationships before beginning her story. She begins by saying that everyone, regardless of class or station, lives by deception. Moreover, Filis questions whether women are, in fact, deceived or whether they permit themselves to become so. Even without drawing wisdom from ancient exempla, we see everyday women who are the victims of great deception. In the novella we learn of the tale of Don Martín, accompanied by his crew and his friend, blown off course by a violent tempest and shipwrecked on Grand Canary Island. Soon after their arrival, a gentleman named Don Jaime graciously invites them to stay at his home while they recuperate from their harrowing voyage—an invitation they willingly accept. The guests are unprepared, however, for the grim spectacle that lies in store for them.[42] While being seated for dinner, Jaime opens a small, locked door, from which a beautiful but very pale woman, no more than twenty-six years old, named Elena, emerges, carrying a human skull.

Soon thereafter, juxtaposing the haggard, young white woman, the narrator shares with us more important details about another woman who also enters the room: she is black and described as follows:

> La otra que por la puerta salió era una negra, tan tinta, que el azabache era blanco en su comparación, y sobre esto, tan fiera, que juzgó don Martín que si no era el demonio, que debía ser retrato suyo, porque las narices eran tan romas, que imitaban los perros bracos que ahora están tan válidos, y la boca, con tan grande hocico y bezos tan gruesos, que parecía boca de león, y lo demás a esta

propoción. Pudo muy bien don Martín notar su rostro y costosos aderezos en lo que tardó en llegar a la mesa, por venir delante de ella las dos doncellas, con dos candeleros de plata en la manos, y en ellos dos bujíos de cera encendidas. Traía la fiera y abominable negra vestida una saya entera con manga en punta, de un raso de oro encarnado, tan resplandeciente y rica, que una reina no la podía tener mejor: collar de hombros y cintura de resplandecientes diamantes; en su garganta y muñecas, gruesas y albísimas perlas, como lo eran las arracadas que colgaban de sus orejas; en la cabeza, muchas flores y piedras de valor, como lo eran las sortijas que traía en sus manos. Que como llegó, el caballero, con alegra rostro, la tomó por la mano y la hizo sentar a la mesa diciendo:

—Seas bien venida, señora mía.

[The other woman who had come in through the kitchen door was black, so black that jet would pale in comparison. She was of such fierce aspect that don Martin thought if she wasn't the devil, she was his very likeness. Her nose was as broad as the nose of the highly prized bloodhound. Her mouth, or snout, had thick protruding lips resembling the gaping maw of a lion and the rest of her was similarly repulsive. It took her so long to get to the table that don Martin was able to take careful note of her face and her costly dress. She was led in by two maids, each bearing a silver candelabra with twin lighted candles. The fierce and abominable [black woman] was wearing a dress all of one piece made of scarlet brocade with long sleeves falling to a point resplendent and so lavish that a queen could want no better. She wore a necklace and belt of glittering diamonds and at her throat and wrists were large glistening pearls, as were the matching earrings dangling from her ears. In her hair she wore flowers and precious gems like the ones that bedecked her fingers. When she drew near the table the gentleman, with happy expression, took her hand and seated her at the table with this greeting:

"Welcome, my lady."][43]

Filis's description of the nameless black woman functions as an antithetical foil to Elena's victimized white womanhood. We learn from Filis that the formerly enslaved black woman—along with four *"esclavas blancas"* who were branded on their faces—lived in Jaime's household. Internal family affairs went awry when the black woman told Jaime that Elena was unfaithful to him with her cousin, whom Jaime had taken in and treated like his own son.[44] Zayas repurposes and unhinges Cervantes's trope of the "*cuatro esclavas blancas*" (four enslaved Moriscas) from *El celoso extremeño*, who bore facial brands and spoke no Spanish. Zayas's configuration of the branded "*esclavas blancas*" involves a cognitive play on words that attends to the perceptions and sensibilities of those aware of and sympathetic to the horrific abuses suffered by white women and nonblack women. Surely, her "*esclavas blancas*" could be enslaved Moriscas, but, given Zayas's proclivity to defend white womanhood and underscore its purported innocence, I take the trope of the "*esclavas blancas*" to reflect Zayas's firm admonishment of the violations wrought against white (European) women. While they may not play a prominent role in the story, they foreshadow, I argue, the assortment of contradictions and moral dilemmas encoded in the novella's nebulous, anonymous black woman dubbed as "Negra." As such, to display the interconnected themes of blackness, gender, slavery, and violence in *Desengaño Cuarto*, Zayas follows the literary tradition of these topics after Cervantes (e.g., *Don Quijote* and *Novelas ejemplares*) and Lope de Vega (e.g., *Los melindres de Belisa* and *Servir a su señor discreto*). Zayas's application of the "Negra" moniker, coupled with her abject and contentious representation of black women more broadly, reflects her inheritance of a long Spanish Golden Age aesthetic and literary tradition that has cast unnamed "Negra" operates in their works.[45]

In the pages ahead, as I develop my analysis of *Desengaño Cuarto*, I wish not to regurgitate conventional readings of this notorious banquet scene. To be frank, overemphasizing Zayas's indisputable antiblack racism bores me. Instead, by shedding light on the machinations of interracial intimacy in wealthy Spanish households, I can thus direct our attention to the significance of the unnamed black woman's highly visible proximity to Don Jaime. If the overarching focus of this meditation concentrates on interracial intimacies, then the frottage—also conceived as a form of close contact, close rubbing, or exchanges of body parts, clothing, food, sounds, thoughts, and words—between the black woman and Jaime invites us to unpack this perceived taboo that seems to bother not only Zayas but also the narrator, those in the room listening to her storytelling, and those hearing the text. In many respects the proximity between the black woman and Jaime—indicative of a kind of frottage predicated on arousals, recognitions, rubbings, and titillation—lingers on a critical and historical desire to highlight the affective conflicts and practices of difference that suture the African diaspora. The unnamed black woman who occupies that central role in the novella, from beginning to end, is the daughter of two enslaved black people who belong to—and are later married by—don Jaime's parents. So this could explain the likelihood of Jaime's proximity in age to the black woman (and even Elena too, perhaps). As opposed to preoccupying my intellectual curiosity with Zayas's abject animalization and dehumanization of this black woman—as well as, for the matter, flatly and reductively arguing for this woman's agency or resistance—I find it more productive to channel the imaginative speculative work and vulnerable wayward reconstructive reading practices of building life and meaning into the unnamed black woman's characterization. Through this methodology I embrace the challenge of imagining and uncovering the origins and symbolism of the clothing and jewels that adorn her body—as well as the stories they could (or would) tell—while she sits at the head of the banquet table, a piece of furniture whose wood could have originated from Africa, Asia, or the Atlantic world.

Zayas's portrayal of the unnamed black woman riffs off the *romance* (ballad), or poem, "Boda de negros" (1643), composed by her contemporary Francisco de Quevedo. Conjoined as one ideological force, Quevedo and Zayas catapult—and thus concretize and weaponize—a literary production of antiblackness in their writings. Known for their dark, sinister, and violent literary treatments of sub-Saharan Africans and their blackness, the works of Quevedo and Zayas still remain insufficiently historicized, theorized, and underimagined. In the broader scheme of the so-called representation of blackness in early modern Spain, scholars seldom place the two in conversation with each other. I treat them as, let's say, two cultural and literary powerhouses that often regurgitate and remix hackneyed antiblack racist anxieties and tropes running rampant in Counter-Reformation Spain. I even wager to assert that Quevedo and Zayas, albeit debatable and dubious to some, depart from—or *unhinge*—Cervantes in their cultural activity in constructing, defending, and disseminating an archaeology of antiblackness in late seventeenth-century Spain.

In many respects my method of unhinging therefore *hinges* on framing the antiblack literary enterprises of Quevedo and Zayas as a vestige to assess the legacy of their aesthetics and sensibilities. Philological sources such as the *Oxford English Dictionary* and the *Diccionario de Autoridades* define the word "vestige," or *vestigio* in Spanish, as a "mark, trace, or visible sign," which no longer exists.[46] I suggest that a vestige correlates to, on the one hand, and conjugates, on the other hand, Michel Foucault's concept of "archaeology."[47] As such, I employ the method of Foucault's archaeology to sift through the racialized discourse and sentimentality of the antiblackness operative in the writings of Quevedo and Zayas. In their rich and vast oeuvre, antiblackness operates in dark, sinister, and violent ways. I argue that the so-called archaeology of their *antiblackness*, in Foucauldian terms, constitutes the deathly, ghostly, and uncanny enunciations of black Africans' purported animality, enslavement, subordination, and vulgarity. Identifying the practice of antiblackness does not suffice. The traces and signs of antiblack aesthetics, politics, and sentiments operative in Quevedo's and Zayas's texts temper Foucault's archaeology. As a kind of grammar or logic, these two writers' negation of their black literary figures' existence, intellect, and voice becomes codified in their elite, Counter-Reformationist society's seventeenth-century discourses and systems of thought.

The deprecating messages and severe warnings articulated in Quevedo's "Boda de negros" do not fall on deaf ears and do not disappear in Zayas's tales of exemplarity. A mise-en-scène of black people playing with customs out of their reach, Quevedo's poem inventories a surplus of ornate inanimate objects, foodstuffs, and other material goods employed to describe that which is animate and living: a group of black Africans celebrating a wedding on the steps of the San Pedro el Viejo Church in Madrid. The text's classical reference to *"el infierno"* from line 6, for instance, analogizes blackness to hell and the diabolic. Similar constructions that equate blackness, black people, and black things to the devil and infernal hellscapes appear in Teresa de Ávila de Jesús's *Libro de la vida* (1588) and Quevedo's narrative work *La hora de todos* (1645). Conceptually, resonating with the light/dark binary found in the language of chiaroscuro from art history, as well as with the good/evil dichotomy found in Christianity, *"infierno"* functions as a hyperbolic reiteration that bonds chromatic blackness to infernal values (e.g., Pluto's remark from *La hora de todos* that "dios dado a los diablos, con una cara afeitada con hollín y pez" (God [had] given to hell's demons a face painted of black dust, soot, and fish scales).[48] Like Zayas, Quevedo marginalizes blackness through grotesque imagery. Philip Thomson characterizes the grotesque as simultaneously conveying the notion of the laughable and the horrifying, as expressed by way of hyperbole.[49] If, as Mikhail Bakhtin maintains, "exaggeration, hyperbolism, excessiveness are generally considered fundamental attributes of the grotesque style," then "Tarde llega el desengaño" inaugurates grotesque imagery through words that qualitatively and quantitatively overshadow the presence of the black woman in the text. If, as Bakhtin also argues—and in light of Antonio's scars—the grotesque is an expression of social and cultural rebellion against order, then the black female body in Zayas's *Desengaño Cuarto* reaffirms its messiness against the strictures of what Norbert Elias defines as the "civilizing process."⁵⁰

Zayas's dinner episode in *Desengaño Cuarto* mirrors the banquet scene in "Boda de negros." Quevedo's poeticizes a banquet table adorned with black foodstuffs and black objects: "donde también les pusieron / negros manteles y platos, / negra sopa y manjar negro" (where the blacks were served black soup and black delicacies set atop black tablecloths and black plates; vv. 45–48).⁵¹ The "manjar negro" parodies the traditional *manjar blanco*, which during Quevedo's time consisted of a stew made of shredded hen breast mixed with sugar, milk, and rice flour. The episode proceeds with a blessing of the meal by "un negro veintidoseno, / con un rostro de azabache / y manos de terciopelo" (a black male minister with a jet-black face and furry hands like velvet; vv. 50–53). With limited information about this man blessing the table and the meal laid atop it, key words such as "*azabache*" (anondyne jet) and "*terciopelo*" (velvet) render a textured embodiment into his body. Like the black woman showcased in "Tarde llega el desengaño," jet—as a color and a raw material (the semiprecious form of lignite, or brown coal)—eroticizes, materializes, and spectacularizes both the minister's and the unnamed black woman's skin and clothing. Velvet perverts the luxuriousness of the fabric to facetiously animalize and denigrate blacks who wear it. Quevedo's reference to velvet analogizes the black body with the texture of animal fur, thereby morphing the minister and his "manos de terciopelo" (velvet-like, furry hands) into a fuzzy animal or beast. Zayas's narrative description of the black woman from "Tarde llega el desengaño" carries the same weight of destructive abstraction of animalizing discourse.

As the narrative intensity gains momentum in "Tarde llega el desengaño," Filis's racially charged language alerts us to the luxurious garments that glisten on the black woman's body that belonged to Elena. As illustrated in figure 13, the heft and size of the pearls hanging from the unnamed black woman's earlobes and those draped around her neck have a fraught history. Contrapuntal to their appearance in "El prevenido engañado," to racialize doña Beatriz's beauty, rank, and whiteness, the textual reference to pearls on the black woman's body carries a different meaning for the audience. Historically, over the course of Iberian colonization and imperial dominion across oceans and other bodies of salty and sweet waters, sub-Saharan Africans and their ancestors across the diaspora executed their skill as deepwater divers and swimmers to expertly cultivate and process pearls concealed in

Fig. 13. Eric Fraser, illustration of *Desengaño Cuarto*, 1963. Sturrock, *Shameful Revenge and Other Stories*, 181.

the flesh of clams, oysters, or any mollusk. Across the shores of the Canary Islands to Caribbean waters and the South American coastline to the Indian and Pacific Oceans, pearls served not only cultural and literary purposes but also legal and transactional ones that transcend the racialized trope of color inherited by Petrarch or Neoplatonism.[52] Writing approximately a century before María de Zayas, on the social impact and flux of the abundance of pearls, Spanish Jesuit missionary and naturalist José de Acosta wrote in his *Historia natural y moral de las Indias* (1588–90) that "even black women wear strands [of pearls]."[53] Prescient in its antiblackness, Acosta's visceral reaction to black women donning pearl necklaces—a jewel that formerly had been hard to obtain and was associated with white European elite consumption—reflects a contiguous astonishment that bubbles just beneath the surface of Zayas's broader discomfort with and distaste for black people (especially black women). As I've demonstrated in my previous work on Francisco de Quevedo, for example, such disapproval and discomfort revolve around deep-seated antiblack feelings and discriminatory convictions for black people who dare approximate, disavow, and dupe the fictitious, systematic, and purported exclusivity of whiteness.

To invoke the legal and sociological legacies and traditions of Cheryl L. Harris and George Lipsitz, the issue at hand pertains to the sociocultural and sociopolitical realities—or the unquestioned and taken-for-granted-truths—of "whiteness as property" and the "possessive investment in whiteness."[54] Such political investments in and legal proprietary claims about pearls' chromatic whiteness in the artistic, literary, material, and visual production of early modern Europe and its imperial reaches transcend the mere innocence of the object's white color. In this vein, according to Francisco Zamora Loboch, an Equatorial Guinean thinker and writer living in exile in Madrid, Quevedo and those who hold onto his anti-Semitism, negrophobia, and xenophobia uphold the tenets of intolerance.[55] To that end, frottage-like in a masturbatory quality to this self-fulfillment, note 215: "Hysterical Whiteness," from Christina Sharpe's *Ordinary Notes*, corroborates, clutches, and sums up my position on Quevedo's and Zayas's corpora. Sharpe reminds us of how "hysterical whiteness makes blackness the provoking agent of mass hysteria that is the province of whiteness itself. Hysterical whiteness is conquest pedagogy."[56]

As a cross-reference with my alchemical and metallurgical intervention on Sancho Panza from meditation 2, I invoke Arjun Appadurai and Molly A. Warsh to ideate how pearls were "things-in-motion" and were carried by people *in motion* who invested with diverse values, expectations, and associations. I believe this to be the case with Zayas's message about the unnamed black woman we meet at the beginning of "Tarde llega el desengaño." A baroque pearl of sorts, the black woman costarring in this work exists as a symbolic *black* pearl who spectacularizes the marvel and grotesqueness of her anomaly. How dare *she* wear them? As a chastising critique of black form and black womanhood—attempting to ratify and dispute the grammars of what theorist and media studies scholar Rizvana Bradley terms "*Anteaesthetics*"—how dare *she* touch them?[57] How dare *they* rest on her black sentient flesh? There's a large and pervasive maritime and oceanic history that cannot be severed from the unique connection between pearls and black people—especially black women. While not a prized medallion or jewel in Zayas's nor the narrator's eyes, the white pearls resting atop the black woman's chest and hanging from her ears retain their long-standing associations with allure, danger, mystery, violence, and the wealth of the sea.[58]

Literary scholars tend to overlook the crucial role the Canary Islands have played historically in the interracial matrix between Don Jaime and his black companion. Let's take, for instance, David Wheat's examination of the interaction between Iberian mariners and sub-Saharan African women in West Africa. Wheat finds that "in the late-sixteenth-century Canary Islands, at least one Spanish man and several Portuguese men were married to women of African descent. Other Portuguese men failed to marry their partners but left goods in their wills to daughters born of sexual unions with black women."[59] My point here insists that Zayas's "Tarde llega el desengaño" illustrates, on the one hand, and admonishes, on the other hand, a culture and society of white Iberian men who either wed or have sustained sexual unions with black Africans and mixed-race black woman. Therefore, in this regard I do not fully subscribe to the notion that Zayas's audience beyond and within the *sarao* would not have been aware of these interracial relationships. This instantiation of the intimate proximity of blackness stirs up an aesthetics of disgust. Describing Don Martín's emotional response in the story, Steven Wagschal notes Martín's visceral reaction that "seems somewhat akin to Vives's 'offensa': it is not the sight of Elena on all fours eating scraps fit for a dog that provokes the emotion . . . but he feels indignation that a black slave is seated at the table, regaled by a white nobleman, when she is, according to his appraisal, better suited to be on the floor."[60] Concerning frottage, the case of Don Martín's "disgust" toward not only the black woman but also Don Jaime's intimate affection for and connection to her underscores Zayas's construction of morally reprehensible critiques about interracial bonds between white men and black women. As such, this serves as a place in the text where Zayas unhinges Cervantes's aesthetic and style insofar as she avoids humor, thereby transforming the elegance of Cervantes's irony and subtleties into volatile bluntness.

As the novella closes, the black woman confesses later that night that Elena was not having an affair. She admits she had lied because she loved Elena's cousin, and Elena had punished her for being disrespectful. Zayas writes that her death was a God-given reward to Elena, further aligning her white characters with God while aligning her nonwhite characters with the devil. If Antonio, from "El prevenido engañado," is portrayed as having corrupted Beatriz and having disrupted Fadrique's love interests, then "Tarde llega el desengaño" also frames the black woman as a traitor who ruins the lives of an innocent aristocratic white woman, whereby an aristocratic white man remains at fault for having acted without evidence. Though Zayas could have written a story that condemns Don Jaime for his gall, hubris, and violence, she instead crafted a story that collapses black womanhood with deceit, jealously, and recklessness. Put another way, the unnamed black woman has duped the system of white supremacy. A jezebel of some sorts, Zayas maintains a stereotypical controlling image of the novella's black woman protagonist to make an example out of her.

After Don Martín witnesses such a spectacle, the narrator, Filis, reiterates how he and his companion were "tan admirados y divertidos en mirarla, que casi no se acordaban de comer" (so amazed and distracted by the sight of [the black woman] that they could hardly eat).[61] Grieving and dying, the black woman cries for a confession, calling out for the maids by name and begging each one to bring her master to her: "¡Jesús, que me muero, confesión!" (Jesus, I'm dying! Confession!). She lies in a lavish bed of "damasco azul, goteras de terciopelo con franjas y flecos de plata" (blue damask with velvet hangings fringed in silver).[62] In Don Martín's eyes, this the "abominable" black woman had been occupying Elena's bed. As the narrator recounts, the black woman confessed that she fell in love with Elena's cousin and tried to persuade him to become her lover. Noting that he always conversed with Elena, she suspected they were in love. Combined with the fact that Elena and the cousin physically and verbally abused the black woman for having sassed them, she sought revenge for their violence by concocting a ruse.[63] In her soliloquy, understood by scholars such as Cornesha Tweede as a textual site of resistance, the unnamed black woman implores that Don Jaime forgive her, yet Elena's honor must be restored for her to occupy her rightful place in the home. And so, it is done: Don Jaime stabs the black woman three to four times to her death with a dagger and runs to his disgraced wife, Elena, who he soon discovers has died.[64]

Even after her death, Zayas's *Desengaño Cuarto* reifies stereotypical clichés of the time. Status quo mythologies reestablish binarized racially dichotomies. Elena, whose honor has been restored, grows more beautiful: "El rostro, aunque flaco, y macilento, tan hermoso, que parecía un ángel" (her face, although gaunt and pallid, was as lovely as an angel's visage).[65] The black woman, whose corpse was buried and taken from the city, represents "un retrato de Lucifer" (the very portrait of Lucifer).[66] Filis ends her disenchantment—or story—with the following warning: "Y es bien mirar que, en la era que corre, estamos en tan adversa opinión con los hombre, que ni con el sufrimiento los vencemos, ni con la inocencia los obligamos" (We should also take into account the fact that in these times we women have such a bad name among men that we can't change their minds through our innocence, nor through our suffering shall we overcome).[67] The moral of the story seems to suggest that white women's bodies are the only bodies subjugated to and abused by patriarchal forces. While the novella's conclusion dismisses black women, it also rules out women who are not high-born nor who embody Filis's—as proscribed by Zayas—preferred ideation of angelic, chaste, and unadulterated whiteness.

I close this meditation by asking how we continue to make meaning out of Zayas's portrayal of interracial intimacy. Drawing from my coauthored work with Chad Leahy in *Pornographic Sensibilities*, I am interested in thinking about Zayas's short stories as proxies that configure blackness—through the constellations of intimacy and miscegenation—as a form of pornotroping, to use Hortense Spillers's useful term.[68] Antonio and the anonymous black woman we've met in this meditation ideate Spillers's theorization of the pornotrope as linked to slavery and sexuality. In *Habeas Viscus*, Alexander Weheliye illuminates for us an understanding of the pornotrope as radically unstable. As an early modern Spanish writer who pornotropes not only blackness but also the interracial intimacies disclosed in the ethnic, literary, racial, and sexual fictions of that racialized blackness, Zayas's portrayal of black people animates a representational dilemma of ambivalence. My ideation of pornotroping in Zayas's two novellas thus stages what Christina Sharpe has termed a "monstrous intimacy," an inhuman relation that is produced out of acts of intimacy, care, and passion.[69] As I have argued elsewhere, the end of Toni Morrison's *Beloved* beckons, "This is not a story to pass on."[70] As opposed to hiding and silencing the archive and story of the traumas of slavery, Morrison implores us to confront the debt assumed by the horrors of slavery to enable us to transform this inheritance into a beloved future. Morrison's declaration that we *must* pass this story down has invigorated me over the course of *Cervantine Blackness* to reimagine a concealed past as a reparative starting point. In a necromantic way, such a reparative starting point not only summons the necrocapitalistic and necropolitical foundations of the West but also awakens the memory and souls of black folk and their descendants, as well as the visible *and* invisible worlds they inhabited. Suspending optimism and pessimism in the critical air of scholarly conflict and debate, my necromantic work would—and should—call us to remember that black women, like the black woman of Zayas's *Desengaño Cuarto*, were forced to innovate new conceptions of home. If nothing else, as I take inspiration from the incomparable Shoniqua Roach, it behooves me, as a literary critic, to stoke fresh imaginaries of black freedom through Zayas's black woman protagonist in "Tarde llega el desengaño."[71] This short story has invited me to reimagine a history of slavery that reconceptualizes what resistance is and where it can—or could—take place. This book ends with an epilogue that takes inspiration from a Morrisonian heuristic of beloved futures. This ending of *Cervantine Blackness* doesn't bespeak finality but marshals the futurity of subjunctive hypotheticals and the freedom to reconcile some things that are not yet over.

EPILOGUE
To Cervantes with Love

I am uninterested in investigating, documenting, theorizing, and inhabiting my own negation—black negation.

I am uninterested in remaining within the dynamics of oppression and resistance, oppression and agency, as the dominant frames within which black life is to be thought and theorized.

I am uninterested in the brief glimpses of something call *black agency* found in colonial archives.
    —Keguro Macharia, "Black (Beyond Negation)"

I could end this book how I began: citing an excerpted passage from the prologue of part 2 of *Don Quixote* (1615). But such a move would be too easy. It would be too predictable. In its obviousness it would foreclose a logical progression that reprises the dearth of ideas, materials, and polemics treated in this volume. Such a move would reproduce the most oppressive logic of any genealogy of ideas. Riffing off the adjectival "Cervantine," I characterize the progression of my closing thoughts as "serpentine." In what follows we coil, slither, and undulate around, under, and in between the conceptual crevices and theoretical contours and confluences examined throughout *Cervantine Blackness*.

This epilogue, affectionately titled "To Cervantes with Love," isn't a farewell—an *Adiós*, if you will—but a beginning. It inaugurates Cervantine futures that designate black culture as critical culture, to use the theoretical conjuring of Hortense Spillers, at the forefront of the future yet to come for (a new kind of) early modern studies and early modern black diaspora studies.[1] To talk about an ending as a *beginning*, one must conceive of *futures*. Under the rubric of futures—collective and capacious yet also subjunctive and transtemporal—my comingling of black futures and Cervantine futures conterminously, creatively, and imaginatively encourages us to make projections about how early modern texts, cultural modes of expression, and visual ideations during Cervantes's life and his legacy resonate with our present times. While the effort to make projections about our cultural, intellectual, and social futures might expose wounds and stir up disagreements, it is my hope that this necessary work may reconcile systemic issues that are not yet over.

Cervantine Blackness stands with the charges outlined by Keguro Macharia in the opening epigraph. Vibing with Macharia's brilliant and shrewd maneuver of black negation, I have set out, over the course of this project, to analyze, demonstrate, and theorize—as well as, at times, conjecture surreptitiously—for an incisive refusal of the dominant frames within which blackness and its adjacent proxies become studied in not just early modern Spanish but also early modern studies writ large. As fomented by my embrace of the artistic, political, and social act of defacing statues in San Francisco's Golden Gate Park, I leave you, my dear reader, with a book whose closing ruminations catapult and sustain my unhinged and unruly affect, fervent tempestuousness, and unabashed vulnerability.

Speaking back to this book's prologue and its four essayistic meditations, this epilogue serves as a beacon of theoretical hope and light for taking seriously the study of blackness in its capaciousness found in the works of Miguel de Cervantes and the dearth of critical reception bestowed on his legacy and name. I channel my deep admiration for Cervantes, his image and legacy, his ethos and ethic, and his *pulcritud* (neatness) and *tiquismiquis* (nitpicky) attention given to contradictions and details through the phrase "To Sir, with Love," a 1967 British drama film starring Sidney Poitier. The social and racial issues revealed and tackled in this movie still resonant with the many forms of activism, social unrest, and protest with which we're dealing in the twenty-first century.[2] If, as I've already disclosed to you, my dear reader, the genesis of *Cervantine Blackness* was sparked during a protest that happened in 2020 on Juneteenth (which commemorates liberation and is a Freedom Day for the formerly enslaved and their ancestors), I'd be remiss to discredit such symbolic origins. The pursuits of freedom and liberation cannot be easily disentangled from the interests and rights of those activists, agents, and protestors who defaced and toppled statues in San Francisco's Golden Gate Park. If that Juneteenth event hadn't had happened, maybe none of us would be holding this book. The red spray paint that marred the bronze bust of Miguel de Cervantes and the red "X" that flagged Sancho Panza's back got me here, in the first place, to meditate on these not-so-easily resolvable conversations.

✢ ✢ ✢

Freedom. Reparative work. Futures. *Cervantine Blackness* constitutes a labor of love that guided me in a journey of (self)liberatory work. My serpentine embrace of West and Central African derived serpent gods has empowered me to slough and shed sheaths of skin of my former intellectual self. Just as much as this book has empowered to me surmount such metamorphoses, this project has also infused me with an insurmountable courage to speak *my truth*, a truth that doesn't easily or neatly map out onto the Cartesian nor lexicographical grids of black agency and black joy or black dehumanization and black stereotype. In the act of speaking my truth, *Cervantine Blackness* has compelled me to make meaning out of African diasporic black life that follows proudly in the footsteps of the black critics, community builders, ethnographers, performers, and writers such as Daphne A. Brooks, Kinitra D. Brooks, Keisha N. Blain, Fatima El-Tayeb, Yinka Esi Graves, Tiffany Florvil, Robert Reid-Pharr, Keeanga-Yamahtta Taylor, and Todne Y. Thomas.

Katherine McKittrick's philosophy on liberation, as the ongoing collaborative expression of black community and black livingness, becomes executed in these thinkers' influences on my work. In *Dear Science and Other Stories*, McKittrick teleports us to a universe where "liberation is an already existing and unfinished and unmet possibility."[3] In tandem with McKittrick's methodological intervention, Yinka Esi Graves's new three-part solo-act production, *The Disappearing Act*, challenges its spectators to negotiate the various ways in which freedom may emerge from the ongoing collaborative expression of black humanity and black livingness. A recent articulation of this kind of creative, liberatory work has unfolded in the image, legacy, and life of Juan de Pareja (ca. 1608–70). In their quest of Pareja in the exquisite curation of the painter's life held by the Metropolitan Museum, my dear colleagues and interlocutors David Pullins and Vanessa K. Valdés have taught me—and, for that matter, have shown the world—what freedom, black futures, and Cervantine futures can look like. As illustrated by Pullins and Valdés, alongside the intellectual fellowship of Luis Méndez Rodríguez and Erin Kathleen Rowe, in their catalog, *Juan de Pareja: Afro-Hispanic Painter in the Age of Velázquez*, we, as an audience, come to see that all around Pareja reverberated a rich black social and cultural life that produced its own carols and poetry and venerated an Africanized Christianity exemplified by figures such as the sixteenth-century Sicilian Franciscan known as Benedict of Palermo.[4] This is the kind of reparative work conducted by the Metropolitan Museum in New York City that has revolved around and reflected the vision of black German studies (I'm thinking of, for example, Jeff Bowersox, Robbie Aitken, Fatima El-Tayeb, Tiffany Florvil, Kira Thurman, and Michelle Wright, among many others); the timely work of Benita Sampedro and scholars of the Global Hispanophone; and Rosalía Cornejo-Parriego and her roster of contributors in *Black USA and Spain: Shared Memories in the Twentieth Century*. Each scholarly, social justice–oriented collective has marshaled new methods and methodologies of linking the black European pasts with our present times and projected futures. Each exemplifies the precipice and futurity of historicizing and examining blackness across geographies, space, and time. The work each has achieved breaks ground and clears paths for future contemplation and work from which Cervantine studies and early modern studies can benefit and grow.

Cervantine Blackness closes shop with two powerful images from Kara Walker's photogravure *Testimony: A Narrative of a Negress Burdened by Good Fortune*. These pieces hypnotize my black gaze insomuch as the black art forms mounted atop horses set in motion for me a personal priority in assessing the consequences of the paradoxical antinomies of slavery and freedom, agency and abjection, and joy and suffering. Walker's equine figures—a black silhouette reminiscent of Master Peter's Puppet Show from *Don Quixote* 2.22–27 and a skeletal form glaring at us with its hollow eyes (which also conjures for me the Reaper entity from the Angulo el Malo theater troupe from *Don Quixote* 2.11—encodes the thematic content and theoretical concerns conveyed in this epilogue's epigraph. Like Cervantes, Walker puts herself in the position of being the controller or the puppet master of imaginary black people. In Cervantine irony, the vexing impact of the black paper image is particularly compelling to Walker. Powerful, disturbing, and controversial, figures 14 and 15 from *Testimony* bear witness to the trauma of slavery that persists in contemporary culture—most notably in the citational and intellectual politics of academe, when it comes to the so-called study of blackness.

Fig. 14. Kara Walker, *Testimony: A Narrative of a Negress Burdened by Good Fortune*, print 2, 2005. Suite of five prints. Photogravure, 16.5 × 22.2 cm. Artwork © Kara Walker. Courtesy of Sikkema Jenkins and Company and Sprüth Magers.

Fig. 15. Kara Walker, *Testimony: A Narrative of a Negress Burdened by Good Fortune*, print 3, 2005. Suite of five prints. Photogravure, 16.5 × 22.2 cm. Artwork © Kara Walker. Courtesy of Sikkema Jenkins and Company and Sprüth Magers.

I utilize these visual texts as a visual exercise to task ourselves with thinking more ethically and morally about exchanges of power and one's—or a faction's—attempts to steal power away from others. This is precisely what Walker's art instantiates for us. Walker's work, like mine throughout *Cervantine Blackness*, challenges us viewers and readers with characters, events, and scenes that are bizarre, graphic, puzzling, and shocking. Known for its controversy, Kara Walker's work activates and encourages our dialogue, engagement, and interpretation that makes works of art truly socially and politically relevant. Herein I seek to execute a similar move with my interventions in the book.

In *The Fire Next Time*, James Baldwin's thoughts resonate with and resound in the critical and political urgency that *Cervantine Blackness* has laid bare: "It is certainly sad that the awakening of one's senses should lead to such a merciless judgment of oneself—to say nothing of the time and anguish one spends in the effort to arrive at any other."[5] I hope this book serves as a reparative starting point for healing, honesty, and repair within my immediate home(s) of scholarly training. Baldwin has reminded me that "*every good-bye ain't gone*: human history reverberates with violent upheaval, uprooting, arrival and departure, hello and good-bye. Yet, I'm not certain that anyone ever leaves home."[6] *Cervantine Blackness* is my catharsis. Having returned home to new pursuits of intellectual curiosity, I have made my peace and now await the fruits of its labor. Ain't no feelin' like bein' free! *Vale*.

Notes

Prologue

Unless otherwise noted, all citations from *El ingenioso hidalgo Don Quijote de la Mancha* come from Luis Andrés Murillo's 1978 Castalia edition. Also, unless otherwise stated, all English translations originate from Edith Grossman's 2005 translation of *Don Quixote*. The Spanish text translated in the epigraph is as follows:

> Desocupado lector: Sólo quisiera dártela monda y desnuda, sin el ornato de prólogo. Porque te sé decir que, aunque me costó algún trabajo componerla, ninguno tuve por mayor que hacer esta prefación que vas leyendo. Muchas veces tomé la pluma para escribille, y muchas la dejé, por no saber lo que escribiría; y estando una suspenso, con el papel delante, la pluma en la oreja, el codo en el bufete y la mano en la mejilla, pensando lo que diría, entró a deshora un amigo mío, gracioso y bien entendido, el cual, viniéndome tan imaginativo, me preguntó la causa, y no encubriéndosela yo, le dije que pensaba en el prólogo que había de hacer. *Vale*.

1. For a theoretically rich exploration of the "Prologue," see Lezra, *Unspeakable Subjects*. At the opening of *El celoso extremeño* (1613), the narrator comments on the leisurely and slaker-like idleness of one sector of Seville's *gente de barrio*, or "neighborhood boys." The exact passage reads as follows: "Hay en Sevilla un género de gente ociosa y holgazana, a quien comúnmente suelen llamar gente de barrio. Estos son los hijos de vecino de cada colación, y de los más ricos della; gente baldía, atildada y *meliflua*, de la cual y de su traje y manera de vivir de su condición y de las leyes que guardan entre sí, había mucho que decir; pero por buenos respectos se deja" ("There are in Sevilla idle, indolent people commonly called *neighborhood boys*. These are the sons of the residents in each parish, the richest among them: useless, well dressed, well spoken, well mannered; there is a great deal to be said about them and their clothing and their way of life, their character and the laws they obey among themselves, but for good reasons we shall put all that aside"). Cervantes, *Novelas ejemplares II*, 106–7; Grossman, *Exemplary Novels*, 218–19.

2. Throughout I channel my own experiences of alienation and solidarity. Drawing from the antisocial turn in queer theory and queer-of-color critique, black apathy, disaffection, and unfeeling undergird the positionality and theoretical in *Cervantine Blackness*. For more on this framework, see Yao, *Disaffected*; Edelman, *No Future*; Edelman, *Bad Education*; Muñoz, "Ephemera as Evidence"; and Muñoz, *Sense of Brown*. I see perturbances could be provoked by a host of issues and phenomena raised in Dubrofsky, *Authenticating Whiteness*.
3. Kondo, *Worldmaking*, 12. For additional scholarship of liberalism, see also L. Lowe, *Intimacies of Four Continents*; and Yao, *Disaffected*.
4. To delve deeper into these problematic expectations, consult Myers, *Of Black Study*, and K. Mitchell, "Identifying White Mediocrity." For a recent, field-changing intervention on education and pedagogy revolving around class, gender, race, and sexuality, see Kendrick and Lawson, "Theorizing Education." Refer also to Kendrick, *Humanizing Childhood*.
5. See Zamora Loboch, *Cómo ser negro*, 101. Zamora Loboch deepens his framing of Cervantes as an antiracist in the poem "Estefanía," from the collection *Memoria de laberintos*, 49–50. For a fuller analysis of Zamora Loboch's interventions in Cervantine thought and *Don Quixote*, refer to Repinecz's erudite study, "Don Quijote in Africa."
6. For further clarity and insight into my political situatedness with these terms, see Táíwò, *Against Decolonisation*. The emergence of "decolonial," as a concept, idea, and theory, began circulating in the 1990s with Trouillot's landmark work *Silencing the Past*. The bibliography on decolonization and its theoretical apparati, approaches, and strategies is vast. My references to those sources in this endnote only touch the tip of the iceberg. However, as a point of entry into this scholarship, I provide a limited bibliography. In African studies, see also Falola, *Decolonizing African Studies*. Concerning Indigeneity, refer to L. Smith, *Decolonizing Methodologies*. On the "global turn," as it addresses and intersects with antiracist and decolonial paradigms in early modern studies, consult the following works: Subrahmanyam, *Connected Histories*; McManus, "Decolonizing Renaissance Humanism"; Biedermann, "(Dis)connected History"; Strathern, "Global Early Modernity"; Cohen-Aponte, "Decolonizing the Global Renaissance"; Zemon Davis, "Decentering History"; and Elkins, Valiavicharska, and Kim, *Art and Globalization*. See also Campbell and Porras, *Routledge Companion*.
7. Keeling, *Queer Times, Black Futures*, 25.
8. Táíwò, *Elite Capture*, 2–3.
9. Táíwò, *Elite Capture*, 30–31.
10. To mobilize my ideation of the "scramble for blackness," I borrow language from Nash's essay "Citational Desires," 77. Commemorating DuCille's now-canonical article, "Occult of True Black Womanhood," Nash's tour de force "Citational Desires" encapsulates what underpins my frustration with the scramble for blackness in early modern Spanish literary criticism and its adjacent interlocutor, or field, of colonial Latin American studies.
11. The Berlin Conference, also known as the Congo Conference (Kongokonferenz) or West Africa Conference (Westafrika-Konferenz), regulated European colonization and trade in Africa during the New Imperialism period and coincided with Germany's sudden emergence as an imperial power.
12. Tallie, "On Black Autonomy." I'd also venture to say that, if nothing else, there's still much to wrestle with on the matter when considering Dan Hicks's game-changing account, *Brutish Museums*. The overemphasis on "black agency," "black joy," and "black

resistance" function as terminological placeholders that edify and monumentalize fleeting, generalized, and less precise conceptualizations of blackness.
13. Katherine McKittrick (@demonicground), "Theorizing should not be a scramble," Twitter, September 20, 2021, https://twitter.com/demonicground/status/1439936161175179267.
14. W. Johnson, "On Agency," 113–15.
15. Bennett, *African Kings*, 24–25.
16. Fuentes, *Dispossessed Lives*, 143. Fuentes's problematizes agency throughout the entirety of this work. Morgan, in her new book *Reckoning with Slavery*, also beautifully advances the bounds and limits of agency and resistance through the category of Orlando Patterson's theory of "social death." On "social death" and related topics, consult V. Brown's masterful essay, "Social Death and Political Life."
17. Miller-Young, *Taste for Brown Sugar*, 16–18.
18. Quashie's *Black Aliveness*, 11. Refer specifically to the introduction, "Aliveness," 1–13, for an overview. Freeburg's *Counterlife* helps us sift through a rich array of cultural forms—comedy, film, literature, music, and sketches—that "conceptualize slave social life and art discourse as *counterlife*." As such, this term "unsettles singular narratives, teloses, fixed categories, oppositions, and what it means to be or have a self" (3).
19. Quashie's *Black Aliveness*, 1. Quashie continues by further elucidating that "this black world is not one where the racial logics and harming predilections of antiblackness are inverted but one where blackness is totality, where every human question and possibility is of people who are black" (2).
20. M. Wright, *Physics of Blackness*, 3, quoted in Quashie, in *Black Aliveness*, 11.
21. Pickens, *Black Madness*, x.

22. See J. Brown's edited collection, *How We Do It*.
23. Christian, "Race for Theory," 52. See also Nash, "Citational Desires." For those who hold grievances with an author's freedom to experiment with form, genre, and style, as I do in this book, I cite at length Quashie's methodological intervention to contextualize and elucidate my deliberate stylistic choices and freedoms: "The black essay as I am explicating it here does not pursue optimism or achievement; it does not respond urgently to the social peril of blackness; it is not a celebration of the yield of hard work, since there is nothing promised by hard work other than more hard work. It is of the working that is of pleasure, just the doing . . . the difficult beauty of being, the beauty of doing one's work." *Black Aliveness*, 93–105. If there are reservations about the freedom I am advocating through the essay as a black genre, perhaps they generate from the anxiety of audience and representation.
24. Christian, "Race for Theory," 61. These ideas are from chapter 5 in Quashie's *Black Aliveness*, 133–34n36, 212–13. See Lorde's argument in "Poetry Is Not a Luxury" and Spillers's essay "Crisis of the Negro Intellectual." Addressing the essay genre, Quashie in chapter 4 of *Black Aliveness* references Morrison's *Playing in the Dark* to underscore "another complication for the black writing subject." Paraphrasing Morrison, he explains that "the very words we might use to portray transformative experiences are racialized, that 'blackness' itself becomes a metaphor of encounter for the nonblack subject. Conceptually, blackness functions as 'excitable speech' and therefore is always addressable externally, a figuring that warps how we understand black writing as an encounter with chaos, ignorance, inexpressibility. These entanglements

of audience leave little room for relationality in the personal essay, a genre that scholar Gerald Early describes as being overwhelmed by the doubleness of insider-outsider as well as of writer-reader" (94).
25. Ortega y Gasset, *Meditations on Quixote*, 41. Refer also to Close, *Romantic Approach*.
26. On recent scholarship on medieval contemplative and medieval philosophy, consult Dyke's *Hidden Wisdom*.
27. I acknowledge and give tremendous thanks to my dear colleague, Matylda Figlerowicz, at Harvard University, for her swift assistance and guidance in translating and providing a fuller culture context for these passages. Additionally, Professor Figlerowicz explained to me that the last translated phrase comes from a ballad starting with "Ach wyjdź na balkon dziewico, nie zważaj na nocy chłód," which means "Oh, come out to the balcony, maiden, don't care about the cold of the night."
28. For more on serpentine metaphors and African diasporic religions and spiritualities, see Strongman, *Queering Black Atlantic Religions*; and Tinsley, *Ezili's Mirrors*. Concerning serpents in the Kongo spirituality of the Bakongo people, consider water spirits known as *bisimbi*, who can appear as calabash vines, human beings, serpents, or kalungas. In the varieties of Hoodoo beliefs and practices throughout the US South, *bisimbi* inhabit brooks, pools of water, streams, and rocks. They are also linked to women's fertility and the natural well-being of the living.
29. Hartman, *Wayward Lives*, xiv–xv.
30. On black geographies, see McKittrick, *Demonic Grounds*; Roane, *Dark Agoras*; Woods and McKittrick, *Black Geographies*; and Hawthorne and Lewis, *Black Geographic*.
31. Raengo, "Introduction," 7.
32. See specifically the introduction from Sharpe, *In the Wake*. Refer also to Mandela Gray's complete development and theorization of *sitting with* in *Black Life Matter*, 7–10.

Meditation 1
1. Malcolm X, "Chickens Coming Home To Roost: Malcolm X," interview, 1963, YouTube video, 1:16, https://www.youtube.com/watch?v=0D6aX3dHR2k.
2. Baldwin, "Talk to Teachers," 678. On politics and scholarly interventions, see Robbins, *Criticism and Politics*.
3. José Manuel Rodríguez Uribes (@jmrdezuribes), "Me resulta incomprensible el ataque," Twitter, June 20, 2020, https://twitter.com/jmrdezuribes/status/1274340766358347776.
4. Ken Salazar (@USAmbMex), "Gracias Sr. Ministro por su defensa de estos símbolos," Twitter, June 21, 2020, https://twitter.com/USAmbMex/status/1274817750729441287.
5. For a complete and rich examination of this subject matter, see Laguna, *Battle for Cultural Identity*. Also refer to Leahy's two-volume collection, tentatively titled *On the Uses and Abuses of Early Modern Spanish Culture*, forthcoming with Amsterdam University Press.
6. Jones and Leahy, "Cervantes y la materia." For a transformative and outstanding study on the literary history and politics of the op-ed, see Séguin's *Op-ed Novel*.
7. Close, in chapter 2 of in *Romantic Approach*, "The Romantics," offers very a thorough literary history and critical literary review of the German Romantics, who "completely transformed the interpretation handed down to them by eighteenth-century neo-classicism" (29). Close identifies the "pioneers" of the Romantic approach as "Friedrich and August Wilhelm Schlegel, F. W. J. Schelling, Ludwig Tieck, and Jean Paul Richter" (29). Egginton's "So-Called Historical Approach" also provides very useful ideas that clearly resonate with my main point.

The idolizing, or romanticizing, of Miguel de Cervantes as a historic figure and physical persona—and by extension his *Don Quijote de la Mancha*—serves to monumentalize and legitimate social orders that convert Cervantes into a monument *of* Spain in terms of collective and individual memory and national identity. For more on this topic and surrounding debates, refer to Pérez Magallón's indispensable and thoroughly documented *Cervantes, monumento de la nación*. Chapter 5, "El monumento material: La estatua de Cervantes," addresses central concerns and debates surrounding the erection of the statue in 1835 in Madrid. Overlapping content and scholarship appear in Labrador Méndez's "Dynamiting *Don Quijote*"; and Sierra Matute's forthcoming essay, "Tongue of Cervantes."

8. See Rubio, "Cervantes racial." For more on discrimination, race, and xenophobia in contemporary Spain, consult Coleman, *Necropolitical Theater*, and the Black View (https://theblackview.com), an online platform that exposes, debates, and discusses issue of diversity, equity, and inclusion in artistic representation in Spain.
9. Riaño, *Decapitados*, 17–19.
10. Araujo, "Toppling Monuments."
11. Quoted from Bey, *Black Trans Feminism*, 33. See original Malcolm X passage in Antwi, *Words of Power*, 73.
12. "Tupac Shakur Wiki," Fandom, accessed March 17, 2024, https://2pac.fandom.com/wiki/California_Love#Lyrics.
13. The appendix, "The Inside Light: Being a Salute to Friendship," from Hurston's autobiography, *Dust Tracks on a Road*, charts Hurston's travels across the entire state of California. In an entry dated July 20, 1941, in Altadena, California, Hurston uses Spanglish to fondly refer to the state as "'nice'; *Buen* nice!" In this work she also calls Californians "Californiacs." See Hurston, *Folklore, Memoirs, and Other Writings*, 796–803. For historical references to black migration in relation to California history, see Roach's "Black Living Room."
14. Didion, "Slouching Toward Bethlehem," 282.
15. Lethabo King, *Black Shoals*, 38.
16. Alandete, "Cae fray Junípero"; Jones and Leahy, "Cervantes y la materia."
17. Delgado, "Juan Manuel Cao"; Jones and Leahy, "Cervantes y la materia."
18. Levinson, *Written in Stone*, 13.
19. Araujo, "Toppling Monuments."
20. Lethabo King, *Black Shoals*, 40.
21. Yao, *Disaffected*, 1–16, 2–3.
22. The Ohlone are the predominant Indigenous group of the Bay Area, including the Chochenyo and the Karkin in East Bay, the Ramaytush in San Francisco, the Yokuts in South Bay and Central Valley, and the Muwekma tribe throughout the region. Other Indigenous groups include the Graton Ranchería community (Coast Miwok and Southern Pomo), Kashaya, Patwin, and Mishewal Wappo in the North Bay, and the Bay Miwok in the East Bay.
23. On this material, see P. Johnson, "Quixotic Allyship?" See also Salvatore Cordileone and Archdiocese of San Francisco, "Archbishop's Rosary for Saint Junipero Serra," June 27, 2020, YouTube video, 3:40, https://youtu.be/lk2qGgVpClM?.
24. For further details, consult Macdonald, "Blink."
25. Molina, *Burlador de Sevilla*; Judd, "Ghostly Mozart."
26. Quoted from Quashie, *Black Aliveness*, 107. In this line Quashie lovingly adds, "And yet Morrison's comment also maintains that the disavowal of black ethical possibility does not surpass the importance of understanding Sethe as an ethical subject. Pivoting on two different meanings of 'right,' Morrison's summation acknowledges that terrible fate for enslaved children (what makes infanticide potentially a right thing) as it asks us to behold Sethe as human and, as such, responsible to questions about being—an imagining of Sethe's thinking

and doing are philosophical in caliber" (107–8). See also Phelan, "Sethe's Choice." In *Black Aliveness* Quashie provides a thorough reading list related to Toni Morrison's ethics and ethical poetics (205n2).
27. Myers, *Of Black Study*, 2.
28. Morgan, *Reckoning with Slavery*, 22. Green also dedicates considerable attention to this issue in *Fistful of Shells*.
29. Bennett, *African Kings*, 90. For a fuller analysis and commentary on these ideas, consult chapter 4, "Authority," 75–100.
30. Pickens, *Black Madness*, x. See also Cooper's *Beyond Respectability*, 11–32. Within early modern studies and the early black diaspora, consult C. Smith, *Race and Respectability*.
31. Quoted in Alexander, *Black Interior*, 4. More broadly, see also Shange's *For Colored Girls*.
32. Corona Pérez, *Trata atlántica y esclavitud*; Bouza, Cardim, and Feros, *Iberian World*. For additional information on slavery in Valladolid during the sixteenth and seventeenth centuries, see L. Fernández, *Comediantes, esclavos, y moriscos*, 130.
33. Rodríguez-Velasco, *Microliteraturas*, 20 (translation mine).
34. For more on this topic, see Sanjurjo's special issue, "Centring Blackness in European History."
35. Alexander, *Black Interior*, 5.
36. Beyoncé, "Cozy," 2022, https://www.musixmatch.com/lyrics/Beyonc%C3%A9/COZY.
37. Sexton, "Basic Black," 81, 78.
38. Nyong'o, *Afro-Fabulations*, 94. On the topic of queerness and temporality, see Row, *Queer Velocities*; Freeman, *Time Binds*; and Puar, *Terrorist Assemblages*.
39. Cohen, "Punks."
40. Gordon, *Ghostly Matters*, 196, xvi. Ibrahim's method for investigating haunted subjects and the ghosts who haunt them influences my approach to thinking of how the relation between the two does not comprise a tidy or enclosed sphere of influence. See specifically chapter 4, "Ghosts," of Ibrahim's *Black Age*. What I'm getting at here is that Cervantes, through his historical and literary characterizations of black Africans, captures an untimeliness that disturbs hegemonic time (one that is linear, progressive, developmental, and conventionally factual). Refer also to L. Lowe's *Intimacies of Four Continents*. Concerning temporalities and timings, see Puar's commentary on "ghostly matters" and hauntings in the preface to *Terrorist Assemblages*, xxiv–xxx.
41. See Mbembe, *Necropolitics*; and Bennett's refutation of Mbembe and Mudimbe in *Black Kings*. For additional information about Patterson's foundational "social death" paradigm, see *Slavery and Social Death*. Refer also to my response to Beusterien in Jones, "Debt Collecting, Disappearance, Necromancy." Fernando de Roja's *La Celestina* (1499) also offers rich material for thinking about necromancy. See Gerli, "Agora que voy sola"; and *Celestina and the Ends*.
42. See *Oxford English Dictionary*, s.v. "necromancy," accessed August 12, 2023, https://www.oed.com/dictionary/necromancy_n.
43. See Deuteronomy 18:10–22 (New Revised Standard Version). For a more detailed, scholarly commentary, see *New Oxford Annotated Bible*, 280–81. So-called mediums and wizards refer to persons who communicated with the dead. Counternecromantic beliefs and practices appear, and are thus forbidden, in Leviticus 19:31, 20:6, 20:27 and Deuteronomy 18:10 (NRSV).
44. This event occurs in 1 Samuel 28:3–25 (NRSV). For more detailed, scholarly information, consult Coogan's edition of *New Oxford Annotated Bible*, 447–48. Ironically, Saul, who had expelled mediums and sorcerers, now seeks one out—the so-called Witch of Endor—and the results and work were still effective. On death and black subjectivity, see Holland, *Raising the Dead*. In the broader context of Zoroaster and the religion

of Zoroastrianism as it's conceived as "nigromancia" in *Don Quixote* 1.47, see Cervantes, *Don Quijote*, 559.
45. I have infinite gratitude for several colleagues in French and Francophone studies who implored and encouraged me to incorporate the figure of the ghostwriter (*nègre*, in French) to build deeper meaning into ghostly matters, hauntings, and necromancy in my theorization of Cervantine Blackness. For more on the theoretical formations and historiographies of the term, see Calhoun's *Suicide Archive*. In Spanish the word *negro* also means "ghostwriter." See definition n. 17 in the *Real Academia Española*, s.v. "negro," accessed August 12, 2023, https://dle.rae.es/negro. Last, but not least, my phrasing and utilization of "I am not your *negro*" takes inspiration from the 2016 social critique documentary, *I Am Not Your Negro*, which forms the basis of Baldwin's unfinished manuscript and memoir "Remember This House."
46. I'm riffing off Brown's outstanding examination and uncovering of Cervantean notions of falsehood, truth, and originality in literary texts. See K. Brown's "Miguel de Cervantes." Borges figures prominently in my ideation of apocryphal. For a Borgesian reading of apocrypha, see Almeida, "Celebración del apócrifo." Consult also Dopico's classic essay, "Pierre Menard."
47. Greer, "Thine and Mine," 222. See also Johnson and Molineux, "Putting Europe in Its Place."
48. Childers, *Transnational Cervantes*, 234.
49. Dopico, "Canons Afire," 16.
50. Domínguez, *Quixotic Memories*, 4.
51. Ibrahim and Ahad, "Black Temporality," 1.
52. Ibrahim and Ahad, "Black Temporality," 1–3.

Meditation 2

1. I'm thinking of the following works: Chartier, *Cardenio*; Dopico, "Canons Afire"; Foucault, *Archaeology of Knowledge*; and Morgan, *Reckoning with Slavery*.
2. Cervantes, *Don Quijote* 2.24, 229; Grossman, *Don Quixote*, 619.
3. Martínez, *Front Lines*, 177. See also Graf's commentary in "Cervantes's Euclidean Theologies," 106.
4. Cartagena Calderón, "Performance of Aging Masculinities," 339.
5. K. Lowe, "Stereotyping of Black Africans."
6. Fracchia, *"Black but Human,"* 154–94; Woods, "Cultural Crossings"; Rowe, *Black Saints*.
7. Mendo, *De las Órdenes Militares*, 101.
8. L. Wright, *Military Orders*.
9. Linares has published and spoken widely on this topic, especially on medieval and early modern Iberian military orders, diplomacy, and gubernatorial administration. His long-awaited forthcoming article, "Black Knighthood," will break important ground on these interrelated topics. See also Bouza, Cardim, and Feros, *Iberian World*.
10. For further reading on black swordsmen and fencers, see the following three essays by Olmedo Gobante: "In Search of the Black Swordsman," "Del frente a la palestra," and "Mucho número que hay dellos." See also Martín Casares, "Negros y mulatos libres sirviendo."
11. In *Staying with Trouble*, Haraway conceives of "speculative fabulation" as a "mode of attention, a theory of history, and a practice of worlding" (230).
12. Nyong'o, *Afro-Fabulations*, 7.
13. E. Wright, *Epic of Juan Latino*, 178.
14. Translations from E. Wright's *Epic of Juan Latino*, 179. Grossman's translation reads, on page 12, as follows:

> Since it's not the will of hea-
> for you to be quite as cle-
> as Juan Latin the Afri-,
> avoid Latin words and phra-.

15. E. Wright, *Epic of Juan Latino*, 178–79.
16. Historian Olivette Otele builds on this debate in her powerful book,

African Europeans, 52–61. See also Fra-Molinero's "Juan Latino."

17. For an analysis and theorization of blackness and disability studies, see Pickens, "Blackness and Disability," as well as her recent monographic study, *Black Madness*. On speech impediment with respect to habla de negros, see Jones's *Staging* Habla de Negros, 47–50.

18. Davidson, *Distressing Language*, 5. The scholar tells us that the book's title is a "verbal conundrum [that] combines a category of design with a condition of affect. Distressed clothing, pre-ripped jeans, 'aged' leather, rough-textured furniture depend on the simulation of wear and tear, a stylistic marker of use that adds a patina of history to contemporary materials" (4). Davidson also connects stuttering to crip speech and crip time (98–116). For more on this topic within crip studies, see Chen et al., *Crip Genealogies*; and Coráñez Bolton, *Crip Colony*. For more on disability studies within the field of early modern Spanish criticism, refer to Juárez-Almendros, *Disabled Bodies*; and García Piñar's various essays: "Ethics of Staging Crip *Comedia*," "Unstageable Birth," "Irrepresentable Corporealities," and "Weight of Authority."

19. Davidson, *Distressing Language*, 4. In this vein a necessary crip theory analysis can be applied to the term *zambo* ("bow-legged" or "pigeon-toed"), which circulated far and wide in colloquial and vernacular discourses as well as the literary landscapes of early modern Spanish drama and prose fictions. As examined in *Staging* Habla de Negros, I am of the belief that conceptual and philological genealogy of this term racializes, albeit not always exclusively, blacks and black diasporic bodies, dance, and movement through the critical vectors of disability studies and queer studies. Two prime examples for further exploration are Lope de Vega's play *Los locos de Valencia* (1620) and Luis Vélez de Guevara's *El diablo cojuelo* (1641). At the level of the word and its cognitive and conceptual implications, *zambo* undoubtedly developed nefarious and pejorative meanings in the US South at the onset of blackface minstrelsy well into—and after—the era of Jim Crow.

20. Cervantes, *Don Quijote* 1.52, 605; Grossman, *Don Quixote*, 446.

21. Fromont, *Art of Conversion*, 2.

22. Thorton and Windmuller-Luna, "Kingdom of Kongo," 88.

23. For more sources on the representation of Portugal in the study of Cervantes, see Burningham, "Os Manchíadas"; and Fox, "From King Sebastian."

24. See Stackhouse, "'Comedia' as Diplomacy." For a discussion of the historical Bumi Jeleen, Ruler of the Wolof (colloquially and fictionally dubbed as "Rey Bemoi"), see Tymowski, *Europeans and Africans*.

25. For an imperial reading and literary analysis of *Comedia Trofea*, see Vélez-Sainz's forthcoming article in Jones, *Recovering Black Performance*.

26. Lihani, *Bartolomé de Torres Naharro*, 61. The Portuguese would arrive at Ternate and Ambao in the Moluccas in 1512. Like no other theatrical piece, the play reflects a near-faithful mapping of Portugal's colonization of the African and Southeast Asian coasts.

27. Grossman, *Don Quixote*, 128. I also depart from Allen's note, in his edition of the novel, where he suggests "los masílicos" came from Africa (*Don Quijote*, 230n10). Following Grossman's translation, I accept "los masílicos" as "the Massilians," for they were Ionian Greeks from western Anatolia, or present-day Turkey. Murillo's 1978 edition offers a more complete classical historiography and fuller literary history of this term. Cervantes, *Don Quijote*, 218–21nn11–24.

28. Collins and Keene, *Balthazar*, 51.

29. Grossman, *Don Quixote*, 446.

30. There exists a vast bibliography and historiography discussing these men's apprenticeships, expeditions, and

lives. For more information, refer to de Góis, *Chronica*; Paiva Manso, *História do Congo*; Brásio, *Monumenta missionaria africana*; Jadin and Dicorati, *Correspondance de Dom Afonso*; Hilton, "Family and Kinship"; Stackhouse, "'Comedia' as Diplomacy"; and Tymowski, *Europeans and Africans*. For additional sources about the enslavement of blacks in Castile, see González Arévalo, *Vida cotidiana*; and Domínguez Ortiz, *Esclavitud en Castilla*.

31. Fromont, *Art of Conversion*, 29–31.
32. Fromont, *Art of Conversion*, 31.
33. M. Wright, *Physics of Blackness*, 1.
34. Cervantes, *Don Quijote* 1.29, 366; Grossman, *Don Quixote*, 245.
35. For detailed information about the dizzying number of race-based etymologies and terms in Spain and its colonies, refer to Forbes, *Africans and Native Americans*. See also Beusterien, *Canines in Cervantes and Velázquez*.
36. Tompkins, "Sweetness, Capacity, Energy," 855.
37. For up-to-date biographies on Cervantes's life, see Gracia, *Miguel de Cervantes*; and Lucía Megías, *Juventud de Cervantes*. Consult the documentary *Buscando a Cervantes: Los misterios de Cervantes* for additional biographical information and criticism about Cervantes. Teatro, November 8, 201, YouTube video, 46:25, https://youtu.be/lZxBsB2LMrk. Timestamp 4:00 provides discussion of Cervantes's grandfather owning slaves. See also Sliwa, *Documentos*. For essays on Sancho Panza and Princess Micomicona, refer to Fra-Molinero, "Sancho Panza"; Fra-Molinero, "Disfraz de Dorotea"; Fuchs, *Passing for Spain*; and Triplette, "Chivalry and Empire."
38. Almost all readers of *Don Quixote* possess some familiarity with the character Princess Micomicona (*Don Quixote* 1.28–47). As such, to be frank, I wish not to regurgitate nor rehearse other literary interpretations of her. The bibliography abounds, and I can do no justice whatsoever by expounding previous readings with yet another round of plot summaries that squarely and tendentiously overemphasize how the simian-based etymology of *micomicona* dehumanizes black people along the axes of antiblack and colonial logics. Such a finalized conclusion is facile and too easy to ascertain. As far as I'm concerned, especially with respect to the critical and theoretical interventions authorized in this book, I wish not to offer a flat reading of the past, of Cervantes's cunningly slippery yet contradictorily conflicted characterization (*not* caricature) of Africa south of the Sahara.

39. Also consult chapters 22–33 in Rodríguez López-Vázquez's *Quijote apócrifo*.
40. Nemser, "Governor Sancho," 18–19.
41. Bigelow, *Mining Language*, 7. On alchemy during the seventeenth century, consider also Quevedo's "Sueño del infierno," where he discuses and satirizes the representation of the term (240n336).
42. Cervantes, *Don Quijote* 1.29.367.
43. Graf, "Cervantes's Euclidean Theologies," 93.
44. Green, *Fistful of Shells*, 36–38. For an in-depth history on gold, refer to pages 31–148. On the gold-mining industries in Francophone West Africa, consult Avignon, *Ritual Geology*. Concerning the cultural study and literary history of gold in early modern Spain and colonial Latin America, see Vilches, *New World Gold*.
45. Green, *Fistful of Shells*, 38–39.
46. Quoted from Bigelow, *Mining Language*, 7. See also Yang, "Silver, Blackness, and Fugitive Value." With respect to children as the embodiment of silver or gold, see Hall, *Things of Darkness*, 253; and Morgan, *Reckoning with Slavery*, 77–80. For further reading on alchemy, see Bauer, "Blood of the Dragon"; Ryan, *Kingdom of Stargazers*; Bamford, "Talisman, Amulet, and Intention"; and Vega, "Colors of Conquest."

47. Andrés reappears in chapter 31 of part 1 of *Don Quixote*. To no avail, the codes of chivalry fail, whereby neither Don Quixote nor Sancho Panza can dutifully repay Andrés his stolen wages. In hopes of making his way to Seville, the teenager leaves the scene penniless with only a piece of bread and cheese Sancho had given him. *Don Quixote* 1.31 closes with Andrés's stern warning to Don Quixote: "Por amor de Dios, señor caballero andante, que si otra vez me encontrare, aunque vea que me hacen pedazos, no me socorra ni ayude, sino déjeme con mi desgracia; que no será tanta, que no sea mayor la que me vendrá de su ayuda vuestra merced, a quien Dios maldiga, y a todos cuantos caballeros andantes han nacido en elm undo." ("For the love of God, Señor Knight Errant, if you ever run into me again, even if you see them chopping me to pieces, don't help me and don't come to my aid, but leave me alone with my misfortune; no matter how bad it is, it won't be worse than what will happen to me when I'm helped by your grace, and may God curse you and all the knights errant ever born in this world.") *Don Quixote* 1.31, 391; Grossman, *Don Quixote*, 266.
48. With a critical tone, Andrés asks, "¿De qué obras es hijo, pues me niega mi soldada y mi sudor y trabajo?" ("But what deeds is this master of mine the son of if he denies me my wages and my sweat and my labor?") Cervantes, *Don Quijote* 1.4, 97; Grossman, *Don Quixote*, 37. Andrés launches a powerful disquisition that still plagues our present times and speaks to equity and labor rights.
49. Cervantes, *Don Quijote* 1.22, 265; Grossman, *Don Quixote*, 163.
50. Close, "Liberation of the Galley Slaves," 15; Cervantes, *Don Quijote* 1.22, 265; Grossman, *Don Quixote*, 163.
51. Cervantes, *Don Quijote* 1.22, 265; Grossman, *Don Quixote*, 163.
52. For more on Cervantes's life in Algiers, see Garcés, *Cervantes in Algiers*.

53. See Canavaggio, *Cervantes*, 214–18. For more on the Royal Jail of Seville, consult Chaves, *Relación de la cárcel*. Foucault's concept and theory of the panopticon in *Discipline and Punish* is also useful. See also Morgado, *Historia de Sevilla*.
54. Fleetwood, *Marking Time*, 25; Cervantes, *Don Quijote* 1.22.265; Grossman, *Don Quixote*, 163.
55. Martín Casares, *Esclavitud en la Granada*, 150–60 (translation mine).
56. *Recopilación de leyes del Reino*, fol. 152 (translation mine).
57. Martín Casares, *Esclavitud en la Granada*, 160 (translation mine).
58. Núñez Muley, *Memorial*, 205–34 (translation mine). For further reading, see Núñez Muley, *Memorandum*; Fuchs, Brewer-García, and Ilika, "Edicts and Official Documents"; and Kimmel, *Parables of Coercion*.
59. Ximénez de Enciso, *Comedia famosa*.
60. See Sáez's edition of Cervantes, *Información de Argel*; Garcés, *Cervantes in Algiers*; and Haedo, *Topografía e historia general*.
61. Morgan, *Reckoning with Slavery*, 15, 24.
62. Morgan, *Reckoning with Slavery*, 65–67, 21.
63. Murphy, *Econimization of Life*, 24. See also Morgan, *Reckoning with Slavery*, 33. On capitalism, slavery, and the racialization of enslaved blacks, consult Keeling, *Queer Times, Black Futures*.
64. Ogundiran, "Of Small Things Remembered." As Ogundiran states, "Unless otherwise specified, the species of cowries mentioned throughout the text is Cypraea moneta. Moneta is the earliest cowry species recorded in West Africa. Native to the Maldive Islands in the Indian Ocean, moneta cowries have an angular outline because of the four to six nodules on their upper surface, and their length varies from 1.3 cm to 1.9 cm." For an additional selection of sources on cowries, their origins, and fifteenth- and sixteenth-century Portuguese trade in the Bight of Benin and the Bight of Biafra, see Barber,

"Money"; Hogendom and Johnson, *Shell Money*; and Pacheco Pereira, *Esmeraldo de situ orbis*.
65. Ogundiran, "Of Small Things Remembered," 444–45, quoted in Green, *Fistful of Shells*, 17–18. See also Sylvanus, *Patterns in Circulation*.
66. I'm thinking specifically about Copeland's article "Empire" and Sampedro and Campoy's double special issue, "Entering the Global Hispanophone."
67. Correas, *Vocabulario de refranes*, 296.
68. See *Diccionario de Autoridades*, s.v. "ensanchar," accessed March 26, 2024, https://apps2.rae.es/DA.html; and *Real Academia Española*, s.v. "ensanchar," accessed March 26, 2024, https://dle.rae.es/ensanchar.
69. The Spanish engineer and urban planner, Ildefons Cerdà Sunyer, designed the nineteenth-century "extension" of Barcelona, called Eixample. For more on historical and theoretical work on cities, urban planning, and urban studies in the Iberian Peninsula, see Resina, *Iberian Cities*; Panzram, *Power of Cities*; and Fraser, *Obsession*.

Meditation 3

1. Miller, *Slaves to Fashion*, 31. Refer also to chapter 1 in Goldberg, *Sonidos Negros*, 31–49.
2. Forcione, *Cervantes and the Humanist Vision*, 38–49.
3. Ruiz, "Counter-Discursive and Erotic Agency," 194. See also Ruiz, "Cervantes's *Celoso*," 155–58.
4. The direct quote from the narrator in *El celoso extremeño* is "que éste es el nombre del que ha dado materia a nuestra novela." Cervantes, *Novelas ejemplares II*, 100. All English translations, unless otherwise noted, come from Grossman, *Exemplary Novels*, 213.
5. Weheliye, *Phonographies*, 5.
6. Cervantes, *Novelas ejemplares II*, 103–4.
7. Hartman, *Wayward Lives*, 23.
8. Roane, "Plotting the Black Commons," 239–41.
9. Roane, *Dark Agoras*; Roane, "Plotting the Black Commons." On these interventions, refer also to Davidson and Carreira da Silva, "Fear of a Black Planet."
10. Cervantes, *Novelas ejemplares II*, 109; Grossman, *Jealous Extremaduran*, 220.
11. Cervantes, *Novelas ejemplares II*, 102; Grossman, *Jealous Extremaduran*, 215.
12. Cervantes, *Novelas ejemplares II*, 109; Grossman, *Jealous Extremaduran*, 220 (emphasis mine).
13. Wilbourne, *Voice, Slavery, and Race*, 380. For further reading on the *castrato*, refer to Feldman, *Castrato*; and Peritz, *Lyric Myth of Voice*. For correct language on terms such as "cross-dresser" and "transvestite," consult Stryker, *Transgender History*.
14. Cervantes, *Poesías*, 285, vv. 32–34. I offer my deepest gratitude to Adam Mahler for helping me refine this translation.
15. Archivo de Protocolos de Sevilla, 1620, oficio 1, libro 7, fols. 568–69.
16. Bolaños Donoso, *Obra dramática*, 49. For more on the life and family of Felipe Godínez, see Sánchez-Cid, *Familia del dramaturgo*.
17. The original text states, "Francisco 'Plegonamo moyete y mantequiyas, / no sabe el Rey de lo que es Rey, y hermano, / si non viene a Siviya ese verano. / Mira que de galera, y que de barca, / que de gente a Triana que atrambiesa, / que de riqueza esta ribera abarca, / a Seviya del mundo sa, Princesa." Lope de Vega, *El amante agradecido*, accessed August 22, 2023, https://www.cervantesvirtual.com/obra/el-amante-agradecido--0/. Original copy housed in the Biblioteca Nacional in Madrid.
18. Freeburg, *Counterlife*, 4.
19. Archivo de Protocolos de Sevilla, 1602, oficio IV, libro IIm, fol. 309r–v. For more documentation on playbills in Spanish Golden Age theater, see de los Reyes Peña, "Carteles de teatro."

20. Barthes, "Grain of the Voice."
21. Quashie, *Black Aliveness*, 10.
22. Quoted from Quashie, *Black Aliveness*, 10–12. The ethos I want takes inspiration from black thinkers such as Saidiya Hartman, Sharon Patricia Holland, Tavia Nyong'o, Kevin Quashie, Robert Reid-Pharr, and Michelle M. Wright. On the polemic of designating early modern white writers as black, see Jones, "Sor Juana's Black Atlantic."
23. Paraphrased from Quashie, *Black Aliveness*, 10.
24. J. Fernández, "Bonds of Patrimony," 978 (emphasis mine).
25. C. Reed, "Harems and Eunuchs," 207–8. Reed persuasively argues in this study that "Cervantes draws at least in part on the very Ottoman and Islamic models he emulates in his other fictional variations on the theme. Specifically, in his construction of the central symbol of confinement—the imposing, prison-like house in which Carrizales encloses his bride—Cervantes evokes the Ottoman institution of the harem" (207–8). See also *Conquista de Jerusalén*, a theatrical work attributed to Cervantes.
26. Laguna, "In the Name of Love."
27. Betancourt, *Byzantine Intersectionality*, 109.
28. Arvas, "Early Modern Eunuchs," 117–19. Arvas develops and expands many of these ideas in his forthcoming book, *Boys Abducted*.
29. I'm referring to Laguna, "In the Name of Love"; and C. Reed, "Harems and Eunuchs."
30. C. Reed, "Harems and Eunuchs," 200.
31. Forcione addresses the "forbidden" registers throughout *El celoso* several times in chapter 1 of *Cervantes and the Humanist Vision*; see pages 38, 50, 71, and 82n72. Also consult Lad, "Panoptic Bodies," 162; and Peirce, *Imperial Harem*, 11. And, without a doubt, refer to Arvas and Reed for additional information about the intricacies of the harem, particularly pertaining to the Topkapı Palace. Please also note that I've emended Grossman's problematic translation of *bozal* as "simple-minded." While the term refers to any newly arrived sub-Saharan African who isn't proficient in Castilian or Portuguese, I find it improper to equate, in an English translation, nonstandard dialects and speech varieties of *bozales* as "simple-minded." For a further analysis of *bozal*, see Jones, *Staging* Habla de Negros.
32. A supporting detail to consider is a visit by the English organ builder Thomas Dallam in 1599, sent by Elizabeth I, to deliver an elaborate organ clock as a gift to Sultan Murad III. See Nicolas de Nicolay, *Quatre premiers*; Bon, *Descrizione del serraglio*; and Hierosolimitano, *Relazione della gran cittá*.
33. C. Reed, "Harems and Eunuchs," 202, 208. See also Laguna, "In the Name of Love."
34. The ìrùkẹ̀rẹ̀ is used as a symbol of authority and power by chiefs, monarchs, and priests. The object is also used in festivals and rituals.
35. See Amezúa y Mayo, *Cervantes, creador de la novela*, 2:245; and Icaza, *Novelas ejemplares I*, 207–8. On Cervantes's vast knowledge of the nook and crannies of Seville's cityscapes, landscapes, and soundscapes, see García López, *Cervantes, la figura*; and Piñero Ramírez and Reyes Cano, *Imagen de Sevilla*.
36. For provocations concerning black life in early modern Seville, see Jones, "Chocolate City," and Jones, *Staging* Habla de Negros.
37. Campt, *Listening to Images*, 4.
38. Cervantes, *Novelas ejemplares II*, 109–10; Grossman, *Jealous Extremaduran*, 220–21.
39. For more information about Loaysa's musical abilities and his knowledge of the various songs mentioned in *El celoso extremeño*, see *capítulo* 3, "Las canciones mencionada por Cervantes en sus obras," in Querol Gavaldá, *Música en la obra*, 77–108.
40. See specifically chapter 1, "Black Skin Acts," in Jones, *Staging* Habla de Negros.

41. For the most accurate and complete bibliography and sources about the myth of Prester John, consult Simmons, *Nubia*, esp. 105–25; and Krebs, *Medieval Ethiopian Kingship*. For the theoretical frameworks of the black radical tradition and critical black studies, most notably the evolution of the myth and the mythologization of Prester John, see Robinson, *Black Marxism*.
42. Cadamosto, *Voyages of Cadamosto*, 29–50.
43. Álvares, *Do Preste Joam das Indias*, fol. 136r. Refer also to Krebs's *Medieval Ethiopian Kingship*. The full description is given in the English translation of Álvares, *Prester John of the Indies*, 1:267–71. For a fuller exploration of West and Central African instruments, see Cole's forthcoming essay, "Constructing Racial Identity." See also *History of Ethiopia* by Pedro Páez Jaramillo (1564–1622), a Spanish Jesuit missionary who lived in Ethiopia.
44. Álvares, *Prester John of the Indies*, 516–17, 1:127. The widespread practice of playing the harp of David, known as a *bagana*, or a large ten-stringed lyre, existed among accomplished Ethiopian nobility. Ethiopian rulers were widely portrayed in traditional Ethiopian iconography as King David playing the lyre and hence would have circulated widely in courtly circles. The *bagana* was used primarily as an accompaniment during meditation and prayer or played during religious occasions, though not in Ethiopian Orthodox church services. Páez Jaramillo describes in his 1622 *History of Ethiopia* how the king was accompanied by different companies of soldiers, who had their own instruments: "King Susenyos (1607–1632) was preceded by all his captains, each with his troop drawn up in order with men on foot in the vanguard and then those on horseback, all dressed for celebration with many banners and playing their drums, trumpets, shawms and flutes, which they have in their own fashion, and firing many guns so that the whole of that broad plain echoed. Lastly came the emperor with many lords on horseback."
45. Jones, *Staging* Habla de Negros, 51.
46. Budasz, "Black Guitar-Players," 3–4.
47. Cervantes, *Novelas ejemplares I*, 231; Grossman, *Jealous Extremaduran*, 130.
48. For more on early modern objects, see Cooke, *Global Objects*. For sixteenth- and seventeenth-century Spanish footwear, see Carrión's "Balcony of the *Chapín*."
49. For more information on these topics, see Gamechogoicoechea Llopis, *Mito de Orfeo*; and Schliephake, "Orpheus in Black." Refer also to Peritz, *Lyric Myth of Voice*, 53–82. In the realm of the history of ideas, consult Sewell, *Orphic Voice*.
50. See *Oxford English Dictionary*, s.v. "throat," entry no. 4, accessed November 16, 2022, https://www.oed.com/dictionary/throat_n.
51. Weidman, "Voice," 232, 235.
52. Emphasis mine. Loaysa says in the original Castilian, "Lo que siento y puedo juzgar por el órgano de la voz, que es muy atiplada, debéis de cantar muy bien." Cervantes, *Novelas ejemplares II*, 109.
53. Translation mine. Original text cited from Puerto Moro, *Obra conocida*.
54. Cruz, *Color of Kink*, 20–21. See also Miller-Young, "Deviant," 111. On rape, sexual violence, and torture in Brazil, consult Aidoo, *Slavery Unseen*.
55. Freeman, *Time Binds*, 137. See also Hartman, *Scenes of Subjection*.
56. Behrend-Martínez, "Manhood and the Neutered Body," 1075–76. In *Chief Eunuch* Hathaway provides an insightful perspective on the topic, explaining that "even in the kingdoms of western Europe, where such 'guardian' eunuchs were unknown, the eunuch singers known as *castrati*, a possible evolution of castrated church singers in the Byzantine Empire, were performing in the church choirs of the Vatican by the mid-sixteenth century and were wildly popular on opera stages until the 1820s" (5).

57. Tortorici, *Sins Against Nature*, 15–18.
58. Arvas, "Early Modern Eunuchs," 119.
59. Betancourt, *Byzantine Intersectionality*, 109.
60. Cervantes, *Novelas ejemplares II*, 117–18; Grossman, *Jealous Extremaduran*, 227.
61. Miller-Young, *Taste for Brown Sugar*, 27. For additional readings on the gaze, see Browne, *Dark Matters*; Nash, *Black Body in Ecstasy*; and Sigal, Tortorici, and Whitehead, *Ethnopornography*.
62. Miller-Young, *Taste for Brown Sugar*, 27–28.
63. For more information on the public performance, see "Mirar a los mirones," Almagro, accessed February 5, 2024, https://www.festivaldealmagro.com/programa/mirar-a-los-mirones/.
64. Germeten, "Police Voyeurism," 251.
65. Cervantes, *Novelas ejemplares II*, 124; Grossman, *Jealous Extremaduran*, 232.
66. Cervantes, *Novelas ejemplares II*, 124–25; Grossman, *Jealous Extremaduran*, 233.
67. Cervantes, *Novelas ejemplares II*, 125; Grossman, *Jealous Extremaduran*, 233.
68. Cervantes, *Novelas ejemplares II*, 125 (translation mine).
69. For more on queer and raced temporalities, see Edelman, *No Future*; Halberstam, *Queer Time and Place*; Ahmed, *Queer Phenomenology*; Freeman, *Time Binds*; Ibrahim, *Black Age*; and Row, *Queer Velocities*.
70. Olid Guerrero, *Del teatro a la novela*, 69.
71. Betancourt, *Byzantine Intersectionality*, 124.
72. Betancourt, *Byzantine Intersectionality*, 124.
73. Reid-Pharr, *Black Gay Man*, 1–10.
74. Woodard, *Delectable Negro*, 14. See also Foster, *Rethinking Rufus*, 102.

Meditation 4

1. Macharia, *Frottage*, 1–2.
2. Covarrubias, *Tesoro*, 1256; *Diccionario de Autoridades*.
3. See *Oxford English Dictionary*, s.v. "intimacy," March 25, 2024, https://www.oed.com/dictionary/intimacy_n.
4. Berlant, *Intimacy*, 1; Sharpe, *Monstrous Intimacies*, 190.
5. Sharpe, *Monstrous Intimacies*, 190; Stoler, *Race and the Education of Desire*.
6. L. Lowe, *Intimacies of Four Continents*, 17.
7. Greer and Rhodes, *Exemplary Tales*, 17. Refer also to "Sexualidad masculina y negra," where Romero-Díaz explores the race relations between black men and white women, as well as the subordination of women in patriarchal society (95–98). Out of concern for the current state of the critical reception bestowed on blackness in Zayas's oeuvre, I maintain that scholars have yet to sufficiently crack the surface of examining blackness's complexity and depth in her works. In short, the dominant consensus has shown that Zayas sadistically dehumanizes black people in grotesque, racist, and pejorative ways.
8. Boyle, "In Search of a Witness," 187, 188; Vollendorf, "Reading the Body Imperiled," 282.
9. See Blain, "Black Historians Know."
10. The sources I have in mind to substantiate my claims appear in Martín Casares, *Criados y esclavos*; Martín Casares and García Barranco, *Mujeres esclavas y abolicionistas*; Jones, "Black Women"; Jones, *Staging* Habla de Negros, 119–58; Ireton, "Black Africans' Freedom"; and Tweede, "Significance of Black Women."
11. Sharpe, *Monstrous Intimacies*, 190.
12. Jones-Rogers, *They Were Her Property*, xii–xiii.
13. See K. Mitchell's exemplary and new edition of *Incidents in the Life*. For more on torture and slavery, consult the following sources and their bibliographies: Mannix, *Black Cargoes*; Higginbotham, *In the Matter of Color*; Jordan, *White over Black*; Manning, *Slavery and African Life*; Browne, *Dark Matters*; and Aidoo, *Slavery Unseen*.
14. Zayas y Sotomayor, *Novelas amorosas y ejemplares*, 295.

15. Greer, *María de Zayas*, 364. Unless otherwise noted, all plot summaries originate from this work, and English translations come from Greer and Rhodes's *Exemplary Tales*.
16. The *Loa sacramental* was performed during Corpus Christi festivities. For the complete work, see Juana Escabias's edition of Mallén, *Teatro completo*, 309–17.
17. Zayas y Sotomayor, *Novelas amorosas y ejemplares*, 309; Greer and Rhodes, *Exemplary Tales*, 116.
18. The study of medicalized blackness has had a robust growth and influence in the cultural, intellectual, and social histories of the African diaspora. The bibliography is abundant, rich, and vast. For more on this topic, see White, *Ar'n't I a Woman?*; Morgan, *Laboring Women*; Cooper Owens, *Medical Bondage*; Hogarth, *Medicalizing Blackness*; Kettler, *Smell of Slavery*; Downs, *Maladies of Empire*; and E. Mitchell, "Morbid Crossings."
19. On racialized blackness through the concept *pretidão*, see Barletta, *Rhythm*. Blackmore, in *Inner Sea* and in *Moorings*, offers a rich analysis of Adamastor, whom he refers to as the "Monster of Melancholy," in *Moorings*. In this work from 2008, Blackmore triangulates Adamastor, racialized blackness, bodily excess, and rhetorical power. In *Moorings* Blackmore explains that the "Adamastor episode, at the center of Camões's text (in the middle of canto V of the ten-canto poem), comprises stanzas 37–60 and is part of the long narrative delivered to the King of Melinde by Vasco da Gama on the history of Portugal and its imperial enterprise during his stay in East Africa" (105–6). For a detailed analysis of Adamastor in *Moorings*, refer to chapter 3, "The Monster of Melancholy." For a study of the cross-fertilization of historical writing in the sixteenth and early seventeenth centuries, consult Marcocci, *Globe on Paper*. On maps, monsters, and the invention of the human, see Davies, *Renaissance Ethnography*.
20. Lovejoy, "Scarification," 103–7. For more on scarification, especially visual representations, see S. Johnson, *History of the Yorubas*; Moritz Rugendeas, *Viagem através do Brasil*; La Roza Corzo, *Tatuados*; and D. Brown, *Santería Enthroned*.
21. Césaire, *Discourse on Colonialism*, 84; Fanon, *Black Skin, White Masks*, 89.
22. I draw on the work of Browne, in *Dark Matters*, 89–129. For an outstanding study and rigorous analysis of branding in early modern Spanish theater, see the forthcoming essay by Slater, "Branding, Bondage, and Typeface." For more on the surveillance of blackness, refer to Browne, *Dark Matters*; and Monahan, *Crisis Vision*.
23. Zayas y Sotomayor, *Novelas amorosas y ejemplares*, 308; Greer and Rhodes, *Exemplary Tales*, 115.
24. Gamboa, "Architectural Cartography"; Maravall, *Culture of the Baroque*.
25. Zayas y Sotomayor, *Novelas amorosas y ejemplares*, 310; Greer and Rhodes, *Exemplary Tales*, 117.
26. Zayas y Sotomayor, *Novelas amorosas y ejemplares*, 310; Greer and Rhodes, *Exemplary Tales*, 117.
27. Here I'm thinking of Woodard, *Delectable Negro*.
28. Ruiz, "Three Faces/Phases," 154. Romero-Díaz's essay "Sexualidad masculina y negra" follows a similar train of thought, although her study analyzes two examples of the hypersexualization of black men in two archival documents from the late eighteenth century.
29. Ruiz, "Three Faces/Phases," 154.
30. Brownlee, *Cultural Labyrinth*, 38–39.
31. Macharia, *Frottage*, 1–5.
32. Macharia, *Frottage*, 5.
33. We can also read life and subjectivity into Beatriz's relation to her intimacy with Antonio. In line with a possible exemplary lesson ascertained from Cervantes's *El viejo celoso* and *El*

casamiento engañoso, we're prompted to ask, Who can control and impede the human nature of a young woman? In another sense the Antonio-Beatriz episode reminds me of a topsy-turvy perversion of Iberian literary works that feature interracial unions between black men and white women. Let's take, for example, the Valencian knight Joanot Martorell's chivalric romance *Tirant lo Blanch* (1490), where Carmesina slept with the black gardener, Lauseta, who is later decapitated. *Tractado*, from the 1554 *Lazarillo de Tormes*, is where Lazarillo recounts the love and affection that his widowed mother, Antonia Pérez, had received from her black boyfriend, named Zaide.

34. Cervantes, *Coloquio de los perros*, 313–14; Grossman, *Colloquy of the Dogs*, 377–78.
35. Cervantes, *Coloquio de los perros*, 323; Grossman, *Colloquy of the Dogs*, 385.
36. Cervantes, *Coloquio de los perros*, 319–20; Grossman, *Colloquy of the Dogs*, 383–83.
37. Góngora y Argote, *Letrillas*.
38. Cervantes, *Coloquio de los perros*, 322.
39. Beusterien, *Canines in Cervantes and Velázquez*, 52.
40. See Beusterien, *Canines in Cervantes and Velázquez*, and Martín, "Sexy Beasts."
41. Holland, *Other*, 10–12. In response to Jackson's *Becoming Human*, Holland further qualifies and explicates that "while my investigation certainly moves in the direction of the latter part of this statement, my inclination would be to steer away from giving over all manner of animal living to the realm of ontology altogether" (266n28). Also refer to Tremblay, "Black Ecologies."
42. Brownlee, *Cultural Labyrinth*, 145, 146.
43. Zayas y Sotomayor, *Desengaños amorosos*, 237; Boyer, *Disenchantments of Love*, 146–47.
44. As stated by Rhodes, in *Dressed to Kill*, Zayas offers us a "brilliant and startling chiaroscuro moment." Rhodes could not be any more correct in that Zayas "besets her reader with several interpretative dilemmas" (24). For a fuller discussion of this scene, see Rhodes, *Dressed to Kill*, 24.
45. I'm thinking of Diego Sánchez de Badajoz's collection of *farsas* as well as the vast repertoire of anonymous interludes and short-skit comedy sketches that cast both fictional and real-life historical black women. See Cotarelo y Mori, *Colección de entremeses*.
46. Please consult the *Oxford English Dictionary*, s.v. "vestige," accessed March 25, 2024, https://www.oed.com/search/dictionary/?scope=Entries&q=vestige.
47. Foucault, *Archaeology of Knowledge*.
48. Quevedo, *Hora de todos*, 179 (translation mine). Also, in the illustrations found in Alfonso X, *Cantigas de Santa María* (situated between the dates 1257 and 1282), appears the image of the devil in the form of a black man. Teresa de Ávila de Jesús refers to the devil as "un negrillo" in *Libro de la vida*.
49. See Thomson, *Grotesque*, 10–28. James Iffland's two-volume study, *Quevedo and the Grotesque*, also provides compelling close readings of grotesque imagery in Quevedo's body of work.
50. Bakhtin, *Rabelais and His World*, 303; Elias, *Civilizing Process*.
51. Translations of Quevedo's "Boda de negros" are mine. All textual citations of Quevedo's "Boda de negros" come from Blecua's 1971 edition of *Poesía original completa*. In this edition "Boda de negros" appears as number 698, where Blecua documents the romance's date of publication in 1643, in *Romances varios*. In *Parnaso español* "Boda de negros" is number 510.
52. For more information about pearl divers and pearl fisheries in early modern Iberia and the early Spanish Caribbean, see Wheat's *Atlantic Africa*, 3, 10–11, 117–18, 141, 256. See also Dawson, *Undercurrents of Power*, especially 57–84.
53. Acosta, *Historia natural*, 168. See also Warsh, *American Baroque*, 78–127.
54. See Harris, "Whiteness as Property"; and Lipsitz, "Possessive Investment in Whiteness."

55. See Zamora Loboch, *Cómo ser negro*, 101.
56. Sharpe, *Ordinary Notes*, 215
57. Bradley, *Anteaesthetics*, 1–104.
58. Appadurai, "Introduction," 5; Warsh "Unruly Objects," 259.
59. Wheat, *Atlantic Africa*, 167. See also J. Johnson, *Wicked Flesh*.
60. Wagschal, "Aesthetics of Disgust," 115.
61. Zayas y Sotomayor, *Desengaños amorosos*, 237; Boyer, *Disenchantments of Love*, 147.
62. Zayas y Sotomayor, *Desengaños amorosos*, 251–52; Boyer, *Disenchantments of Love*, 160–61.
63. Refer to chapter 3 in my *Staging* Habla de Negros for textual material and theoretical framings for examining black women's agency and authoritative voices.
64. See Tweede's dissertation, "Significance of Black Women."
65. Zayas y Sotomayor, *Desengaños amorosos*, 252; Boyer, *Disenchantments of Love*, 161.
66. Zayas y Sotomayor, *Desengaños amorosos*, 253; Boyer, *Disenchantments of Love*, 163.
67. Zayas y Sotomayor, *Desengaños amorosos*, 255; Boyer, *Disenchantments of Love*, 163.
68. Spillers, *Black, White, and in Color*. For studies on pornography in medieval and early modern Iberia, see Jones and Leahy, "Introduction."
69. See Sharpe, *Monstrous Intimacies*, 1–26.
70. Morrison, *Beloved*, 274.
71. I am specifically citing and thinking of Roach's award-winning essay, "Black Living Room."

Epilogue

1. For the full set of ideas and theories of black culture laid out, see Spillers, "Idea of Black Culture."
2. Clavell, *To Sir, with Love*.
3. McKittrick, *Dear Science*, 13.
4. See McCarthy, "Master's Tools," 21.
5. Baldwin, *Fire Next Time*, 25.
6. Baldwin, "Every Good-Bye Ain't Gone," 778.

Bibliography

Primary Sources

Abraham, Roy Clive. *Dictionary of Modern Yoruba*. 2nd ed. London: Hodder and Stoughton, 1962.

Acosta, José de. *Historia natural y moral de las Indias*. 1588–90. Edited by Edmundo O'Gorman. Mexico City: Fondo de Cultura Económica, 1962.

Alemán, Mateo. *Guzmán de Alfarache, I y II*. Edited by José María Micó. Madrid: Cátedra, 2006.

Alfonso X. *Cantigas de Santa María*. Edited by Walter Mettmann. Madrid: Castalia, 1986.

———. *Cantigas profanas*. Edited by Juan Paredes. Madrid: Castalia, 2010.

———. *General estoria*. Edited by Pedro Sánchez-Prieto Borja. 10 vols. Madrid: Biblioteca Castro, 2001.

———. *Lapidario*. Edited by María Brey Mariño. Odres nuevos. Madrid: Castalia, 1968.

———. *Libro de los juegos: Ajedrex, dados e tablas; Ordenamiento de las tafurerías*. Edited by Raúl Orellana Calderón. Madrid: Biblioteca Castro, 2007.

Álvar, Carlos, ed. *Gran enciclopedia cervantina*. Vol. 2. Madrid: Castalia, 2005.

Álvares, Francisco. *Do Preste Joam das Indias: Verdadera informaçam das terras do Preste Joam*. Lisboa, 1540.

———. *The Prester John of the Indies: A True Relation of the Lands of the Prester John, Being the Narrative of the Portuguese Embassy to Ethiopia in 1520, Written by Father Francisco Alvares*. Edited by Charles F. Beckingham and George W. B. Huntingford. Cambridge: Cambridge University Press, 1961.

Apuleius. *The Golden Ass*. Translated by William Addlington. Cambridge, MA: Harvard University Press, 1965.

Auto de los Reyes Magos. In *Teatro medieval*. Edited by Miguel Ángel Pérez Priego, 119–31. Madrid: Cátedra, 2009.

Ávila de Jesús, Teresa de. *Libro de la vida*. Edited by Otger Steggink. Madrid: Castalia, 1986.

Bon, Ottaviano. *Descrizione del serraglio del gransignore*. Milan: Salerno Editrice, 2002.

Brásio, António. *Monumenta missionaria africana*. 15 vols. Lisbon: Agência Geral do Ultramar, 1952–88.

Cadamosto, Alvise. *The Voyages of Cadamosto and Other Documents on Western Africa* in the Second Half of the Fifteenth Century. Edited by G. R. Crone. London: Hakluyt Society, 1937.

Camões, Luís de. *Os Lusíadas*. 1572. Edited by Emanuel Paulo Ramos. Porto: Porto Editora, 1990.

Cervantes, Miguel de. *El celoso extremeño*. 1613. In Cervantes, *Novelas ejemplares II*, 99–135.

———. *El coloquio de los perros*. In Cervantes, *Novelas ejemplares II*, 297–359.

———. *La conquista de Jerusalén por Godofre de Bullón*. Edited by Héctor Brioso Santos. Madrid: Cátedra, 2009.

———. "Entremés del Viejo celoso." In Cervantes, *Entremeses*, 249–69.

———. *Entremeses*. Edited by Adrián J. Sáez. Madrid: Cátedra, 2020.

———. *La información de Argel*. Edited by Adrián J. Sáez. Madrid: Cátedra, 2019.

———. *El ingenioso hidalgo Don Quijote de la Mancha*. 1605–15. Edited by Luis Andrés Murillo. 2 vols. Madrid: Castalia, 1978.

———. *El ingenioso hidalgo Don Quijote de la Mancha*. 1605–15. 2 vols. Edited by John Jay Allen. Madrid: Cátedra, 2008.

———. "Novela del casamiento engañoso." In Cervantes, *Novelas ejemplares II*, 279–96.

———. *Novelas ejemplares I*. Edited by Harry Sieber. 2 vols. Madrid: Cátedra, 2003.

———. *Novelas ejemplares II*. Edited by Harry Sieber. Madrid: Cátedra, 2003.

———. *Poesías*. Edited by Adrián J. Sáez. Madrid: Cátedra, 2016.

Césaire, Aimé. *Discourse on Colonialism*. New York: Monthly Review Press, 2001.

Chiado, Antonio Ribeiro. *Auto da natural invenção*. Lisbon: Livraria Ferreira, 1917.

Correas, Gonzalo. *Vocabulario de refranes y frases proverbiales*. 1637. Edited by Louis Combet. Madrid: Castalia, 2000.

Cotarelo y Mori, Emilio. *Colección de entremeses, loas, bailes, jácaras, y mojigangas desde fines del siglo XVI a mediados del XVIII*. Vols. 1–2. Madrid: Bailly-Bailliére, 1911.

Covarrubias Horozco, Sebastián de. *Tesoro de la lengua castellana o española*. 1611. Edited by Ignacio Arellano and Rafael Zafra. Madrid: Iberoamericana-Vervuert, 2006.

Descartes, René. *Discourse on Method and Meditations on First Philosophy*. Translated by Donald A. Cress. Indianapolis: Hackett, 1998.

Diccionario de Autoridades. Vols. 1–6. Madrid: Real Academia Española, 1726–39.

Didion, Joan. *Joan Didion: The 1960s and 1970s*. Edited by David L. Ulin. New York: Library of America, 2019.

———. "Notes from a Native Daughter." In Didion, *Joan Didion*, 345–55.

———. "Slouching Toward Bethlehem." In Didion, *Joan Didion*, 282–87.

Du Bois, W. E. B. 1903. *The Souls of Black Folk*. New York: Penguin, 1996.

The English Standard Version Bible: Containing the Old and New Testaments with Apocrypha. Oxford: Oxford University Press, 2009.

Fanon, Frantz. *Black Skin, White Masks*. Translated by Charles Lam Markmann. New York: Grove Press, 1967.

———. *The Wretched of the Earth*. Translated by Constance Ferrington. New York: Grove Press, 1963.

Fernández de Avellaneda, Alonso. *El Quijote aprócrifo*. Edited by Alfredo Rodríguez López-Vázquez. Madrid: Cátedra, 2011.

Godinho, António. *Livro da nobreza e perfeiçam das armas*. Portugal, 1548.

Góis, Damião de. *Chronica do Feliccissimo Rei Dom Emanuel*. Lisbon: Correa, 1566–67.

Góngora y Argote, Luis de. *Letrillas*. Edited by Robert Jammes. Madrid: Castalia 1980.

Goytisolo, Juan. *Disidencias*. Barcelona: Seix Barral, 1977.

Greaves, John, ed. *Description of the Grand Signor's Seraglio, or Turkish Emperour's Court*. London: Ridley, 1653.

Greer, Margaret Rich. *María de Zayas Tells Baroque Tales of Love and the Cruelty of Men*. University Park: Penn State University Press, 2000.

Greer, Margaret Rich, and Elizabeth Rhodes, eds. and trans. *Exemplary Tales of Love and Tales of Disillusion*. Chicago: University of Chicago Press, 2009.

Grossman, Edith, trans. *Colloquy of the Dogs.* In *Exemplary Novels.* By Miguel de Cervantes, 367–416. New Haven, CT: Yale University Press, 2016.

———, trans. *Don Quixote.* By Miguel de Cervantes. New York: HarperCollins, 2005.

———, trans. *Exemplary Novels.* By Miguel de Cervantes. New Haven, CT: Yale University Press, 2016.

———. *The Jealous Extremaduran.* By Miguel de Cervantes. New Haven, CT: Yale University Press, 2016.

Haedo, Fray Diego de. *Topografía e historia general de Argel.* 1578–81. 3 vols. Madrid: Sociedad de Bibliófilos Españoles, 1881.

Hierosolimitano, Domenico. *Relazione della gran cittá di Costantinopoli.* Rome: Fei, 2014.

Hughes, Langston. *I Wonder as I Wander: An Autobiographical Journey.* New York: Reinhart, 1956.

———. *A New Song.* New York: International Workers Order, 1938.

Hurston, Zora Neale. *Folklore, Memoirs, and Other Writings.* New York: Library of America, 1995.

Jacobs, Harriet. *Incidents in the Life of a Slave Girl.* Ontario: Broadview Press, 2023.

Jadin, Louis, and Mireille Dicorati. *Correspondance de Dom Afonso, roi du Congo, 1506–1543.* Brussels: Academie Royale des Sciences D'outre-mer, 1974.

Lazarillo de Tormes. 1554. Edited by Francisco Rico. Madrid: Cátedra, 2003.

Mallén, Ana Caro de. *Teatro completo.* Edited by Juana Escabias. Madrid: Cátedra, 2023.

Manuel, Juan. *El conde Lucanor.* 1335. Edited by Guillermo Serés and Germán Orduna. Barcelona: Galaxia Gutenberg, 2006.

Mármol Carvajal, Luis del. *Historia de la rebelión y castigo de los moriscos del Reino de Granada.* 1600. Málaga: Editorial Agruval, 1991.

Martorell, Joanot, and Martí Joan de Galba. *Tirant lo Blanc i altres escrits de Joanot Martorell.* 1490. Edited by Martí de Riquer. Barcelona: Ariel, 1969.

Mendo, Andrés. *De las Órdenes Militares, de sus principios, gobierno, privilegios, y obligaciones.* Madrid, 1681.

Mitchell, Koritha. ed. *Incidents in the Life of a Slave Girl.* Ontario: Broadview Press, 2023.

Molina, Tirso de. *El burlador de Sevilla.* Edited by Alfredo Rodríguez López-Vázquez. Madrid: Cátedra, 2016.

Morgado, Alonso de. *Historia de Sevilla.* Seville: Pescioni y Leon, 1587.

Morrison, Toni. *Beloved.* New York: Vintage Books, 1987.

———. *Playing in the Dark: Whiteness and the Literary Imagination.* New York: Vintage Books, 1993.

Nicolay de, Nicolas. *Quatre premiers livres des navigations et peregrinations orientales.* Antwerp: Anvers, 1577.

Núñez Muley, Francisco. *A Memorandum for the President of the Royal Audiencia and Chancery Court of the City and Kingdom of Granada.* Edited and translated by Vincent Barletta. Chicago: University of Chicago Press, 2013.

———. *Memorial.* Adapted and modernized by R. Foulché-Delbosc. *Revue Hispanique* 6 (1899): 205–39.

———. "Memorial." In "The Original Memorial of Don Francisco Núñez Muley," edited by Kenneth Garrad. *Atlante* 2 (1954): 168–226.

———. *Memorial en defensa de las costumbres moriscas.* 1566. Reprint, Barcelona: Linkgua, 2014.

Ortega y Gasset, José. *Meditations on Quixote.* Translated by Evelyn Rugg and Diego Marín. New York: Norton, 1963.

Páez Jaramillo, Pedro. *History of Ethiopia.* 1622. Translated by Christopher J. Tribe. 2 vols. Aldershot: Ashgate, 2011.

Paiva Manso, Visconde de. *História do Congo: Obra posthuma.* Lisbon: Typographia da Academia, 1877.

Pérez Galdós, Benito. *Fortunata y Jacinta: Dos historias de casadas.* 1887. Edited by Francisco Caudet. Madrid: Cátedra, 2011.

Puerto Moro, Laura ed. *Obra conocida de Rodrigo de Reinosa.* San Millán de

Cogolla: Fundación de San Millán de la Cogolla/Cilengua, 2010.
Quevedo, Francisco de. "Boda de negros." 1971. In *Poesía original completa*, edited by José Manuel Blecua, 769–71. Barcelona: Planeta, 1999.
———. *La hora de todos*. 1645. Edited by Luisa López-Grigera. Madrid: Castalia, 1975.
———. *Poesía original completa*. Edited by José Manuel Blecua. 1971. Reprint, Barcelona: Planeta, 1999.
———. *Poesía varia*. Edited by James O. Crosby. Madrid: Cátedra, 2007.
———. *Prosa festiva completa*. Edited by Carmen Celsa García-Valdés. Madrid: Cátedra, 2007.
———. "Sueño del infierno." In *Los sueños*, edited by Ignacio Arellano, 170–269. Madrid: Cátedra, 2019.
Recopilación de leyes del Reino. 1567. Reprint, Alcalá de Henares: Ángulo, 1581.
Reinosa, Rodrigo de. "Gelofe, Mandinga." 1516–24. In Puerto Moro, *Obra conocida*, 168–77.
Rodríguez de Montalvo, Garci. *Las sergas de Esplandián*. 1510. Edited by Carlos Sainz de la Maza. Madrid: Castalia, 2003.
Rodríguez López-Vázquez, Alfredo, ed. *El Quijote apócrifo*. Madrid: Cátedra, 2011
Tirso de Molina (attributed). *El burlador de Sevilla*. Edited by Alfredo Rodríguez López-Vázquez. Madrid: Cátedra, 2016.
Vega Carpio, Félix Lope de. *Arte nuevo de hacer comedias*. Edited by Enrique García Santo-Tomás. Madrid: Cátedra, 2009.
———. *Obras*. Edited by Marcelino Menéndez y Pelayo. 15 vols. Madrid: Real Academia Española, 1894–1913.
Visconde de Paiva Manso. *História do Congo: Obra posthuma*. Lisbon: Typographia da Academia, 1877.
Ximénez de Enciso, Diego. *Comedia famosa de Juan Latino*. Edited by Juliá Martínez. Madrid: Aldus, 1951.
Yllera, Alicia, ed. *Desengaños amorosos*. Madrid: Cátedra, 2006.
Zayas y Sotomayor, María de. "La esclava de su amante." In Yllera, *Desengaños amorosos*, 127–69.
———. "El prevenido engañado." 1637. In *Novelas amorosas y ejemplares compuestas por Doña María de Zayas y Sotomayor*. Edited by Julián Olivares, 295–342. Madrid: Cátedra, 2007.
———. "Tarde llega el desengaño" or *Desengaño Cuarto*. In Yllera, *Desengaños amorosos*, 227–55.

Secondary Sources

Aguilar, Ignacio, Luis Gómez Canseco, and Adrián J. Sáez, eds. *El teatro de Miguel de Cervantes*. Madrid: Visor, 2016.
Ahmed, Sara. *Queer Phenomenology*. Durham, NC: Duke University Press, 2006.
Aidoo, Lamonte. *Slavery Unseen: Sex, Power, and Violence in Brazilian History*. Durham, NC: Duke University Press, 2018.
Alandete, David. "Cae fray Junípero: El odio a lo hispano arrecia en Estados Unidos." ABC Cultura. June 21, 2020. https://www.abc.es/cultura/abci-fray-junipero-odio-hispano-arrecia-estados-unidos-202006210138_noticia.html.
Alexander, Elizabeth. *The Black Interior*. Saint Paul, MN: Graywolf Press, 2004.
Almeida, Ivan. "Celebración del apócrifo en 'Tlön, Uqbar Tertius.'" *Variaciones Borges* 15 (2003): 181–206.
Amezúa y Mayo, Agustín González de. *Cervantes, creador de la novela corta española*. 2 vols. Madrid: Consejo Superior de Investigaciones Científicas, 1956–58.
Antwi, George. *The Words of Power*. Bangkok: Booksmango, 2012.
Appadurai, Arjun. "Introduction: Commodities and the Politics of Value." In *The Social Life of Things: Commodities of Cultural Perspective*, edited by Arjun Appadurai, 3–63. Cambridge: Cambridge University Press, 1986.
Araujo, Ana Lucia. "Toppling Monuments Is a Global Movement. And It Works." *Washington Post*, June 23, 2020. https://www.washingtonpost.com/outlook/2020/06/23/toppling-monuments-is-global-movement-it-works/.

Arvas, Abdulhamit. *Boys Abducted: The Homoerotics of Empire and Race in Early Modernity*. Durham, NC: Duke University Press, forthcoming.

———. "Early Modern Eunuchs and the Transing of Gender and Race." *Journal for Early Modern Cultural Studies* 19, no. 4 (2019): 116–36.

Avalle-Arce, Juan Bautista. "'El celoso extremeño,' de Cervantes." In *Homenaje a Ana María Barrenechea*, edited by Lía Schwartz and Isaías Lerner, 199–205. Madrid: Castalia, 1984.

Avignon, Robyn d'. *A Ritual Geology: Gold and Subterranean Knowledge in Savanna West Africa*. Durham, NC: Duke University Press, 2022.

Bakhtin, Mikhail. *Rabelais and His World*. Translated by Hélène Iswolsky. Bloomington: Indiana University Press, 1984.

Baldwin, James. *Collected Essays*. New York: Library of America, 1998.

———. "Every Good-Bye Ain't Gone." In Baldwin, *Collected Essays*, 773–78.

———. *The Fire Next Time*. 1962. Reprint, New York: Vintage, 1993.

———. *I Am Not Your Negro*. Directed by Raoul Peck. New York: Magnolia Pictures; Culver City, CA: Amazon Studios, 2016.

———. "A Talk to Teachers." 1963. In Baldwin, *Collected Essays*, 678–87.

Bamford, Heather. "Talisman, Amulet, and Intention in Medieval and Early Modern Iberia." *Revista Hispánica Moderna* 74, no. 2 (2021): 133–48.

Barber, Karin. "Money, Self-Realization, and the Person in Yòrúba Texts." In Guyer, *Money Matters*, 205–24.

Barletta, Vincent. *Rhythm: Form and Dispossession*. Chicago: University of Chicago Press, 2020.

Barthes, Roland. "The Grain of the Voice." In *The Sound Studies Reader*, edited by Jonathan Sterne, 504–10. London: Routledge, 2012.

Bauer, Ralph. "The Blood of the Dragon: Alchemy and Natural History in Nicolás Monardes's *Historia medicinal*." In Slater, *Medical Cultures*, 67–88.

Behrend-Martínez, Edward. "Manhood and the Neutered Body in Early Modern Spain." *Journal of Social History* 38, no. 4 (2005): 1073–93.

Bennett, Herman L. *African Kings and Black Slaves: Sovereignty and Dispossession in the Early Modern Atlantic*. Philadelphia: University of Pennsylvania Press, 2019.

Berlant, Lauren. *Intimacy*. Durham, NC: Duke University Press, 2000.

Betancourt, Roland. *Byzantine Intersectionality: Sexuality, Gender, and Race in the Middle Ages*. Princeton, NJ: Princeton University Press, 2020.

Bethencourt, Francisco. *Racisms: From the Crusades to the Twentieth Century*. Princeton, NJ: Princeton University Press, 2015.

Beusterien, John. *Canines in Cervantes and Velázquez: An Animal Studies Reading of Early Modern Spain*. Burlington, VT: Ashgate, 2013.

———. *An Eye on Race: Perspectives from Theater in Imperial Spain*. Lewisburg, PA: Bucknell University Press, 2006.

Bey, Marquis. *Black Trans Feminism*. Durham, NC: Duke University Press, 2022.

Bickman Berzock, Kathleen. *Caravans of Gold, Fragments in Time: Art, Culture, and Exchange Across Medieval Saharan Africa*. Princeton, NJ: Princeton University Press, 2019.

Biedermann, Zoltán. "(Dis)connected History and the Multiple Narratives of Global Early Modernity." *Modern Philology* 119, no. 1 (2021): 13–32.

Bigelow, Allison Margaret. *Mining Language: Racial Thinking, Indigenous Knowledge, and Colonial Metallurgy in the Early Modern Iberian World*. Chapel Hill: University of North Carolina Press, 2020.

Blackmore, Josiah. *The Inner Sea: Maritime Literary Culture in Early Modern Portugal*. Chicago: University of Chicago Press, 2022.

———. *Moorings: Portuguese Expansion and the Writing of Africa*. Minneapolis: University of Minnesota Press, 2008.

Blain, Keisha N. "Black Historians Know There's No Such Thing as Objective History." *New Republic*, September 9, 2022. https://newrepublic.com/article/167680/presentism-history-debate-black-scholarship.

———, ed. *Until I Am Free: Fannie Lou Hamer's Enduring Message to America*. Boston: Beacon Press, 2021.

———. *Wake Up America: Black Women on the Future of Democracy*. New York: Norton, 2024.

Bolaños Donoso, Piedad. *La obra dramática de Felipe Godínez: Trayectoria de un dramaturgo marginado*. Seville: Diputación de Sevilla, 1983.

Bouza, Fernando, Pedro Cardim, and Antonio Feros, eds. *The Iberian World, 1450–1820*. New York: Routledge, 2019.

Boyer, H. Patsy, ed. and trans. *The Disenchantments of Love: A Translation of the Desengaños Amoroso*. Albany: State University of New York Press, 1997.

Boyle, Margaret E. "In Search of a Witness: Violence and Women in María de Zayas." In Jones and Leahy, *Pornographic Sensibilities*, 187–98.

Bradley, Rizvana. *Anteaesthetics: Black Aesthesis and the Critique of Form*. Stanford, CA: Stanford University Press, 2023.

Branche, Jerome C., ed. *Trajectories of Empire: Transhispanic Reflections on the African Diaspora*. Nashville: Vanderbilt University Press, 2022.

Brown, David. *Santería Enthroned: Art, Ritual, and Innovation in an Afro-Cuban Religion*. Chicago: University of Chicago Press, 2003.

Brown, Jericho, ed. *How We Do It: Black Writers on Craft, Practice, and Skill*. New York: Amistad, 2023.

Brown, Katherine L. "Miguel de Cervantes, Author of the Apocryphal *Quijote*: Borges, 'Pierre Menard,' and Literary Creation as Apocrypha." *Romance Notes* 39, nos. 2–3 (2021): 110–25.

Brown, Vincent. "Social Death and Political Life in the Study of Slavery." *American Historical Review* 114, no. 5 (2009): 1231–49.

Browne, Simone. *Dark Matters: On the Surveillance of Blackness*. Durham, NC: Duke University Press, 2015.

Brownlee, Marina S. *The Cultural Labyrinth of María Zayas*. Philadelphia: University of Pennsylvania Press, 2000.

Budasz, Rogério. "Black Guitar-Players and Early African-Iberian Music in Portugal and Brazil." *Early Music* 35, no. 1 (2007): 3–21.

Burningham, Bruce. "Os Manchíadas." In Dopico and Layna Ranz, *USA Cervantes*, 247–72.

Caballero Bonald, José Manuel. *Sevilla en tiempos de Cervantes*. Barcelona: Planeta, 1991.

Calhoun, Doyle. *The Suicide Archive: Reading Resistance in the Wake of French Empire*. Durham, NC: Duke University Press, 2024.

Campbell, Stephen J., and Stephanie Porras, eds. *The Routledge Companion to Global Renaissance Art*. New York: Routledge, 2024.

Campt, Tina M. *A Black Gaze: Artists Changing How We See*. Cambridge, MA: MIT Press, 2021.

———. *Listening to Images*. Durham, NC: Duke University Press, 2017.

Canavaggio, Jean. *Cervantes*. Translated by Mauro Armiño. 1986. Reprint, Madrid: Austral, 2015.

Carrión, María M. "The Balcony of the *Chapín*, or the Vain Architecture of Shoes in Early Modern Spain." *Journal of Spanish Cultural Studies* 14, no. 2 (2013): 143–58.

Cartagena Calderón, José R. "*Don Quixote* and the Performance of Aging Masculinities." In Fernández and Martín, *Drawing the Curtain*, 331–53.

Castellano López, Abigail, and Adrián J. Sáez, eds. *Vidas en armas: Biografías militares en la España del Siglo de Oro*. Huelva: Universidad de Huelva, 2019.

Chartier, Roger. *Cardenio Between Cervantes and Shakespeare: The Story of a Lost Play.* New York: Polity, 2013.

Chaves, Cristóbal de. *Relación de la cárcel de Sevilla.* Madrid: Clásicos el Arbol, 1983.

Chen, Mel Y., Alison Kafer, Eunjung Kim, and Julie Avril Minich, eds. *Crip Genealogies.* Durham, NC: Duke University Press, 2023.

Childers, William. *Transnational Cervantes.* Toronto: University of Toronto Press, 2006.

Christian, Barbara. "The Race for Theory." In "The Nature and Context of Minority Discourse." Special issue, *Cultural Critique* 6 (1987): 51–63.

Christian, Kathleen, and Leah Clark, eds. *European Art and the Wider World, 1350–1550.* Manchester: Manchester University Press, 2018.

Clavell, James, dir. *To Sir, with Love.* Culver City, CA: Columbia Pictures, 1967.

Close, Anthony. *Cervantes and the Comic Mind of His Age.* Cambridge: Cambridge University Press, 2000.

———. "The Liberation of the Galley Slaves and the Ethos of *Don Quijote.*" Part 1. *Cervantes: The Bulletin of the Cervantes Society of America* 27, no. 1 (2007): 11–30.

———. *Romantic Approach to "Don Quixote."* Cambridge: Cambridge University Press, 1978.

Cohen, Cathy. "Punks, Bulldaggers, and Welfare Queens: The Radical Potential of Queer Politics." *GLQ* 3, no. 4 (1997): 437–65.

Cohen-Aponte, Ananda. "Decolonizing the Global Renaissance: A View from the Andes." In Savoy, *Globalization of Renaissance Art,* 67–94.

Cole, Janie. "Constructing Racial Identity and Power in Music, Ceremonial Practices, and Indigenous Instruments in Early Modern African Kingdoms." In Jones, Lee, and Polanco, *Routledge Companion to Race.*

Coleman, Jeffrey K. *The Necropolitical Theater: Race and Immigration on the Contemporary Stage.* Evanston, IL: Northwestern University Press, 2020.

Collins, Kristen, and Bryan C. Keene, eds. *Balthazar: A Black African King in Medieval and Renaissance Art.* Los Angeles: Getty Museum, 2023.

Cooke, Edward S., Jr. *Global Objects: Toward a Connected Art History.* Princeton, NJ: Princeton University Press, 2022.

Cooper, Brittney. *Beyond Respectability: The Intellectual Thought of Race Women.* Urbana: University of Illinois Press, 2017.

Cooper Owens, Deirdre. *Medical Bondage: Race, Gender, and the Origins of American Gynecology.* Athens: University of Georgia Press, 2017.

Copeland, Eva Maria. "Empire, Nation, and the *Indiano* in Galdós's *Tormento* and *La loca de la casa.*" *Hispanic Review* 80, no. 2 (2012): 221–42.

Coráñez Bolton, Sony. *Crip Colony: Mestizaje, US Imperialism, and the Queer Politics of Disability in the Philippines.* Durham, NC: Duke University Press, 2023.

Cornejo-Parriego, Rosalía, ed. *Black USA and Spain: Shared Memories in the Twentieth Century.* New York: Routledge, 2020.

Corona Pérez, Eduardo. *Trata atlántica y esclavitud en Sevilla (c. 1500–1650).* Seville: Editorial Universidad de Sevilla, 2022.

Corzo, Gabino La Roza. *Tatuados: Deformaciones étnicas de los cimarrones en Cuba.* Havana: Fundación Fernando Ortiz, 2011.

Cruz, Ariane. *The Color of Kink: Black Women, BDSM, and Pornography.* New York: New York University Press, 2016.

Davidson, Joe P. L., and Filipe Carreira da Silva. "Fear of a Black Planet: Climate Apocalypse, Anthropocene Futures, and Black Social Thought." *European Journal of Social Theory* 25, no. 4 (2022): 521–38.

Davidson, Michael. *Distressing Language: Disability and the Poetics of Error.* New York: New York University Press, 2022.

Davies, Surekha. *Renaissance Ethnography and the Invention of the Human: New Worlds, Maps, and Monsters.* Cambridge: Cambridge University Press, 2017.

Dawson, Kevin. *Undercurrents of Power: Aquatic Culture in the African Diaspora.* Philadelphia: University of Pennsylvania Press, 2018.

de C. M. Saunders, A. C. *A Social History of Black Slaves and Freedman in Portugal, 1441–1555.* Cambridge: Cambridge University Press, 1982.

Delgado, Grethel. "Juan Manuel Cao: 'Derribar nuestros símbolos es un modo de discriminarnos.'" *Diario las Américas* (Miami), June 21, 2020. https://www.diariolasamericas.com/eeuu/juan-manuel-cao-derribar-nuestros-simbolos-es un-modo-discriminarnos-n4201532.

de los Reyes Peña, Merecedes. "Los carteles de teatro en el Siglo de Oro." *Criticón* 59 (1993): 99–118.

Derbew, Sarah F. *Untangling Blackness in Greek Antiquity.* Cambridge: Cambridge University Press, 2022.

Descartes, René. *Discourse on Method and Meditations on First Philosophy.* Translated by Donald A. Cress. Indianapolis: Hackett, 1998.

Domínguez, Julia. *Quixotic Memories: Cervantes and Memory in Early Modern Spain.* Toronto: University of Toronto Press, 2022.

Domínguez Búrdalo, José. "Del ser (o no ser) hispano: Unamuno frente la negritud." *MLN* 121 (2006): 322–42.

Domínguez Ortiz, Antonio. *La esclavitud en Castilla en la edad moderna y otros estudios marginados.* Granada: Comares, 2003.

Dopico, Georgina. "Canons Afire: Libraries, Books, and Bodies in *Don Quixote*'s Spain." In González Echeverría, *Cervantes' Don Quixote*, 95–124.

———. "Pierre Menard, Traductor del Quijote, or Echo's Echoes." *Cervantes: Bulletin of the Cervantes Society of America* 31, no. 1 (2011): 27–49.

Dopico, Georgina, and Francisco Layna Ranz, eds. *USA Cervantes: Treinta y nueve Cervantistas en Estados Unidos.* Madrid: Polifemo, 2009.

Downs, Jim. *Maladies of Empire: How Colonialism, Slavery, and War Transformed Medicine.* Cambridge, MA: Belknap Press of Harvard University Press, 2021.

DuBois Shaw, Gwendolyn. *Seeing the Unspeakable: The Art of Kara Walker.* Durham, NC: Duke University Press, 2004.

Dubrofsky, Rachel E. *Authenticating Whiteness: Karens, Selfies, and Pop Stars.* Jackson: University Press of Mississippi, 2022.

DuCille, Ann. "The Occult of True Black Womanhood: Critical Demeanor and Black Feminist Studies." *Signs* 19, no. 3 (1994): 591–629.

Dwyer, Erin Austin. *Mastering Emotions: Feelings, Power, and Slavery in the United States.* Philadelphia: University of Pennsylvania Press, 2021.

Dyke, Christina van. *A Hidden Wisdom: Medieval Contemplatives on Self-Knowledge, Reason, Love, Persons, and Immortality.* Oxford: Oxford University Press, 2022.

Earle, T. F., and Kate Lowe, eds. *Black Africans in Renaissance Europe.* Cambridge: Cambridge University Press, 2005.

Edelman, Lee. *Bad Education: Why Queer Theory Teaches Us Nothing.* Durham, NC: Duke University Press, 2023.

———. *No Future: Queer Theory and the Death Drive.* Durham, NC: Duke University Press, 2004.

Egginton, William. "The So-Called Historical Approach to *Don Quixote*." Stanford Humanities Center. February 4, 2013. https://shc.stanford.edu/arcade/interventions/so-called-historical-approach-don-quixote.

Egginton, William, and David Castillo. *What Would Cervantes Do? Navigating Post-truth with Spanish Baroque Literature.* Ottawa: McGill-Queen's University Press, 2022.

Elias, Norbert. *The Civilizing Process.* Rev. ed. Hoboken, NJ: Blackwell, 2000.

Elkins, James, Zhivka Valiavicharska, and Alice Kim, eds. *Art and Globalization.* University Park: Penn State University Press, 2010.

Escribano, Francesc, dir. *Buscando a Cervantes.* Madrid: ArtesMedia and Minoría

Absoluta, 2016. https://www.atresplayer.com/lasexta/documentales/buscando-a-cervantes.

Falola, Toyin. *Decolonizing African Studies: Knowledge Production, Agency, and Voice.* Rochester, NY: University of Rochester Press, 2022

Falola, Toyin, and Matt D. Childs, eds. *The Yoruba Diaspora in the Atlantic World.* Bloomington: Indiana University Press, 2004.

Feldman, Martha. *Castrato: On Natures and Kinds.* Berkeley: University of California Press, 2016.

Fernández, Esther, and Adrienne L. Martín, eds. *Drawing the Curtain: Cervantes's Theatrical Revelations.* Toronto: University of Toronto Press, 2022.

Fernández, James D. "The Bonds of Patrimony: Cervantes and the New World." *PMLA* 109, no. 5 (1994): 969–81.

Fernández, Luis. *Comediantes, esclavos, y moriscos en Valladolid: Siglos XVI y XVII.* Valladolid: Secretariado de Publicaciones, Universidad de Valladolid, 1988.

Few, Martha, and Zeb Tortorici, eds. *Centering Animals in Latin American History.* Durham, NC: Duke University Press, 2013.

Findlen, Paula, ed. *Early Modern Things: Objects and Their Histories.* 2nd ed. New York: Routledge, 2021.

Fleetwood, Nicole R. *Marking Time: Art in the Age of Mass Incarceration.* Cambridge, MA: Harvard University Press, 2020.

Foa, Sandra M. *Feminismo y forma narrativa: Estudio del tema y las técnicas de María de Zayas y Sotomayor.* Madrid: Hispanofila, 1979.

Forbes, Jack D. *Africans and Native Americans: The Language of Race and the Evolution of Red-Black Peoples.* Urbana: University of Illinois Press, 1993.

Forcione, Alban K. *Cervantes and the Humanist Vision: A Study of Four Exemplary Novels.* Princeton, NJ: Princeton University Press, 1982.

———. *Cervantes, Aristotle, and the "Persiles."* Princeton, NJ: Princeton University Press, 1970.

Foster, Thomas A. *Rethinking Rufus: Sexual Violation of Enslaved Men.* Athens: University of Georgia Press, 2019.

Foucault, Michel. *The Archaeology of Knowledge and the Discourse of Language.* Translated by A. M. Sheridan Smith. New York: Pantheon Books, 1972.

———. *Discipline and Punish.* Translated by A. M. Sheridan Smith. New York: Pantheon Books, 1972.

———. *The Order of Things: An Archaeology of the Human Sciences.* New York: Vintage Books, 1994.

———. *Power/Knowledge: Selected Interviews and Other Writings, 1972–1977.* Edited by Colin Gordon. Translated by Colin Gordon, Leo Marshall, John Mepham, and Kater Soper. New York: Pantheon Books, 1972.

Fox, Dian. "From King Sebastian of Portugal to Miguel de Cervantes and *Don Quijote*: A Genealogy of Myth and Influence." *Modern Language Notes* 135, no. 2 (2020): 387–408.

Fracchia, Carmen. *"Black but Human": Slavery and Visual Art in Hapsburg Spain, 1480–1700.* Oxford: Oxford University Press, 2019

———. "Sancho Panza y la esclavización de los negros." *Afro-Hispanic Review* (Fall 1994): 25–31.

Fra-Molinero, Baltasar. "'El disfraz de Dorotea': Usos del cuerpo negro en la España de Cervantes." *Indiana Journal of Hispanic Literatures* 2, no. 2 (1994): 63–85.

———. *La imagen de los negros en el teatro del Siglo de Oro.* Madrid: Siglo Veintiuno, 1995.

———. "Juan Latino and His Racial Difference." In Earle and Lowe, *Black Africans,* 326–44.

———. "Sancho Panza y la esclavización de los negros." *Afro-Hispanic Review* 13, no. 2 (Fall 1994): 25–31.

Franco Silva, Alfonso. *La esclavitud en Sevilla y su tierra a fines de la Edad Media.* Seville: Diputación Provincial de Sevilla, 1979.

———. *Los esclavos de Sevilla*. Seville: Diputación Provincial de Sevilla, 1980.

———. *Registro documental sobre la esclavitud sevillana (1453–1513)*. Seville: Universidad de Sevilla, 1979.

Fraser, Benjamin. *Obsession, Aesthetics, and the Iberian City*. Nashville: Vanderbilt University Press, 2022.

Freeburg, Christopher. *Counterlife: Slavery After Resistance and Social Death*. Durham, NC: Duke University Press, 2021.

Freeman, Elizabeth. *Time Binds: Queer Temporalities, Queer Histories*. Durham, NC: Duke University Press, 2010.

French, Howard W. *Born in Blackness: Africa, Africans, and the Making of the Modern World, 1471 to the Second World War*. New York: Norton, 2021.

Fromont, Cécile. *The Art of Conversion: Christian Visual Culture in the Kingdom of Kongo*. Chapel Hill: University of North Carolina Press, 2014.

———. *Images on a Mission in Early Modern Kongo and Angola*. University Park: Penn State University Press, 2022.

Fuchs, Barbara. *Passing for Spain: Cervantes and the Fictions of Identity*. Urbana: University of Illinois Press, 2003.

Fuchs, Barbara, Larissa Brewer-García, and Aaron J. Ilika, eds. and trans. "Edicts and Official Documents Concerning the Moriscos." In *"The Abencerraje" and "Ozmín and Daraja": Two Sixteenth-Century Novellas from Spain*, 111–29. Philadelphia: University of Pennsylvania Press, 2014.

Fuentes, Marisa J. *Dispossessed Lives: Enslaved Women, Violence, and the Archive*. Philadelphia: University of Pennsylvania Press, 2016.

Gamboa, Yolanda. "Architectural Cartography: Social and Gender Mapping in María de Zayas's Seventeenth-Century Spain." *Hispanic Review* 71, no. 2 (2003): 189–203.

Gamechogoicoechea Llopis, Ane. *El mito de Orfeo en la literatura barroca española*. Valladolid: Universidad de Valladolid, 2011.

Garcés, María Antonia. *Cervantes in Algiers*. Ithaca, NY: Cornell University Press, 2005.

García-Arenal, Mercedes, and Gerard Wiegers. *Los moriscos: Expulsión y diaspora; Una perspectiva internacional*. Valencia: Universidad de València, 2013.

García López, Jorge. *Cervantes, la figura en el tapiz: Itinerario personal vivencia intelectual*. Barcelona: Marcial Pons, 2015.

García Piñar, Pablo. "The Ethics of Staging Crip *Comedia*." *Arizona Journal of Hispanic Cultural Studies* 27 (2023): 147–65.

———. "Irrepresentable Corporealities: The Staging of *Las Paredes Oyen* in the Nineteenth and Twentieth Centuries." *Comedia Performance* 19 (2022): 40–59. https://doi.org/10.5325/COMEPERF.19.1.0040.

———. "The Optics of Bodily Deviance: Juan Ruiz de Alarcón's Path to Public Office." In *Extraordinary Bodies in Early Modern Nature and Culture*, edited by Maja Bondestam, 85–102. Amsterdam: University of Amsterdam Press, 2020. https://doi.org/10.1515/9789048552375-005.

———. "The Unstageable Birth of the Crip *Galán*: Juan Ruiz de Alarcón's *Las paredes oyen*." *Symposium: A Quarterly Journal in Modern Literatures* 77, no. 2 (2023): 72–88. https://doi.org/10.1080/00397709.2023.2200098.

———. "The Weight of Authority: Sancho's Fat Body in Barataria (2.45)." In *Don Quijote*, edited by Diana de Armas Wilson, 797–805. New York: Norton, 2020.

García Santo-Tomás, Enrique. *Espacio urbano y creación literaria en el Madrid del Felipe IV*. Madrid: Iberoamericana, 2004.

Gaylord, Mary Malcolm. "Don Quixote's New World Language." *Cervantes: Bulletin of the Cervantes Society of America* 27, no. 1 (2007): 71–94.

———. "Pulling Strings in Master Peter's Puppets: Fiction and History in *Don Quijote*." In "Frames for Reading:

Cervantes Studies in Honor of Peter N. Dunn," edited by M. M. Gaylord. Special issue, *Cervantes* 18, no. 2 (1998): 117–47.

Gerli, E. Michael. "'Agora que voy sola': Celestina, Magic, and the Disenchanted World." *eHumanista* 19 (2011): 157–71.

———. *Celestina and the Ends of Desire.* Toronto: University of Toronto Press, 2011.

———. *Cervantes: Displacements, Inflections, and Transcendence.* Newark, DE: Cuesta, 2019.

Germeten, Nicole von. "Police Voyeurism in Enlightenment Mexico City." In Jones and Leahy, *Pornographic Sensibilities*, 248–63.

Giles, Ryan, and Steven Wagschal, eds. *Beyond Sight: Engaging the Senses in Iberian Literature and Cultures, 1200–1750*, Toronto: University of Toronto Press, 2018.

Gilroy, Paul. *The Black Atlantic: Modernity and Double Consciousness.* Cambridge, MA: Harvard University Press, 1993.

Goldberg, K. Meira. *Sonidos Negros: On the Blackness of Flamenco.* Oxford: Oxford University Press, 2019.

Gomez, Michael A. *African Dominion: A New History of Empire in Early and Medieval West Africa.* Princeton, NJ: Princeton University Press, 2018.

González Arévalo, Raúl. *La vida cotidiana de los esclavos en la Castilla del Renacimiento.* Barcelona: Marcial Pons, 2022.

González Echevarría, Roberto, ed. *Cervantes' Don Quixote: A Casebook.* Oxford: Oxford University Press, 2005.

Gordon, Avery F. *Ghostly Matters: Haunting and the Sociological Imagination.* Minneapolis: University of Minnesota Press, 2008.

Gracia, Jordi. *Miguel de Cervantes: La conquista de la ironía.* Barcelona: Taurus, 2016.

Graf, Eric Clifford. "El Greco's and Cervantes's Euclidean Theologies." In Laguna and Beusterien, *Goodbye Eros*, 83–116.

Graullera Sanz, Vicente. *La esclavitud en Valencia en los siglos XVI y XVII.* Valencia: Instituto Valenciano de Estudios Históricos, 1978.

Green, Toby. *A Fistful of Shells: West Africa from the Rise of the Slave Trade to the Age of Revolution.* New York: Penguin, 2020.

Greer, Margaret Rich. "Thine and Mine: The Spanish 'Golden Age' and Early Modern Studies." *PMLA* 126, no. 1 (2011): 217–24.

Gutarra Cordero, Dannelle. *She Is Weeping: An Intellectual History of Racialized Slavery in the Atlantic World.* Cambridge: Cambridge University Press, 2022.

Guyer, Jane ed., *Money Matters: Instability, Values, and Social Payments in the Modern History of West African Communities.* Portsmouth, NH: Currey, 1995.

Halberstam, Jack J. *In a Queer Time and Place: Transgender Bodies, Subcultural Lives.* New York: New York University Press, 2005.

Hall, Kim F. *Things of Darkness: Economies of Race and Gender in Early Modern England.* Ithaca, NY: Cornell University Press, 1995.

Hannaford, Ivan. *Race: The History of an Idea.* Baltimore: Johns Hopkins University Press, 1995.

Haraway, Donna. *Staying with Trouble: Making Kin in the Chthulucene.* Durham, NC: Duke University Press, 2016.

Harris, Cheryl L. "Whiteness as Property." *Harvard Law Review* 106, no. 8 (1993): 1707–91.

Hartman, Saidiya V. *Scenes of Subjection: Terror, Slavery, and Self-Making in Nineteenth-Century America.* New York: Norton, 2022.

———. *Wayward Lives, Beautiful Experiments: Intimate Histories of Riotous Black Girls, Troublesome Women, and Queer Radicals.* New York: Norton, 2019.

Hathaway, Jane. *The Chief Eunuch of the Ottoman Harem.* Cambridge: Cambridge University Press, 2018.

Hawthorne, Camilla, and Jovan Scott Lewis, eds. *The Black Geographic: Praxis, Resistance, Futurity.* Durham, NC: Duke University Press, 2023.

Hegel, Georg Wilhelm Friedrich. *Hegel's Phenomenology of Spirit.* 1807. Translated by A. V. Miller. Oxford: Oxford University Press, 1977.

———. *Introduction to the Philosophy of History*. Translated by Leo Rauch. Indianapolis: Hackett, 1988.

———. "Lordship and Bondage." In Hegel, *Hegel's Phenomenology of Spirit*, 111–19.

Hicks, Dan. *The Brutish Museums: The Benin Bronzes, Colonial Violence, and Cultural Restitution*. London: Pluto Press, 2021.

Higginbotham, A. Leon, Jr. *In the Matter of Color: Race and the American Legal Process*. New York: Oxford University Press, 1978.

Hilton, Anne. "Family and Kinship Among the Kongo South of the Zaire River from the Sixteenth to the Nineteenth Centuries." *Journal of African History* 24, no. 2 (1983): 189–206.

Hobson, Janell, ed. *The Routledge Companion to Black Women's Cultural Histories*. New York: Routledge, 2021.

Hogarth, Rana A. *Medicalizing Blackness: Making Racial Difference in the Atlantic World, 1780–1840*. Chapel Hill: University of North Carolina Press, 2017.

Hogendom, Jan, and Marion Johnson, eds. *The Shell Money of the Slave Trade*. Cambridge: Cambridge University Press, 1986.

Holland, Sharon Patricia. *An Other: A Black Feminist Consideration of Animal Life*. Durham, NC: Duke University Press, 2023.

———. *Raising the Dead: Readings of Death and (Black) Subjectivity*. Durham, NC: Duke University Press, 2000.

Ibrahim, Habiba. *Black Age: Oceanic Lifespans and the Time of Black Life*. New York: New York University Press, 2021.

Ibrahim, Habiba, and Badia Ahad, eds. "Black Temporality in Times of Crisis." Special issue, *South Atlantic Quarterly* 121, no. 1 (2022): 1–10.

Icaza, Francisco de. *Las "Novelas ejemplares" de Cervantes: Sus críticos, sus modelos literarios, sus modelos vivos, y su influencia en el arte*. 1901. Reprint, Madrid: Real Academia Española 1928.

Iffland, James. *Quevedo and the Grotesque*. 2 vols. London: Támesis, 1978.

Ireton, Chloe L. "Black Africans' Freedom Litigation Suits to Define Just War and Just Slavery in the Early Spanish Empire." *Renaissance Quarterly* 73, no. 4 (2020): 1277–319.

Irigoyen-Garcia, Javier. "'La música ha sido hereje': Pastoral Performance, Moorishness, and Cultural Hybridity in *Los baños de Argel*." *Bulletin of Comediantes* 62, no. 2 (2010): 45–62.

———. *The Spanish Arcadia: Sheep Herding, Pastoral Discourse, and Ethnicity in Early Modern Spain*. Toronto: University of Toronto Press, 2013.

Jackson, Zakiyyah Iman. *Becoming Human: Matter and Meaning in an Antiblack World*. New York: New York University Press, 2020.

Johnson, Carina L., and Catherine Molineux. "Putting Europe in Its Place: Material Traces, Interdisciplinarity, and the Recuperation of the Early Modern Extra-European Subject." *Radical History Review* 130 (January 2018): 62–99.

Johnson, Carroll B. *Cervantes and the Material World*. Urbana: University of Illinois Press, 2000.

Johnson, E. Patrick. *Appropriating Blackness: Performance and the Politics of Authenticity*. Durham, NC: Duke University Press, 2003.

———, ed. *No Tea, No Shade: New Writings in Black Queer Studies*. Durham, NC: Duke University Press, 2016.

Johnson, Jessica Marie. *Wicked Flesh: Black Women, Intimacy, and Freedom in the Atlantic World*. Philadelphia: University of Pennsylvania Press, 2020.

Johnson, Paul Michael. "Quixotic Allyship? The Colonial, Transnational, and Racialized Legacies of Cervantes's Statues." In Leahy, *Uses and Abuses*.

Johnson, Samuel. *The History of the Yorubas from the Earliest Time to the Beginning of the British Protectorate*. Edited by Obadiah Johnson. 1921. Reprint, Lagos: Routledge, 1937.

Johnson, Walter. "On Agency." *Journal of Social History* 37, no. 1 (2003): 113–24.
Jones, Nicholas R. "Black Women in Early Modern Spanish Literature." In Hobson, *Routledge Companion*, 57–65.
———. "Chocolate City, Chessboard City: Black Vitality in Renaissance Seville." *Black Perspectives* (blog). African American Intellectual History Society, October 16, 2018. https://www.aaihs.org/chocolate-city-chessboard-city-black-vitality-in-renaissance-seville.
———. "Cosmetic Ontologies, Cosmetic Subversions: Articulating Black Beauty and Humanity in Luis de Góngora's "En la fiesta del Santísimo Sacramento." *Journal for Early Modern Cultural Studies* 15, no. 1 (2015): 25–54.
———. "Debt Collecting, Disappearance, Necromancy." In *Early Modern Black Diaspora Studies: A Critical Anthology*, edited by Cassander L. Smith, Nicholas R. Jones, and Miles P. Grier, 211–21. New York: Palgrave, 2018.
———. "Nuptials Gone Awry, Empire in Decay: Crisis, *Lo Cursi*, and the Rhetorical Inventory of Blackness in Quevedo's 'Boda de negros.'" *Arizona Journal of Hispanic Cultural Studies* 20 (2016): 29–47.
———, ed. *Recovering Black Performance in Early Modern Iberia*. Double special issue, *Bulletin of the Comediantes* 74, nos. 1–2 (2022–23).
———. "Sor Juana's Black Atlantic: Colonial Blackness and the Poetic Subversions of *Habla de Negros*." *Hispanic Review* 86, no. 3 (2018): 265–85.
———. Staging Habla de Negros: *Radical Performances of the African Diaspora in Early Modern Spain*. University Park: Penn State University Press, 2019.
Jones, Nicholas R., and Chad Leahy. "Cervantes y la materia de las vidas negras." *Ctxt: Contexto y acción*, July 3, 2020. https://ctxt.es/es/20200701/Firmas/32774/cervantes-estatua-blacklives-matter-nick-jones-chad-leahy.htm.
———. "Introduction: Rethinking the Pornographic in Premodern and Early Modern Spanish Cultural Production." In Jones and Leahy, *Pornographic Sensibilities*, 1–16.
———, eds. *Pornographic Sensibilities: Imagining Sex and the Visceral in Premodern and Early Modern Spanish Cultural Production*. New York: Routledge, 2021.
Jones, Nicholas R., Christina H. Lee, and Dominique E. Polanco, eds. *The Routledge Companion to Race in Early Modern Artistic, Material, and Visual Production*. New York: Routledge, forthcoming.
Jones-Rogers, Stephanie. *They Were Her Property: White Women as Slave Owners in the American South*. New Haven, CT: Yale University Press, 2020.
Jordan, Winthrop. *White over Black: American Attitudes Toward the Negro, 1550–1812*. Chapel Hill: University of North Carolina Press, 1968.
Juárez-Almendros, Encarnación. *Disabled Bodies in Early Modern Spanish Literature: Aging Women and Saints*. Liverpool: University of Liverpool Press, 2018.
Judd, Timothy. "Ghostly Mozart: The 'Commendatore Scene' from 'Don Giovanni.'" *Listeners Club* (blog). October 30, 2020. https://thelistenersclub.com/2020/10/30/ghostly-mozart-the-commendatore-scene-from-don-giovanni/.
Keeling, Kara. *Queer Times, Black Futures*. New York: New York University Press, 2019.
Kendrick, Anna Kathryn. *Humanizing Childhood in Early Twentieth-Century Spain*. Cambridge, UK: Legenda, 2020.
Kendrick, Anna Kathryn, and Parker Lawson, eds. "Theorizing Education in the Global Hispanophone." *Bulletin of Hispanic Studies* 100, no. 1 (2023): 5–13.
Kettler, Andrew. *The Smell of Slavery: Olfactory Racism and the Atlantic World*. Cambridge: Cambridge University Press, 2020.

Kimmel, Seth. *Parables of Coercion: Conversion and Knowledge at the End of Islamic Spain*. Chicago: University of Chicago Press, 2015.

Kondo, Dorinne. *Worldmaking: Race, Performance, and the Work of Creativity*. Durham, NC: Duke University Press, 2018.

Krebs, Verena. *Medieval Ethiopian Kingship, Craft, and Diplomacy with Latin Europe*. Cham, Switzerland: Palgrave Macmillan, 2021.

Labrador Méndez, Germán. "Dynamiting *Don Quijote*: Literature, Colonial Memory, and the Crisis of the National Subject in the Monumental Poetics of the Cervantine Tercentenary (Spain 1915–1921)." *Journal of Iberian and Latin American Studies* 19, no. 3 (2013): 185–209.

Lad, Jateen. "Panoptic Bodies: Black Eunuchs as Guardians of the Topkapı Harem." In *Harem Histories: Envisioning Places and Living Spaces*, edited by Marilyn Booth, 136–76. Durham, NC: Duke University Press, 2010.

Laguna, Ana María G. *Cervantes, the Golden Age, and the Battle for Cultural Identity in Twentieth-Century Spain*. New York: Bloomsbury, 2021.

——— . "In the Name of Love: Cervantes's Play on Captivity in *La gran sultana*." In Fernández and Martín, *Drawing the Curtain*, 150–75.

Laguna, Ana María G., and John Beusterien, eds. *Goodbye Eros: Recasting Forms and Norms of Love in the Age of Cervantes*. Toronto: University of Toronto Press, 2020.

La Roza Corzo, Gabino. *Tatuados: Deformaciones étnicas de los cimarrones en Cuba*. Havana: Fundación Fernando Ortiz, 2011.

Leahy, Chad. *On the Uses and Abuses of Early Modern Spanish Culture*. Amsterdam: Amsterdam University Press, forthcoming.

Lethabo King, Tiffany. *The Black Shoals: Offshore Formations of Black and Native Studies*. Durham, NC: Duke University Press, 2019.

Levinson, Sanford. *Written in Stone: Public Monuments in Changing Societies*. Durham, NC: Duke University Press, 2018.

Lezra, Jacques. *Unspeakable Subjects: The Genealogy of the Event in Early Modern Europe*. Stanford, CA: Stanford University Press, 1997.

Lihani, John. *Bartolomé de Torres Naharro*. Detroit: Twayne, 1979.

Linares, Héctor. "Visualizing Black Knighthood in Early Modern Iberia." In Jones, Lee, and Polanco, *Routledge Companion to Race*.

Lipsitz, George. "The Possessive Investment in Whiteness: Racialized Social Democracy and the 'White' Problem in American Studies." *American Quarterly* 47, no. 3 (1995): 369–87.

Little, Arthur. *Shakespeare Jungle Fever: National-Imperial Re-visions of Race, Rape, and Sacrifice*. Stanford, CA: Stanford University Press, 2000.

Lorde, Audre. "A Burst of Light: Living with Cancer." In *A Burst of Light: Essays by Audre Lorde*, 49–134. Ithaca, NY: Firebrand, 1988.

——— . "Poetry Is Not a Luxury." In Lorde, *Sister Outsider*, 24–27.

——— . *Sister Outsider: Essays and Speeches by Audre Lorde*. Freedom, CA: Crossing Press, 1984.

Lovejoy, Paul E. "Scarification and the Loss of History in the African Diaspora." In *Activating the Past: History and Memory in the Black Atlantic World*, edited by Andrew Apter and Lauren Derby, 98–138. Newcastle, UK: Cambridge Scholars.

Lowe, Kate. "The Stereotyping of Black Africans." In Earle and Lowe, *Black Africans*, 17–57.

Lowe, Lisa. *The Intimacies of Four Continents*. Durham, NC: Duke University Press, 2015.

Lucía Megías, José Manuel. *La juventud de Cervantes: Una vida en construcción*. 3 vols. Madrid: Edaf, 2016–19.

———. *La madurez de Cervantes: Una vida en la corte (1580–1604)*. Madrid: Edaf, 2019.
———. *La plenitud de Cervantes: Una vida en papel (1604–1616)*. Madrid: Edaf, 2019.
Macdonald, Hattie, dir. "Blink." In *Doctor Who*. Cardiff: BBC Wales, 2007.
Macharia, Keguro. "Black (Beyond Negation)." *New Inquiry* (blog). May 26, 2018. https://thenewinquiry.com/blog/black-beyond-negation/.
———. *Frottage: Frictions of Intimacy Across the Black Diaspora*. New York: New York University Press, 2019.
Mandela Gray, Biko. *Black Life Matter: Blackness, Religion, and the Subject*. Durham, NC: Duke University Press, 2022.
Manning, Patrick. *Slavery and African Life: Occidental, Oriental, and African Slaver Trades*. Cambridge: Cambridge University Press, 1990.
Mannix, Daniel. *Black Cargoes: A History of the Atlantic Slave Trade, 1518–1865*. New York: Viking, 1962.
Maravall, José Antonio. *Culture of the Baroque: Analysis of a Historical Structure*. Translated by Terry Cochran. Minneapolis: University of Minnesota Press, 1986.
Marcocci, Giuseppe. *The Globe on Paper: Writing Histories of the World in Renaissance Europe and the Americas*. Oxford: Oxford University Press, 2020.
Martín, Adrienne L. "Sexy Beasts: Women and Lapdogs in Baroque Satirical Verse." In Laguna and Beusterien, *Goodbye Eros*, 157–76.
Martín Casares, Aurelia. *Criados y esclavos de nobles y reyes de España: Siglos XVI–XVIII*. Valencia: Tirant Humanidades, 2020.
———. *La esclavitud en la Granada del siglo XVI: Género, raza, y religión*. Granada: Universidad de Granada, 2000.
———. "Negros y mulatos libres sirviendo en las tropas reales españolas." In Martín Casares, *Criados y esclavos*, 147–74.
Martín Casares, Aurelia, and Margarita García Barranco, eds. *La esclavitud negroafricana en la historia de España: Siglos XVI y XVII*. Granada: Comares, 2010.
———. *Mujeres esclavas y abolicionistas en la España de los siglos XVI al XIX*. Madrid: Iberoamericana, 2014.
———. "The Musical Legacy of Black Africans in Spain: A Review of Our Sources." *Anthropological Notebooks* 15, no. 2 (2009): 51–60.
———. "Popular Depictions of Black African Weddings in Early Modern Spain." *Renaissance and Reformation/Renaissance et Réforme* 32, no. 1 (2008): 107–21.
Martínez, Miguel. *Front Lines: Soldiers' Writing in the Early Modern Hispanic World*. Philadelphia: University of Pennsylvania Press, 2016.
———, ed. *Vida y sucesos de la Monja Alférez*. Madrid: Castalia, 2021.
Martínez-Góngora, Mar. "Más allá del islam: África en *Don Quijote*." *eHumanista* 2 (2013): 362–78.
———. "La sombra de Isabel la Católica en *Don Quijote*: Cervantes, Dorotea, y la princesa Micomicona." *eHumanista* 44 (2020): 220–35.
Mbembe, Achille. *Necropolitics*. Durham, NC: Duke University Press, 2019.
McCarthy, Jesse. "The Master's Tools." In *Who Will Pay Reparations on My Soul?*, 3–21. New York: Liveright, 2021.
McKinley, Michelle A. *Fractional Freedoms: Slavery, Intimacy, and Legal Mobilization in Colonial Lima, 1600–1700*. Cambridge: Cambridge University Press, 2016.
McKittrick, Katherine. *Dear Science and Other Stories*. Durham, NC: Duke University Press, 2021.
———. *Demonic Grounds: Black Women and the Cartographies of Struggle*. Minneapolis: University of Minnesota Press, 2006.
McManus, Stuart Michael. "Decolonizing Renaissance Humanism." *American Historical Review* 127, no. 3 (2022): 1131–61.
Méndez Rodríguez, Luis. *Esclavos en la pintura sevillana de los Siglos de Oro*. Seville:

Universidad de Sevilla/Ateneo de Sevilla, 2011.

Miller, Monica. *Slaves to Fashion: Black Dandyism and the Styling of Black Diasporic Identity*. Durham, NC: Duke University Press, 2009.

Miller-Young, Mireille. "The Deviant and the Defiant Art of Black Women Porn Directors." In *The Feminist Porn Book: The Politics of Producing Pleasure*, edited by Tristan Taormino, Constance Penley, Celine Perrenas Shimizu, and Mireille Miller-Young, 105–20. New York: Feminist Press at the City University of New York, 2013.

———. *A Taste for Brown Sugar: Black Women in Pornography*. Durham, NC: Duke University Press, 2014.

Mitchell, Elise A. "Morbid Crossings: Surviving Smallpox, Maritime Quarantine, and Gendered Geography of the Early Eighteenth-Century Intra-Caribbean Slave Trade." *William and Mary Quarterly* 79, no. 2 (2022): 177–210.

Mitchell, Koritha. "Identifying White Mediocrity and Know-Your-Place Aggression: A Form of Self-Care." *African American Review* 51, no. 4 (2018): 253–62.

Monahan, Torin. *Crisis Vision: Race and the Cultural Production of Surveillance*. Durham, NC: Duke University Press, 2022.

Morgan, Jennifer L. *Laboring Women: Reproduction and Gender in New World Slavery*. Philadelphia: University of Pennsylvania Press, 2004.

———. *Reckoning with Slavery: Gender, Kinship, and Capitalism in the Early Black Atlantic*. Durham, NC: Duke University Press, 2021.

Moritz Rugendeas, Johann. *Viagem através do Brasil*. 1835. São Paulo: Itatiaia/USP, 1979.

Morrison, Matthew D. *Blacksound: Making Race and Popular Music in the United States*. Berkeley: University of California Press, 2024.

Moten, Fred. *In the Break: Aesthetics of the Black Radical Tradition*. Minneapolis: University of Minnesota Press, 2003.

Muñoz, José Esteban. "Ephemera as Evidence: Introductory Notes to Queer Acts." *Women and Performance* 8, no. 2 (1996): 5–16.

———. *The Sense of Brown*. Edited by Joshua Chambers-Letson and Tavia Nyong'o. Durham, NC: Duke University Press, 2020.

Murphy, Michelle. *The Econimization of Life*. Durham, NC: Duke University Press, 2017.

Murray, Pauli. "The Liberation of Black Women." In *Voices of the New Feminism*, edited by Mary Lou Thompson, 87–102. Boston: Beacon Press, 1970.

Myers, Joshua. *Of Black Study*. London: Pluto Press, 2022.

Nash, Jennifer C. *The Black Body in Ecstasy: Reading Race, Reading Pornography*. Durham, NC: Duke University Press, 2014.

———. "Citational Desires: On Black Feminism's Institutional Longings." *Diacritics* 48, no. 3 (2020): 76–91.

Nemser, Daniel. "Governor Sancho and the Politics of Insularity." *Hispanic Review* 78, no. 1 (2010): 1–23.

The New Oxford Annotated Bible, New Revised Standard Version, with the Apocrypha. Edited by Michael D. Coogan. Oxford: Oxford University Press, 2018.

Nyong'o, Tavia. *Afro-Fabulations: The Queer Drama of Black Life*. New York: New York University Press, 2019.

Ogundiran, Akinwumi. "Of Small Things Remembered: Beads, Cowries, and Cultural Translations of the Atlantic Experience in Yorubaland." *International Journal of African Historical Studies* 35, nos. 1–2 (2022): 427–57.

———. *The Yoruba: A New History*. Bloomington: Indiana University Press, 2020.

Olid Guerrero, Eduardo. *Del teatro a la novela: El ritual del disfraz en la Novelas ejemplares de Cervantes*. Alcalá de Henares: Universidad de Alcalá Servicios de Publicaciones, 2015.

Olmedo Gobante, Manuel. "Del frente a la palestra: Esgrima y ejército en la carrera autorial de Jerónimo Sánchez de Carranza." In Castellano López and Sáez, *Vidas en armas*, 101–14.

———. "'El mucho número que hay dellos': El valiente negro en Flandes y los esgrimistas afrohispanos de Grandezas de la espada." *Bulletin of the Comediantes* 70, no. 2 (2018): 67–91.

———. "In Search of the Black Swordsman: Race and Martial Arts Discourse in Early Modern Iberia." In Branche, *Trajectories of Empire*, 46–78.

Otele, Olivette. *African Europeans: An Untold History*. London: Hurst, 2020.

Pacheco Pereira, Duarte. *Esmeraldo de situ orbis*. Lisbon: Edição de Joaquim Barradas de Carvalho, 1991.

Panzram, Sabine, ed. *The Power of Cities: The Iberian Peninsula from Late Antiquity to the Early Modern Period*. Leiden: Brill, 2019.

Patterson, Orlando. *Slavery and Social Death: A Comparative Study*. Cambridge, MA: Harvard University Press, 1985.

Peirce, Leslie P. *The Imperial Harem: Women and Sovereignty in the Ottoman Empire*. Oxford: Oxford University Press, 1993.

Pérez Magallón, Jesús. *Cervantes, monumento de la nación: Problemas de identidad y cultura*. Madrid: Cátedra, 2015.

Peritz, Jessica Gabriel. *The Lyric Myth of Voice: Civilizing Song in Enlightenment Italy*. Berkeley: University of California Press, 2022.

Phelan, James. "Sethe's Choice: *Beloved* and the Ethics of Reading." *Style* 32, no. 2 (1998): 318–33.

Pickens, Therí Alyce. *Black Madness :: Mad Blackness*. Durham, NC: Duke University Press, 2019.

———, ed. "Blackness and Disability." Special issue, *African American Review* 50, no. 2 (2017).

———. "Blue Blackness, Black Blueness: Making Sense of Blackness and Disability." In "Blackness and Disability." Special issue, *African American Review* 50, no. 2 (2017): 93–103.

Piñero Ramírez, Pedro M., and Rogelio Reyes Cano. *La imagen de Sevilla en la obra de Cervantes: Espacio y paisaje humano*. Seville: Universidad de Sevilla, 2013.

Poupeney Hart, Catherine, Alfredo Hermenegildo, and César Oliva Olivares, eds. *Cervantes y la puesta en escena de la sociedad de su tiempo (Actas del Coloquio de Montreal, 1997)*. Murcia: Universidad de Murcia, 1999.

Puar, Jasbir K. *Terrorist Assemblages: Homonationalism in Queer Times*. 10th anniversary exp. ed. Durham, NC: Duke University Press, 2017.

Pullins, David, and Vanessa K. Valdés, eds. *Juan de Pareja: Afro-Hispanic Painter in the Age of Velázquez*. New York: Metropolitan Museum of Art, 2023.

Quashie, Kevin. *Black Aliveness, or A Poetics of Being*. Durham, NC: Duke University Press, 2021.

Querol Gavaldá, Miguel. *La música en la obra de Cervantes*. Alcalá de Henares: Centro de Estudios Cervantinos, 2005.

Raengo, Alessandra. "Introduction: Blackness as Process." *Liquid Blackness: Journal of Aesthetics and Black Studies* 5, no. 2 (2021): 5–18.

Reed, Anthony. *Soundworks: Race, Sound, and Poetry in Production*. Durham, NC: Duke University Press, 2021.

Reed, Cory A. "Harems and Eunuchs: Ottoman-Islamic Motifs of Captivity in *El celoso extremeño*." *Bulletin of Hispanic Studies* 76, no. 2 (1999): 199–214.

Reid-Pharr, Robert. *Archives of Flesh: African America, Spain, and Post-Humanist Critique*. New York: New York University Press, 2016.

———. *Black Gay Man: Essays*. New York: New York University Press, 2001.

Repinecz, Martin. "Don Quijote in Africa: Fictionality as an Antidote to Racism." *Bulletin of Hispanic Studies* 94, no. 6 (2017): 607–23.

Resina, Joan Ramón, ed. *Iberian Cities*. New York: Routledge, 2001.

Rhodes, Elizabeth. *Dressed to Kill: Death and Meaning in Zayas's Desengaños*. Toronto: University of Toronto Press, 2011.

Riaño, Peio H. *Decapitados: Una historia contra los monumentos a racistas*, *esclavistas, e invasores*. Madrid: Penguin, 2021.

Roach, Joseph. *Cities of the Dead: Circum-Atlantic Performance*. New York: Columbia University Press, 1996.

Roach, Shoniqua. "The Black Living Room." *American Quarterly* 74, no. 3 (2022): 791–811.

Roane, J. T. *Dark Agoras: Insurgent Black Social Life and the Politics of Place*. New York: New York University Press, 2023.

———. "Plotting the Black Commons." *Souls: A Critical Journal of Black Politics, Culture, and Society* 20, no. 3 (2018): 239–66.

Robbins, Bruce. *Criticism and Politics: A Polemical Introduction*. Stanford, CA: Stanford University Press, 2022.

Robinson, Cedric. *Black Marxism: The Making of the Black Radical Tradition*. Chapel Hill: University of North Carolina Press, 2021.

Rodríguez, Dylan. "The Pitfalls of White Liberal Panic." In *Making Abolitionist Worlds: Proposal for a World on Fire*, edited by Abolition Collective, 122–26. New York: Common Notions, 2020.

Rodríguez-Velasco, Jesús R. *Microliteraturas*. Madrid: Cátedra, 2022.

Rogério, Budasz. "Black Guitar Players and Early African-Iberian Music in Portugal and Brazil." *Early Music* 35, no. 1 (2007): 3–21.

Romero-Díaz, Nieves. "La sexualidad masculina y negra a debate en la España de la temprana modernidad." *Romance Notes* 58, no. 1 (2018): 95–104.

Row, Jennifer Eun-Jung. *Queer Velocities: Time, Sex, and Biopower on the Early Modern Stage*. Evanston, IL: Northwestern University Press, 2022.

Rowe, Erin Kathleen. *Black Saints in Early Modern Global Catholicism*. Cambridge: Cambridge University Press, 2019.

———. "Race in Early Modern Iberia." *Bulletin for Spanish and Portuguese Historical Studies* 47, no. 1 (2022): 173–91.

Rubio, Rebeca. "Cervantes racial: Humanidad, identidad, y libertad a la luz de un reparto diverso." *eHumanista/Cervantes* 8 (2020): 115–31.

Ruiz, Eduardo. "Cervantes's *Celoso*: A Tale of Colonial Lack." *Hispanic Review* 81, no. 2 (2013): 145–63.

———. "Counter-Discursive and Erotic Agency: The Case of the Black Slaves in Miguel de Cervantes's 'El celoso extremeño.'" *Hispania* 97, no. 2 (2014): 194–206.

———. "Three Faces/Phases of Male Desire: Veiled Woman, Passive Virgin, and African Devil in María de Zayas's 'Tarde llega el desengaño.'" *Symposium: A Quarterly Journal in Modern Literatures* 72, no. 3 (2018): 149–62.

Ryan, Michael A. *A Kingdom of Stargazers: Astrology and Authority in the Late Medieval Crown of Aragon*. Ithaca, NY: Cornell University Press, 2011.

Sáez, Adrián J. "El factor Cervantes: Anatomía de los prólogos de *La Galatea* al *Persiles*." In Valentín Núñez Rivera, *Paratextos y prosa*, 163–77.

Sampedro, Benita, and Adolfo Campoy, eds. "Entering the Global Hispanophone." Special issue, *Journal of Spanish Cultural Studies* 20, nos. 1–2 (2019).

Sánchez-Cid, Francisco Javier. *La familia del dramaturgo Felipe Godínez: Un clan judeoconverso en la época de la Contrarreforma*. Huelva: Universidad de Huelva, 2016.

Sanjurjo, Jesús. "Centring Blackness in European History: A *European History Quarterly* Forum." Special issue, *European History Quarterly* 53, no. 1 (2023).

Santos, Antonio. "Caracterización del negro en la literatura española del XVI." *Lemir* 15 (2011): 23–46.

Savoy, Daniel, ed. *The Globalization of Renaissance Art*. Leiden: Brill, 2017.

Schliephake, Christopher. "Orpheus in Black: Classicism and Cultural Ecology in Marcel Camus, Samuel R. Delany, and Reginald Shepherd." *Anglia* 134, no. 1 (2016): 113–35.

Schwartz, Lía, and Isaías Lerner, eds. *Homenaje a Ana María Barrenechea*. Madrid: Castalia, 1984.

Séguin, Bécquer. *The Op-ed Novel: A Literary History of Post-Franco Spain.* Cambridge, MA: Harvard University Press, 2024.

Selden, Daniel L. "*Aithiopika* and Ethiopanism." In *Studies in Heliodorus*, edited by Richard Hunter, 182–217. Cambridge, UK: Cambridge Philological Society, 1998.

Sewell, Elizabeth. *The Orphic Voice.* 1960. New York: New York Review Books, 2022.

Sexton, Jared. "Basic Black." *Liquid Blackness: Journal of Aesthetics and Black Studies* 5, no. 2 (2021): 74–83.

Shange, Ntozake. *For Colored Girls Who Have Considered Suicide When the Rainbow Is Enuf.* New York: Macmillan, 1977.

Sharpe, Christina. *In the Wake: On Blackness and Being.* Durham, NC: Duke University Press, 2016.

———. *Monstrous Intimacies: Making Post-slavery Subjects.* Durham, NC: Duke University Press, 2010.

———. *Ordinary Notes.* New York: Farrar, Straus, and Giroux, 2023.

Sierra Matute, Víctor. "The Tongue of Cervantes: Addressing Quixotic Monumentalization in the Global Hispanophone." In Leahy, *Uses and Abuses*.

Sigal, Pete, Zeb Tortorici, and Neil Whitehead, eds. *Ethnopornography: Sexuality, Colonialism, and Archival Knowledge.* Durham, NC: Duke University Press, 2020.

Simmons, Adam. *Nubia, Ethiopia, and the Crusading World, 1095–1402.* New York: Routledge, 2023.

Slater, John. "Branding, Bondage, and Lope's Typeface." In Jones, *Recovering Black Performance*, 225–47.

———, ed. *Medical Cultures of the Early Modern Spanish Empire.* New York: Routledge, 2014.

Sliwa, Krzysztof. *Documentos de Miguel de Cervantes Saavedra.* Navarra, Spain: Ediciones Universidad de Navarra, 1999.

Smallwood, Stephanie. *Saltwater Slavery: A Middle Passage from Africa to American Diaspora.* Cambridge, MA: Harvard University Press, 2008.

Smith, Cassander L. *Black Africans in the British Imagination: English Narratives of the Early Atlantic World.* Baton Rouge: Louisiana State University Press, 2016.

———. *Race and Respectability in an Early Black Atlantic.* Baton Rouge: Louisiana State University Press, 2023.

Smith, Linda Tuhiwai. *Decolonizing Methodologies: Research and Indigenous Peoples.* London: Zed Books, 2021.

Soto, Isabel. "'I Knew That Spain Once Belonged to the Moors': Langston Hughes, Race, and the Spanish Civil War." *Research in African Literatures* 45, no. 3 (2014): 130–46.

Spicer, Joaneath, ed. *Revealing the African Presence in Renaissance Europe.* Baltimore: Walters Art Gallery, 2013.

Spillers, Hortense J. "'All the Things You Could Be by Now, If Sigmund Freud's Wife Was Your Mother': Psychoanalysis and Race." In Spillers, *Black, White, and in Color*, 376–427.

———. *Black, White, and in Color: Essays on American Literature and Culture.* Chicago: University of Chicago Press, 2003.

———. "The Crisis of the Negro Intellectual: A Post-date." In Spillers, *Black, White, and in Color*, 428–70.

———. "The Idea of Black Culture." *CR: The Centennial Review* 6, no. 3 (2006): 7–28.

———. "Mama's Baby Papa's Maybe: An American Grammar Book." In Spillers, *Black, White, and in Color*, 203–29.

———. "Peter's Pans: Eating in the Diaspora." In Spillers, *Black, White, and in Color*, 1–64.

Stackhouse, Kenneth A. "The 'Comedia' as Diplomacy: Lope de Vega's Portuguese Plays and Union with Castile." *Mediterranean Studies* 11 (2002): 103–13.

Stoler, Ann Laura. *Race and the Education of Desire: Foucault's History of Sexuality and the Colonial Order of Things.* Durham, NC: Duke University Press, 1995.

Strathern, Alan. "Global Early Modernity and the Problem of What Came Before." *Past and Present* 238, no. 13 (2018): 317–44.

Strongman, Roberto. *Queering Black Atlantic Religions: Transcorporeality in Candomblé,*

Santería, and Vodou. Durham, NC: Duke University Press 2019.

Stryker, Susan. *Transgender History*. Berkeley, CA: Seal Press, 2017.

Sturrock, John, trans. *A Shameful Revenge and Other Stories*. London: Folio Society, 1963.

Subrahmanyam, Sanjay. *Connected Histories: Essays and Arguments*. London: Verso, 2022.

Sylvanus, Nina. *Patterns in Circulation: Cloth, Gender, and Materiality in West Africa*. Chicago: University of Chicago Press, 2016.

Táíwò, Olúfẹ́mi. *Against Decolonisation: Taking African Agency Seriously*. London: Hurst, 2022.

Táíwò, Olúfẹ́mi O. *Elite Capture: How the Powerful Took Over Identity Politics (and Everything Else)*. Chicago: Haymarket Books, 2022.

Tallie, T. J. "On Black Autonomy and Responding to Abstract, Genteel Contempt." Tumblr. August 17, 2022. https://theteej.tumblr.com/post/692882482112151552/on-black-autonomy-and-responding-to-abstract.

Thomson, Philip. *The Grotesque*. London: Metuchen, 1972.

Thorton, John K., and Kristen Windmuller-Luna. "The Kingdom of Kongo." In *Kongo: Power and Majesty*, edited by Alisa LaGamma, 87–118. New York: Metropolitan Museum of Art, 2015.

Tinsley, Omise'eke Natasha. "Black Atlantic, Queer Atlantic: Queer Imaginings of the Middle Passage." *GLQ: A Journal of Gay and Lesbian Studies* 14, no. 2 (2008): 191–215.

———. *Ezili's Mirrors: Imagining Black Queer Genders*. Durham, NC: Duke University Press 2018.

Tompkins, Kyla Wazana. "Sweetness, Capacity, Energy." *American Quarterly* 71, no. 3 (2019): 849–56.

Tortorici, Zeb. *Sins Against Nature: Sex and Archives in Colonial New Spain*. Durham, NC: Duke University Press, 2018.

Tremblay, Jean-Thomas. "Black Ecologies (Humanity, Animality, Property)." *GLQ* 29, no. 1 (2023): 129–39.

Triplette, Stacey. "Chivalry and Empire: The Colonial Argument of the Princess Micomicona Scene in *Don Quijote*, Part I." *Cervantes: Bulletin of the Cervantes Society of America*, Spring 2010, 163–86.

Trouillot, Michel-Rolph. *Silencing the Past: Power and the Production of History*. 20th anniversary ed. Boston: Beacon Press, 2015.

Tweede, Cornesha. "The Significance of Black Women to Early Modern Iberian Literature." PhD diss., University of Oregon, 2022.

Tymowski, Michał. *Europeans and Africans: Mutual Discoveries and First Encounters*. Leiden: Brill, 2021.

Valentín Núñez Rivera, José, ed. *Paratextos y prosa de ficción en el Siglo de Oro: Los entresijos de la escritura*. Sielae, Spain: Coruña, 2024.

Vélez-Sainz, Julio. "Silencio de reyes negros: *La Comedia Trofea* de Torres Naharro y la cartografía de la colonización africana." In Jones, *Recovering Black Performance*, 179–95.

Vega, Martín. "Colors of Conquest: Perceptions of Gold, Whiteness, and Skin in Mexico's Early Colonial Histories." *Journal for Early Modern Cultural Studies* 21, no. 1 (2021): 1–25.

Vilches, Elvira. *New World Gold: Cultural Anxiety and Monetary Disorder in Early Modern Spain*. Chicago: University of Chicago Press, 2010.

Vollendorf, Lisa. "Reading the Body Imperiled: Violence Against Women in María de Zayas." *Hispania* 78, no. 2 (1995): 272–82.

———. *Reclaiming the Body: María de Zayas's Early Modern Feminism*. Chapel Hill: University of North Carolina Press, 2001.

Wagschal, Steven. "The Aesthetics of Disgust in Miguel de Cervantes and María de Zayas." In Giles and Wagschal, *Beyond Sight*, 94–120.

Warsh, Molly A. *American Baroque: Pearls and the Nature of Empire, 1492–1700*. Chapel Hill: University of North Carolina Press, 2018.

———. "Unruly Objects: Baroque Fantasies and Early Modern Realities." In Findlen, *Early Modern Things*, 255–72.

Weheliye, Alexander G. *Feenin' R&B Music and the Materiality of BlackFem Voices and Technology*. Durham, NC: Duke University Press, 2023.

———. *Habeas Viscus: Racializing Assemblages, Biopolitics, and Black Feminist Theories of the Human*. Durham, NC: Duke University Press, 2014.

———. *Phonographies: Grooves in Sonic Afro-Modernity*. Durham, NC: Duke University Press, 2005.

Weidman, Amanda. "Voice." In *Keywords in Sounds*, edited by David Novak and Matt Sakakeeny, 232–45. Durham, NC: Duke University Press, 2015.

Wheat, David. *Atlantic Africa and the Spanish Caribbean, 1570–1640*. Chapel Hill: University of North Carolina Press, 2016.

White, Deborah Gray. *Ar'n't I a Woman? Female Slaves in the Plantation South*. New York: Norton, 1999.

Wilbourne, Emily. "Little Black Giovanni's Dream: Black Authorship and the 'Turks, and Dwarves, and the Bad Christians' of the Medici Course." In Wilbourne and Cusick, *Acoustemologies in Contact*, 135–65.

———. "*Lo Schiavetto* (1612): Travestied Sound, Ethnic Performance, and the Eloquence of the Body." *Journal of the American Musicological Society* 63, no. 1 (2010): 1–43.

———. *Voice, Slavery, and Race in Seventeenth-Century Florence*. Oxford: Oxford University Press, 2023.

Wilbourne, Emily, and Suzanne G. Cusick, eds. *Acoustemologies in Contact: Sounding Subjects and Modes of Listening in Early Modernity*. Cambridge, UK: Open Book, 2021.

Williamsen, Amy R., and Judith A. Whitenack. *María de Zayas: The Dynamics of Discourse*. Madison, NJ: Fairleigh Dickinson University Press, 1995.

Woodard, Vincent. *The Delectable Negro: Human Consumption and Homoeroticism within U.S. Slave Culture*. New York: New York University Press, 2014.

Woods, Clyde, and Katherine McKittrick, eds. *Black Geographies and the Politics of Place*. Roseville, MN: Between the Lines, 2007.

Woods, Kim. "Cultural Crossings in Spain and in the New World, 1350–1550." In Christian and Clark, *European Art*, 63–100.

Woubshet, Dagmawi. *The Calendar of Loss: Race, Sexuality, and Mourning in the Early Era of AIDS*. Baltimore: Johns Hopkins University Press, 2015.

Wright, Elizabeth R. *The Epic of Juan Latino: Dilemmas of Race and Religion in Renaissance Spain*. Toronto: University of Toronto Press, 2016.

Wright, L. P. *The Military Orders in Habsburg Spain: An Economic and Social Study*. Cambridge: Cambridge University Press, 1970.

Wright, Michelle M. *Physics of Blackness: Beyond the Middle Passage Epistemology*. Minneapolis: University of Minnesota Press, 2015.

Yang, Chi-Ming. "Silver, Blackness, and Fugitive Value, 'from China to Peru.'" *Eighteenth Century* 59, no. 2 (2018): 141–66.

Yao, Xine. *Disaffected: The Cultural Politics of Unfeeling in Nineteenth-Century America*. Durham, NC: Duke University Press, 2021.

Yussuf, Kathryn. *A Billion Black Anthropocenes of None*. Minneapolis: University of Minnesota Press, 2018.

Zamora Loboch, Francisco. *Cómo ser negro y no morir en Aravaca*. Barcelona: Ediciones B, 1994.

———. *Memoria de laberintos*. Madrid: SIAL, 1999.

Zemon Davis, Natalie. "Decentering History: Local Stories and Cultural Crossings in a Global World." *History and Theory* 50, no. 2 (2011): 317–44.

Index

Page references to images are indicated with italics.

Abindarráez, 84–86
  See also Jarifa
abjection, 2, 35, 47, 112, 123–24, 126–27, 140
abolition, 25, 38, 75
academe, 3, 9–11, 23, 31, 33, 35–36, 41, 58, 140
  academic departments, 23, 41
  bandwagonism, 8
  cervantistas, 41–42
  Eurocentrism, 4, 22, 24
  gatekeeping, 32
  MLA, 3
  trendy, 4–5, 8, 40
Acosta, José de, 130
activism, 24–25, 28–29, 32, 138–39
aesthetics, 10, 15, 24, 37, 64–65, 127, 132
  anteaesthetics, 131
  antiblack, 128
  Baroque, 5, 101–2, 104, 109, 131
  black queer, 36–37
  black trans, 36
  carceral, 64–65
  grotesque, 41, 109, 128, 131, 158n49
African Diaspora, 2, 5–6, 8, 10, 15–17, 34–37, 39, 42–43, 49, 76–77, 79, 83, 86, 104, 110, 126, 139, 146n28, 150n19, 157n18
African diasporic religions, 146n28

Afro-Brazil, 88
Afro-Cuba, 15
Afro-European, 55
Afro-Hispanic, 70, 140
African ethnonyms,
  Aden, 54
  Akan, 62
  Bakongo, 146n28
  Çapa, 53–54
  Kongo, 15, 48–49, 52, 55–57, 146n28
  Kikongo-language, 52
  Mandinga, 19, 54, 78
  Milindo, 54
  monicongo, 49, 52–54, 56–58
  Wolof, 150n24
  Yorùbá, 15, 82, 110, 157n20
African monarchs,
  Afonso I of Kongo, 56–57, 151n30
  Bemoy, 53, 150n24
  Bumi Jeleen, 150n24
  King Susenyos, 155n44
  manicongo, 18, 48–49, 51–52, 55–57
African spiritual systems
  despojo, 40
  divination, 39
  Haitian Vodou, 15

African spiritual systems (*continued*)
    Hoodoo, 146n28
    Palo Mayombe, 15
    See also serpentine metaphors; Yorùbá òrìṣà
Africanized Iberian languages. See *habla de negros*
agency, 2–3, 5–10, 12, 17–18, 40–41, 73, 127, 137, 139–40,144n12, 145n16, 159n63
Aguado, Simón, 53
Ahad, Badia, 43.
Ahmed, Sara, 156n69
Aidoo, Lamonte, 155n54, 156n13
Alandete, David, 27
alchemy, 62, 68–69, 151n41, 151n46
    gold, 7, 57–59, 61–62, 68–70, 96, 151n44
    See also blackness: as alchemical
Aldana, Francisco de, 19
Alexander, Elizabeth, 35–36
Algiers, 46, 59, 62–63, 69
Alpujarras Rebellion, 59, 65
Álvares, Francisco, 87, 155n43–n44
Amadís de Gaula, 50.
    See also *libros de caballerías*
Angola, 52, 54
animal studies, 11, 42, 119, 122–24, 128–29, 158n41
    dogs, 116, 118, 121–23
    domestication, 71, 122
antiblackness, 7, 9, 21–22, 24, 32–33, 36, 41, 45, 49, 78, 108, 119, 122–23, 126–28, 130–31, 145n19, 151n38
    See also blackness
apocrypha, 40, 60, 149n46
Appadurai, Arjun, 131
Araujo, Ana Lucia, 25, 28
architecture, 2, 75, 79–81
archive, 16, 19, 40, 76–77, 94, 100, 110, 137, 149n45, 157n28
Arguijo family, 19, 60, 118.
    Arguijo, Gaspar de, 19, 118
    Arguijo, Juan Bautista de, 118
    See also Felipe Godínez; slave owners; slave trade
Aristotle, 10
Arvas, Abdulhamit 80, 94–95, 154n28, 154n31
Augustine, Saint, 13
auto-de-fé, 97
autobiography, 17, 26, 46, 59, 147n13

Avalle-Arce, Juan Bautista, 73
Avellaneda, Alonso Fernández de, 60
azabache, 124, 129
    jet, 125, 129

Bakhtin, Mikhail, 128
Baldwin, James, 10, 21, 29, 142
Balthazar (mage), 55, 60
Barletta, Vincent, 110, 157n19
Barthes, Roland, 78
BDSM, 12, 74, 93, 95
Benedict of Palermo, 140
Benin, 15, 62, 70, 152n64
Bennett, Herman, 8, 10, 33, 54, 57, 69
Berlant, Lauren, 102
Berlin Conference, 7, 144n11
Betancourt, Roland, 95, 99
Beusterien, John, 97, 115, 123, 148n41
Bey, Marquis, 10
Beyoncé, 37
Biafra, 62, 152n64
Bible, 39, 42, 148n43–44
    Deuteronomy, 39
    Leviticus, 148n43
    1 Samuel, 148n44
Bigelow, Allison Margaret, 60, 151n41
Bismark, Otto von, 7
black Africans, 2, 5, 7, 17, 34, 42, 46, 49, 61, 65, 68, 79, 86, 116, 128, 132; 148n40
    guitar players, 74, 83, 85, 87–88, 96, 99
    erudite men, 49–50, 56
    dehumanization of, 2, 127, 139, 151n38, 156n7
    musicians, 86–87
    horsemen, 46, 47, 140, 155n44 (*see also* João de Sá)
    swordsmen, 47, 49
    soldiers, 18, 46–49
    sovereignty, 4, 8, 54, 59, 62
black aliveness, 9, 11, 74, 145n18–n19, 145n23–n24, 147n26, 154n22
black feminism, 9, 11, 33, 48, 123
black futures, 4, 12, 42, 138
black interior, 36, 75, 78, 86
black thinkers, 9, 154n22
black skin, 37, 59, 82, 109, 113, 115, 119, 123, 129, 139
    bocací, 108–10, 112
    branding, 112, 125–26, 157n22
    cicatrization, 110–12

184   INDEX

keloids, 109
scarification, 107, 109–11, 110, 157, 128 (see also African spiritual systems: Yorùbá)
velvet, 129, 133
blackface, 69, 73, 150n19
Blackmore, Josiah, 110, 157n19
blackness,
   animalization, 41, 123, 127 (see also: animal studies)
   granular, 12, 48–49, 55, 58
   liquid, 17–19, 32–33, 37, 74
   phenomenology of, 3, 9–13, 40
   pretidão 157n19 (see also Vincent Barletta)
   racialized, 5–6, 12–13, 24, 33, 35, 41, 101, 107, 134
   sub-Saharan African, 18, 21, 38, 41–42, 45, 58, 101, 103
Blain, Keisha N., 104, 139
"Boda de negros." *See* Francisco de Quevedo y Villegas
Borbón, María Cristina de, 105
Borges, Jorge Luis, 149n46
   Pierre Menard (character), 149n46
Bouza, Fernando, 65
Boyle, Margaret E., 103–4
bozal, 51, 78, 95, 154n31
Bradley, Rizvana, 131
Brásio, Padre Antonio, 56, 151n30
Brazil, 15, 88
Brooks, Kinitra, 139
Brown, Katherine L., 149n46
Brownlee, Marina S., 103, 114
Byzantium, 95, 99, 155n56

Cadamosto, Alvise, 86
California, 25–26, 29, 147n13
Canals, Ricard, 105, 107,
Cairo, 62, 87
Camões, Luís Vaz, 110
   See also *Os Lusíadas*
Campt, Tina, 10, 83
Camus, Marcel, 88
Canavaggio, Jean, 64
Cantigas de Santa María, 158n48
Cao, Juan Manuel, 27
Cape Verde, 19, 54, 67
capitalism, 8, 33, 62, 69, 71, 102, 105, 119
capón, 90
   See also eunuch
Cardim, Pedro, 149n9

Cartagena Calderón, José R., 46
castration, 74, 79, 88–89, 92, 94, 100
   neutering, 83, 155n56
   See also eunuch; castration; castrato
castrato, 76
   See also eunuch; Jessica Peritz; music
Celestina, La, 148n41
Celoso extremeño, El (Cervantes), 12, 18–19, 73–75, 78–79, 81–83, 88–89, 93–95, 99, 112, 122, 126, 143n1, 153n4, 154n31, 154n39, 157n33
   Carrizales, Felipo de (character), 74–76, 79–81, 83, 85, 87, 94, 96, 98, 154n25
   Guiomar (character), 18, 74–75, 95, 97–98
   homosocial bond, 85
   Loaysa (character), 74–76, 83–87, 89, 94–100, 154n39
Cerdà Sunyer, Ildefons, 153n69
Cervantes y Saavedra, Miguel de, 1–5, 9, 12–24, 23, 26–43, 45–65, 68–71, 73–83, 85–89, 94–103, 107, 112, 116, 118–19, 122–23, 126–27, 132, 137–40, 157n33
   New World, and the, 59, 70–71, 87, 130
   Don Quijote de la Mancha (see *Don Quijote de la Mancha*)
   Celoso extremeño (see *Celoso extremeño, El*)
   Coloquio de los perros (see *Coloquio de los perros, El*)
   Galatea, 19
   Persiles y Segismunda (Cervantes), 65
   Rinconete y Cortadillo (see *Rinconete y Cortadillo*)
   Viaje del Parnaso, El (Cervantes), 19–20, 76
Cervantine blackness, 2–5, 8–13, 15–17, 19–22, 25, 32–33, 35–36, 38–43, 45, 47, 49–50, 74, 78, 83, 134–35, 137–40, 142
Cervantine futures, 138–40
Cervantine-serpentine, 15, 18
errantry, 16
and ghostwriting, 149n45
positionality of, 144n2
serpentine, 14–15, 18–19, 32–33, 36, 40, 137, 139
Césaire, Aimé, 112
Céspedes, Eleno/a, 112
Chafariz d'el-Rei, 47
   See also João de Sá
Chartier, Roger, 45
chattel slavery. *See* slavery
chivalric romance. *See libros de caballerías*

cicatrization. *See* black skin: cicatrization
citational politics, 56, 104, 140, 144n10, 145n23
Claramonte, Andrés de, 47
Close, Anthony, 24, 63
clothing, 86, 117, 126–27, 129
   gregüescos, 97, 120
   ìrùkẹrẹ, 82, 154n34
Cohen, Cathy, 38, 113, 129
colonialism, 22, 24, 28, 53, 57, 60, 62, 67, 79, 102, 112
colonization, 7, 29, 53, 129
Coloquio de los perros, El (Cervantes), 18, 53, 65, 116, 119, 122–23
   Berganza (character), 116–23
   Cañizares (character), 65
   Cipión (character), 117–23
colorism, 16
Columbus, Christopher, 5, 28, 71
Conde Lucanor, 60
Congo, 54–55, 67
   See also African ethnonyms: Kongo
conquest, 28, 71, 103, 131
Constantinople. *See* Ottoman Empire
Coráñez Bolton, Sony, 150n18
Cordileone, Salvatore, 29
   See also necromancy: exorcism
Cornejo-Parriego, Rosalía, 140
Correas, Gonzalo, 71
cosmetics, 111
   aderezos, 117, 125
   afeite, 128
   copete, 98
Cotarelo y Mori, Emilio, 158n45
Covarrubias, Sebastián de, 102
crip studies, 51, 84, 150n18
   See also García Piñar, Pablo
critical fabulation. *See* Saidiya Hartman
Cruz, Ariane, 93
Cuba, 15, 71, 111
   See also African Diaspora: Afro-Cuba

Da Gama, Vasco, 157n19
Dahomey, Kingdom of, 15, 54
Davidson, Michael, 51, 150n18–n19
decolonial, 3–4, 144n6
   See also academe; bandwagoning
defacing statues, 12, 22, 25–32, 43, 138–39, 147n9
   demonumentalize, 24

Golden Gate Park, 12, 22–23, 25–26, 32, 43, 138–39
   See also necromancy: exorcism
Descartes, René, 13, 16, 112, 139
Diablo cojuelo, El, 150n19
Diccionario de Autoridades, 71, 102, 127
Didion, Joan, 26–27, 29
dogcatchers, 122–23
domestic space, 18, 75, 101–2, 107
   hayloft, 18, 75, 78, 81, 86, 98
   domestication. See animal studies
Domínguez, Julia, 42
Don Quijote de la Mancha (Cervantes),
   Alifanfarón, 55
   Alonso Quijano (character), 45
   Andrés (character), 47, 62–63, 152n47–n48
   Angulo el Malo (character), 140
   Dorotea (character), 18, 59–60
   galley slaves, 63–65
   Garamantes, 55
   Ginés de Pasamonte (character), 64
   monicongo académico de Argamasilla, 18, 49, 52, 57–58
   Panza, Sancho (character), 18, 54, 58–63, 65, 68–71, 119, 122, 131, 139, 152n47;
   avarice, 59, 71; gluttony, 58–59, 71
   Princesa Micomicona (character), 18, 59, 69, 151n38
   Micomicón, 61
   Ricote (character), 65
   Rocinante (character), 63
Dopico, Georgina, 42, 45
Dr. Dre, 25–26, 60, 69
Du Bois, W. E. B., 10, 43
Duchess of Alba, 106

Early Modern studies, 2–5, 9, 11, 41, 100, 138, 140
Early Modern Spanish studies, 3, 6, 41
   See also academe
Edelman, Lee, 144n2
Egginton, William, 5, 146n7
El Greco. *See* Greco
"El prevenido engañado" (Zayas), 79, 107–8, 116, 129, 132
   Antonio (character), 87, 107–15, 128, 132, 134
   Doña Beatriz (character), 108, 112–15, 129, 132
   Don Fadrique (character), 108–9, 113, 115, 132

El-Tayeb, Fatima, 139–40
Elias, Norbert, 129
enslaved people, 2, 7–9, 18–19, 29, 34, 46, 51, 59, 61, 64–71, 73, 75, 77–79, 85–86, 94–95, 97, 101, 104–5, 108, 111–12, 115–16, 118–19, 121–23, 125–28, 138
    Berbería, 66–67
    children, 147n26
    esclavas blancas, 125–26
    esclavos blancos, 59
    men, 46, 59, 66–67, 78, 83
    neck, 64, 89, 129
    shackle, 89, 93
    women, 112, 125–26
Equatorial Guinea, 71
Ethiopia, 18, 20, 47–48, 59, 86–87
    nobility, 155n44
eunuch, 12, 18, 37, 73–75, 79–83, 154n25, 155n56
    See also Kızlar Ağası
exemplarity, 60, 119, 128
Ezili, Tinsely, 146n28

face, 109–13, 115, 125, 128–29, 133
    See also black skin
Fanon, Frantz, 112
    epidermalization, 112
feminism, 9, 11, 33, 48, 96, 123
Festival de Almagro. *See* theater companies: Festival de Almagro
fetishes, 36, 97
    See also BDSM
Fleetwood, Nicole R., 64
Floyd, George, 6, 22, 43
folklore, 85, 118
Foucault, Michel de, 45, 127–28
    archaeology, 19, 52, 55, 127–28
Fra-Molinero, Baltasar, 151n37
Freeburg, Christopher, 77, 145n18
Fromont, Cécile, 52, 56–57
frottage, 11, 86, 101–2, 115, 126, 131–32
    See also interracial intimacy
Fuentes, Marisa J., 9

Gamboa, Yolanda, 113
García Barranco, Margarita, 66
García Piñar, Pablo, 150n18
German Romanticism, 146n7
Germeten, Nicole von, 97
Ghana, 62

ghostly matters, 30–31, 38, 40, 71, 128, 148n40, 149n45
    See also necromancy
ghostwriter, 40, 149n45
    nègre, 149n45
Godínez, Felipe, 20, 60, 76–77
    See also Arguijo family; slave owners; slave trader
Godinho, Antonio, 57
Golden Gate Park. *See* defacing statues: Golden Gate Park
Góngora y Argote, Luis de, 34, 122–23
González Arévalo, Raúl, 66
González de Amezúa y Mayo, Agustín, 56, 83
Gordon, Avery F., 38, 148n40
Goya y Lucientes, Francisco de, 105–6, 106
Goytisolo, Juan, 114
Graf, Eric Clifford, 60–61
Greco, Domenikos Theotokopoulos, 60
Green, Toby, 61
Greer, Margaret Rich, 41–42, 108, 156n7
Grossman, Edith, 56, 143, 150n27, 154n31
Guinea, 4, 18, 48, 52–53, 56, 67, 71, 120–22, 131

habla de negros, 2, 6, 10, 40, 48, 50–51, 75, 77, 86, 93, 95, 98, 108, 122, 150n17
    Africanized Iberian languages, 51
    as crip speech, 51, 150n18
    fala da Guiné, 87
    fala de preto, 87
    representation of, 50–51
Haedo, Fray Diego de, 152n60
Haitian Vodou. *See* African spiritual systems
Halberstam, Jack, 156n69
Haraway, Donna, 16, 48, 149n11
harem, 74, 79–81, 154n25, 154n31
    serallo, 80
Harris, Cheryl L., 131
Hartman, Saidiya, 10, 16, 36, 48, 75, 78, 94, 154n22
    critical fabulation, 16–17
Hathaway, Jane, 155n56
Hegel, Wilhelm Friedrich, 9, 33
Hicks, Dan, 144n12
Holland, Sharon Patricia, 11, 123, 148n44, 154n22, 158n41
Holy Office of the Inquisition, 10, 34, 41, 60, 66, 97, 112
homosociality, 80, 85, 99

Honduras, 19
Hughes, Langston, 20

Ibrahim, Habiba, 43, 148n40
idleness, 1–3, 19, 42, 48, 143n1
Ignatius Loyola, Saint, 13
incarceration, 63–65
Indigeneity, 29, 60, 71, 147n22
Inquisition. *See* Holy Office of the Inquisition
interracial intimacy, 12, 49, 89, 93–94, 99, 102, 104–5, 107–8, 114–15, 126, 132, 134, 156n7
  See also frottage
intersectionality, 59, 95
Islam, 41, 54–55, 67
  See also Núñez Muley, Francisco

Jackson, Zakiyyah Iman, 123–24, 158n41
Jacob, Harriet, 105
Jarifa, 84–86
  See also Abindarráez
Joanna of Austria, 106
João de Sá, 47, 53
  See also black Africans, Chafariz d'el-Rei
João III of Portugal, 47, 53, 88
Johnson, Walter, 8
Juan Latino, 18, 48–51, 68, 149n14
Judaism, 55
  Judeo-converso, 76
Juneteenth, 24, 138–39

Kaplan, Amy, 102
Kimmel, Seth, 152n58
kink, 93–94
Kızlar Ağası. *See* Ottoman Empire
Kongokonferenz, 144n11
  See also Berlin Conference

Lad, Jateen, 81
Laguna, Ana María, 5, 79–81
Las sergas de Esplandián, 60
Lazarillo de Tormes, 60, 79, 158n33
Leahy, Chad, 23, 25, 27, 40, 134
Lee, Spike, 115
Lethabo King, Tiffany, 27–28
Levinson, Sanford, 28
Lewis, Jovan Scott, 17
Lezra, Jacques, 143n1

libros de caballerías, 50
  caballeros andantes, 152n47 (*see also* chivalry)
  chivalric romances, 42, 50, 52, 54, 58–59, 152n47, 158n33
  knights, 52, 58, 63, 152n47
Lihani, John, 53
Linares, Héctor, 47, 149n9
literary canon, 11, 23, 28, 33–34, 38, 47, 114
Lorde, Audre, 10–11.
Lovejoy, Paul E., 110–11
Lowe, Lisa, 46, 102, 148n40

MacCade, Tony, 6
Macharia, Keguro, 11, 101, 115, 137–38
Mali, 55
Mallén, Ana Caro de, 108
Mandela Gray, Biko, 11
Manila, 71
Mansa Musa, 61
Mármol Carvajal, Luis del, 68
Martín Casares, Aurelia, 65, 67, 156n10
Martín, Adrienne L., 123
Martínez, Miguel, 46
Marxism, 62
  social class, 6, 19, 29, 38, 98, 102–3, 105, 114–15, 124, 144n4
Mbembe, Achille, 39
McKittrick, Katherine, 8, 17, 139
meditation,
  as methodology, 10–20
  theoretical framework, 10–11
  contemplation and devotion, 13
microliterature. *See* Rodríguez-Velasco, Jesús
Miller-Young, Mireille, 9, 96–97
Mitchell, Koritha, 144n4, 156n13
monicongo. See *Don Quijote de la Mancha* (Cervantes): monicongo académico de Argamasilla,
Montalvo, Garci, 60
Moráis, Cristóvão de, 105–6, *106*
Maravall, José Antonio, 113
Moriscos, 41, 59, 65–68
  See also enslaved people: white slaves; Núñez Muley, Francisco
Morrison, Toni, 10–11, 32–36, 38–39, 134–35, 145n24
  Beloved, 32, 39, 134–35
  Sethe (character), 32; 147n26

188   INDEX

Mozambique, 54
Mozart, Wolfgang Amadeus, 30
   Don Giovanni, 31
Muñoz, Jose Esteban, 144n2
Murphy, Michelle, 70, 152n63
   phantasmagorical, 70
music, 11–12, 30, 74–77, 83, 85–86, 88, 99
music in Africa
   chira-wata, 87
   masinqo, 87
music in Spain
   Pésame dello, 86
   sarabande, 85
   sarao, 132
   seguidillas, 86
   tonada, 84
   zarabanda, 84, 86
Myers, Joshua, 32, 144n4

Naharro, Torres, 53–54, 150n26
necklace, 89, 93, 125, 130
necrocapitalism, 39, 134
necromancy, 38–40, 134, 148n41, 148n43–44, 149n45
   exorcism, 29 (*see also* Salvatore Cordileone)
necropolitics, 39, 124, 134, 148n41
negreros, 60, 70, 118
Niger, 55
Nigeria, 70
Nubia, 55
Núñez Muley, Francisco, 66, 68
   See also Islam; moriscos
Nyong'o, Tavia, 16, 38, 48, 154n22

Ogundiran, Akinwumi, 70, 152n64
Olmedo Gobante, Manuel, 149n10
Oran, 67
Orpheus, 88, 155n49
   Negrorpheus, 88
Os Lusíadas (Camões), 110
   Adamastor, 110, 157n19
Ottoman Empire, 74, 79–81, 86, 154n25
   Constantinople, 56, 81
   Kızlar Ağası, 79, 82 (*see also* eunuch)
   sultan, 80–81, 154n32
   Topkapı Palace, 81, 154n31
   Turks, 41
ouroboros, 13, 15, 36
   See also serpentine metaphors
Oxford English Dictionary, 39, 88, 102, 127

pandemic, 6, 2
Pareja, Juan de, 139–40
Patterson, Orlando, 39, 145n16, 148n41
pearls, 82, 93, 112–13, 125, 129–31
Pérez Galdós, Benito, 70
Peritz, Jessica, 153n13, 155n49
   See also castrato
Petrarca, Francesco, 130
phantom. *See* ghostly matters; Murphy, Michelle: phantasmagorical
picaresque literature, 47, 63, 79
Pickens, Therí Alyce, 10–11, 150n17
Pierre Menard (character). *See* Borges, Jorge Luis
poetry
   burlesque, 47, 50, 56, 57
   canciones, 154n39
   coplas, 86, 93
   jácaras, 47
   letrilla, 122
Poitier, Sidney, 138
policing, 6, 32, 105, 122–23
pornotrope, 93, 134
Portuguese Empire, 47, 52–53, 61, 86, 88
   Evora, 52
   Goa, 54, 61
   Kantora, 61
   Lisbon, 47, 52, 54, 57, 61
   Moluccas, 53, 150n26
   Prester John of the Indies, 59, 86–87, 155n41–n44
Ptolemy, 53–54
Pullins, David, 139–40

Quashie, Kevin, 9–10, 145n18–n24, 147n26, 148, 154n22
queer studies, 4, 12, 16, 24, 33, 36–39, 48, 74–76, 80, 94–95, 98–100
   nonbinary, 80, 94–95
   queering, 15, 94–95, 99
   antisocial turn, 144n2
Quevedo y Villegas, Francisco de, 34, 47, 51, 127–29, 131, 158n48–n51
   "Boda de negros", 127–29, 158n51
Quiñones de Benavente, Luis, 34
quixotic, 10, 39, 42, 48, 63, 103

race and gender, 12, 59, 80, 83, 89, 94, 97, 102, 105, 113, 123
race-play, 93

racial impersonation. *See* blackface
racism, 7, 24, 32, 45, 94, 126
Real Academia Española, 56, 71
Reed, Cory, 79–81
Reid-Pharr, Robert, 99, 139
Reinosa, Rodrigo de, 78, 89, 93–94
   Gelofe Mandinga, 78
   Jorgico (character), 89–93
Renaissance, 37, 50, 55–56
reparative work, 134, 139–40, 142
Repinecz, Martin, 144n5
Rhodes, Cecil John, 7
Riaño, Peio H., 24, 25
Ribeiro Chiado, Antonio, 87
Rinconete y Cortadillo (Cervantes), 47, 88
   Gananciosa (character), 88
Roach, Joseph, 31, 134, 147n13, 159n71
Roach, Shoniqua, 134
Rodríguez-Velasco, Jesús, 34–35
   microliterature, 34–35
Rogério, Budasz, 87
Romero-Díaz, Nieves, 103, 156n7, 157n28
Rubio, Rebeca, 24
Rueda, Lope de, 53
   Coloquio de Gila, 53
   Comedia Eufemia, 53
   Comedia Trofea, 53–54, 150n25
Ruiz, Eduardo, 73, 114

Sade, 65
sadomasochism, 94, 105
Salas Barbadillo, Alonso Jerónimo de, 97
Sampedro, Benita, 140, 153n66
Sánchez de Badajoz, Diego, 158n45
São Tomé, 62, 67
scarification. *See* black skin: scarification
Sedgwick, Eve, 99
Senegal, 53
Senegambia, 54, 86
serpentine metaphors, 15, 36, 146n28
   Aida Wedo, 15
   bisimbi, 146n28
   Dambala, 15
   kalungas, 146n28
   See also Cervantine Blackness: Cervantine-serpentine; Yorùbá òrìṣà
Serra y Ferrer, Fray Junípero, 29
Shakespeare, William, 41, 115
Shange, Ntozake, 34–35
Sharpe, Christina, 10, 102, 104, 131, 134

skin. *See* black skin
Slater, John, 157n22
slave owners, 104–5, 118
   See also Arguijo family; Felipe Godínez
slave trade, 19, 34, 59–62, 65, 67 69, 114, 122
   See also Arguijo family; Felipe Godínez
slavery, 8, 10–11, 22, 24, 32–33, 38, 46, 48,
      54, 58–59, 61–70, 73, 75–76, 84, 86,
      101–5, 112, 114, 119, 122, 126, 134–35,
      140
   chattel slavery, 105
   domestic slaves, 89
soundscape, 77, 88
Spain,
   Andalusia, 77
   Barcelona, 71, 153n69
   Ensanche, 71
   Canary Islands, 19, 124, 130, 132
   Catalonia, 107
   Coordoba, 123
   Granada, 18, 21, 49, 65–68, 108
   Madrid, 24, 104, 108, 128, 131, 147n7
   Seville, 18–19, 34, 54, 61, 63–64, 75–77, 83,
      86, 98, 107–8, 112–13, 117–18, 143n11
   Toledo, 66, 68
   Valladolid, 148n32
Spanish Empire, 46
Spanish Americas, 75
Spanish Golden Age, 3, 23, 41, 126, 153n19
Spillers, Hortense, 11, 69, 134, 138, 145n24
Sri Lanka, 55
Starowieyski, Franciszek, 14
Stoler, Ann Laura, 102
Strongman, Roberto, 15, 146n28
Stryker, Susan, 153n13
sub-Saharan Africa, 18, 21, 23, 38, 41–42, 45,
      52–53, 58–60, 65–66, 68–69, 76, 79,
      86, 101, 103–4, 109, 132, 154n31

Taprobana, 55
Taylor, Breonna, 6, 43
Téllez de Guzmán, Luis, 77
Teresa of Ávila, Saint, 13, 128, 158n48
theater companies,
   Festival de Almagro, 24, 97
   Joven Compañía Nacional de Teatro
      Clásico, 24
   Theater Company Grumelot, 97
theater in Spain,
   auto, 59–60, 87, 102

corral de comedias, 77
farsa, 158n45
mojiganga, 54
playbills, 77, 153n19
pregoneros, 77
Thomas, Todne Y., 139
Thorton, John, 8, 52
Tompkins, Kyla Wazana, 59
Tortorici, Zeb, 94–95
Trouillot, Michel-Rolph, 144n6
Tunis, 62
Tupac Shakur, 25
Tweede, Cornesha, 133

Vega y Carpio, Félix Lope de, 34, 47, 53, 112, 126
   El santo negro Rosambuco, 47
   Los locos de Valencia, 150n19
   El amante agradecido, 77, 153n17
Vélez de Guevara, Luis, 150n19
voice
   atiplada, 76, 84–85, 89, 94, 155n52 (*see also* castrato)
   garganta, 90–91, 112, 125
   throat, 83, 88–90, 92–94, 113, 125
Vollendorf, Lisa, 103–4
voyeurism, 86, 96–98, 103, 113
   scopophilia, 98

Walker, Kara, 140–42, *141*
Weheliye, Alexander, 11, 134
Weidman, Amanda, 88–89

whiteness, 36, 38, 60, 112–13, 129, 131, 134, 144n2
   sartorial, 112–13
   aristocratic white woman, 94, 132
Wilbourne, Emily, 73, 76
Woodard, Vincent, 99
Wright, Elizabeth, 49–51, 140, 149n14
Wright, Michelle, 140, 154n22

Ximénez de Enciso, Diego, 68

Yang, Chi-Ming, 62
Yao, Xine, 29, 144n2
Yorùbá. *See* African ethnonyms
Yorùbá òrìṣà, 15
   Erinlè, 15
   Ọbàtálá, 15
   Olókun, 15
   Yemọja, 15
Yorubaland, 70

Zamora Loboch, Francisco, 4, 32, 131, 144n5
Zayas y Sotomayor, María de, 12, 34, 79, 94, 97, 107–16, 124, 126–34, 156n7, 158n44
   and Cervantes, 101–2, 119–21
   interracial race relations, 102–4
   "La esclava de su amante"; Fajardo, Isabel (character), 112
   "El prevenido engañado" (*see* "El prevenido engañado")
   "Tarde llega el desengaño" (Zayas), 107, 124, 128–29, 130, 131–32, 135